JOURNAL FOR THE STUDY OF THE OLD TESTAMENT SUPPLEMENT SERIES
106

Editors
David J.A. Clines
Philip R. Davies

JSOT Press
Sheffield

GRADED HOLINESS

A Key to the Priestly
Conception of the World

Philip Peter Jenson

Journal for the Study of the Old Testament
Supplement Series 106

Copyright © 1992 Sheffield Academic Press

Published by JSOT Press
JSOT Press is an imprint of
Sheffield Academic Press Ltd
The University of Sheffield
343 Fulwood Road
Sheffield S10 3BP
England

Printed on acid-free paper in Great Britain
by Billing & Sons Ltd
Worcester

British Library Cataloguing in Publication Data

Jenson, Philip Peter
    Graded Holiness: Key to the Priestly
    Conception of the World.—(JSOT
    Supplement Series, ISSN 0309-0787; No. 106)
    I. Title II. Series
    222.1306

    ISBN 1-85075-360-1

CONTENTS

ACKNOWLEDGMENTS

This book is a partial revision of my doctoral dissertation, submitted to Cambridge University in 1988. I have sought to ensure that the main text can be read by those who do not know Hebrew—readers of Leviticus are rare enough as it is! I have been able to interact to a limited extent with more recent literature. The growing number of these studies testifies to an encouraging interest in what has been the Cinderella of biblical traditions. In particular, the magisterial 1100 page commentary on Leviticus 1–16 by Jacob Milgrom arrived too late for consideration, although the influence of his many other works will be evident in the following pages. However, the goal of this work is more to summarize and mediate than to give the last word on any issue of detail.

I am indebted to a number of people and places without which this book could not have been written. I record my deep gratitude to my supervisor, Dr Graham Davies, for his steady encouragement, his careful advice, and his continuing friendship. The inspiration of Professor Menahem Haran, who supervised me during my year at the Hebrew University of Jerusalem, can be found in numerous places. Several discussions with Professor Roy Porter saved me from various errors and omissions. Dr Walter Houston kindly allowed me to read parts of his monograph, soon to be published in this series.

Throughout, my parents have given unstinting support, not least financially. I have special memories of two superb libraries, the Ecole Biblique in Jerusalem, and Tyndale House, Cambridge. A year in Jerusalem at the Hebrew University was made possible by a scholarship from the Israeli Government, and I received a substantial grant from the Tyndale Council, with whom I gladly share a vision for godly and learned scholarship. Two very enjoyable years in a parish ensured that the implications of my study were not confined to the distant past. I thank the Revd Peter Goode for his friendship, wisdom and support, and for generously giving me the time to complete the thesis. I am grateful to Professor David Clines and the Sheffield Academic Press for accepting this volume for publication.

These acknowledgments would not, however, be complete without paying tribute to my wife Ruth. From first to last (and that includes the indexes!) she has remained my most faithful and stimulating critic. She and our two daughters, Kirsten and Charis, have made sure that the Priestly writings do not have the last word, but take their place in a larger and longer story.

ABBREVIATIONS

AB	Anchor Bible
AES	*Archives européenes sociologiques*
AJSL	*American Journal of Semitic Languages and Literature*
AmAnthr	*American Anthropologist*
AnBib	Analecta Biblica
ANET	J.B. Pritchard (ed.), *ancient Near Eastern Texts* (3rd edn, with Supplement)
AOAT	Alter Orient und Altes Testament
ASORDS	American Schools of Oriental Research Dissertation Series
ASTI	*Annual of the Swedish Theological Institute*
ATAbh	Alttestamentliche Abhandlungen
ATS	Arbeiten zu Text und Sprache im Alten Testament
AUSS	*Andrews University Seminary Studies*
AV	Authorized Version
BA	*Biblical Archaeologist*
BARev	*Biblical Archaeology Review*
BASOR	*Bulletin of the American Schools of Oriental Research*
BBB	Bonner biblische Beiträge
BDB	F. Brown, S.R. Driver and C.A. Briggs, *A Hebrew and English Lexicon of the Old Testament.*
BEvT	Beiträge zur evangelischen Theologie
BHS	*Biblia Hebraica Stuttgartensia*
Bib	*Biblica*
BibLeb	*Bibel und Leben*
BR	*Biblical Research*
BJRL	*Bulletin of the John Rylands University Library of Manchester*
BJS	Brown Judaic Studies
BKAT	Biblischer Kommentar: Altes Testament
BT	*The Bible Translator*
BTB	*biblical Theology Bulletin*
BZ	*Biblische Zeitschrift*
BWANT	Beiträge zur Wissenschaft vom Alten und Neuen Testament
BZAW	Beihefte zur *Zeitschrift für die alttestamentliche Wissenschaft*
CBC	Cambridge Bible Commentary
CBQ	*Catholic biblical Quarterly*

CBSC	Cambridge Bible for Schools and Colleges
CTA	A. Herdner (ed.), *Corpus des tablettes en cunéiformes aphabétiques découvertes à Ras Shamra-Ugarit*
CurAnth	*Current Anthropology*
DBSup	*Dictionnaire de la Bible, Supplément*
EncJud	*Encyclopaedia Judaica*
EM	*Encyclopaedia Miqrait (Biblica)*
EncRel	*Encyclopaedia of Religion* (M. Eliade, ed.)
ERE	J. Hastings (ed.), *Encyclopedia of Religion and Ethics*
EvT	*Evangelische Theologie*
ExpTim	*Expository Times*
EvQ	*Evangelical Quarterly*
FRLANT	Forschungen zur Religion und Literatur des Alten und Neuen Testaments
GNB	*Good News Bible*
HAR	*Hebrew Annual Review*
HAT	Handbuch zum Alten Testament
HBT	*Horizons in biblical Theology*
HDB	J. Hastings (ed.), *A Dictionary of the Bible*
HKAT	Handkommentar zum Alten Testament
HR	*History of Religions*
HSM	Harvard Semitic Monographs
HSAT	A. Bertholet (ed.), *Die Heilige Schrift des Alten Testaments*
HTR	*Harvard Theological Review*
HUCA	*Hebrew College Union Annual*
ICC	International Critical Commentary
IDB	*Interpreter's Dictionary of the Bible*
IDBSup	*IDB*, Supplementary Volume
IEJ	*Israel Exploration Journal*
Int	*Interpretation*
ISSE	D.L. Sills (ed.), *International Encyclopedia of the Social Sciences*
JAAR	*Journal of the American Academy of Religion*
JANESCU	*Journal of the Ancient Near Eastern Society of Columbia University*
JAOS	*Journal of the American Oriental Society*
JB	Jerusalem Bible
JBL	*Journal of biblical Literature*
JES	*Journal of Ecumenical Studies*
JewEnc	*The Jewish Encyclopedia*
JJS	*Journal of Jewish Studies*
JNES	*Journal of Near Eastern Studies*
JNSL	*Journal of Northwest Semitic Languages*
JPSV	*Jewish Publication Society Version*

JR	*Journal of Religion*
JQR	*Jewish Quarterly Review*
JRAI	*Journal of the Royal Anthropological Institute*
JSOT	*Journal for the Study of the Old Testament*
JSOTSup	*Journal for the Study of the Old Testament*, Supplement Series
JSS	*Journal of Semitic Studies*
JTS	*Journal of Theological Studies*
KAI	H. Donner and W. Röllig, *Kanaanäische und aramäische Inschriften*
KB	W. Baumgartner, L.H. Köhler, B. Hartmann and E.Y. Kutscher, *Hebräisches und aramäisches Lexicon zum Alten Testament*
KAT	Kommentar zum Alten Testament
KeH	Kurzgefasstes exegetisches Handbuch zum Alten Testament
KHAT	Kurzer Hand-Commentar zum Alten Testament, Tübingen
MT	Masoretic Text
MTZ	*Münchener theologische Zeitschrift*
NASB	*New American Standard Bible*
NCB	New Century Bible
NEB	*New English Bible*
NICOT	New International Commentary on the Old Testament
NIV	*New International Version*
NJB	H. Wansbrough (ed.), *New Jerusalem Bible*
NJPSV	*New Jewish Publication Society Version*
NKZ	*Neue kirchliche Zeitschrift*
NRSV	*New Revised Standard Version*
NRT	*Nouvelle revue théologique*
Numen	*Numen: International Review for the History of Religions*
OBT	Overtures to biblical Theology
OTL	Old Testament Library
OTS	*Oudtestamentische Studiën*
PEQ	*Palestinian Exploration Quarterly*
QSem	Quaderni di semitistica
RB	*Revue Biblique*
REB	Revised English Bible
RelSRev	*Religious Studies Review*
RevExp	*Review and Expositor*
RevQ	*Revue de Qumran*
RHR	*Revue de l'histoire des religions*
RSV	Revised Standard Version
RV	Revised Version
Sam.	Samaritan Pentateuch
SANT	Studien zum Alten und Neuen Testament
SBLDS	Society of biblical Literature Dissertation Series

SBLSP	*Society of biblical Literature Seminar Papers*
SBT	Studies in biblical Theology
SJLA	Studies in Judaism and Late Antiquity
SJT	*Scottish Journal of Theology*
SNTSMS	Society for New Testament Studies Monograph Series
ST	*Studia Theologica*
TBü	Theologische Bücherei
THAT	E. Jenni and C. Westermann (eds.), *Theologisches Handwörterbuch zum Alten Testament*
TOTC	Tyndale Old Testament Commentaries
ThWAT	G.J Botterweck and H.H. Ringgren (eds.), *Theologisches Wörterbuch zum Alten Testament*
TDNT	G. Kittel and G. Friedrich (eds.), *Theological Dictionary of the New Testament*
TynBul	*Tyndale Bulletin*
TZ	*Theologische Zeitschrift*
UF	*Ugarit-Forschungen*
VT	*Vetus Testamentum*
VTSup	*Vetus Testamentum*, Supplements
WBC	Word biblical Commentary
WMANT	Wissenschaftliche Monographien zum Alten und Neuen Testament
ZAW	*Zeitschrift für die alttestamentliche Wissenschaft*
ZTK	*Zeitschrift für Theologie und Kirche*

Chapter 1

THE CULTIC TEXTS OF THE PRIESTLY WRITING

1.1 *Introduction*

The Pentateuchal texts describing the worship of Israel (the cult) in a substantial body of texts are found principally in Exodus 25–31, 35–40, Leviticus and parts of Numbers.[1] The unity of style, language and content in this material has been traced to priestly perspectives and interests,[2] and so it is traditionally called the Priestly Writing (P).[3] P is normally understood also to include narratives in Genesis and Exodus.[4] However, this study is primarily concerned with a theological investigation of the texts describing the cult, although it is hoped that the results will contribute towards a fuller understanding of the Priestly Writing as a whole.

This opening chapter provides an orientation to scholarly debate on

1. The basis for the study is the Masoretic Text as represented by *BHS*. The LXX text lies outside the scope of the discussion (the special problems of Exod. 25–40 are discussed by Finn 1914 and Gooding 1959).

2. Various passages in this corpus exhibit different styles and are normally assigned to other sources. The narrative of the golden calf and the renewal of the covenant (Exod. 32.1–34.28) is one important text, although it is in its own way concerned with the subject of worship. The record of the wanderings in the wilderness (Num. 10.11–36.13) also contains a number of non-Priestly narratives (e.g. Num. 22–24). For details, see the standard introductions and commentaries.

3. Unlike 'Priestly Code' or 'Priestly Narrative', 'Priestly Writing' (*Priesterschrift*) is a useful neutral description of this body of material, which contains both law and narrative (cf. Saebø 1980: 364). I shall use a capital P (denoting the Priestly writing) for the texts assigned to P, and a small letter for that which pertains to priests (e.g. priestly family). Unless the context indicates otherwise, P will refer to the Priestly cultic texts.

4. There are a number of important texts dealing with the cult prior to Exod. 25 that are normally assigned to P. These include Gen. 2.1-3 and Exod. 16.1-20 (the Sabbath), Gen. 9.1-17 (the blood prohibition) and Gen. 17 (circumcision).

P, and a defence of the general approach which has been adopted to this difficult and complex material. It is becoming increasingly clear that the critical study of the Bible has close ties with broader issues of theology and history. An awareness of factors which have affected the interpretation of P in the past is valuable in assessing the history of its investigation and interpreting P anew in the late twentieth century (§1.2). The feasibility and character of a theology of the Priestly cultic texts largely depend on the approach taken to certain critical questions, and so these must be discussed (§1.3). It is possible to discern two approaches to the theology of these texts, one closely linked with a presumed date and setting for P (kerygmatic theologies, §1.4), and the other a more systematic treatment (§1.5). It is proposed that the latter is more suited to the nature of the cultic texts, and a traditional scheme which will provide the structure for the body of the analysis (Chapter 4 to Chapter 7) is introduced (§1.5.2).

1.2 *The Evaluation of the Priestly Writing*

There has been a sad neglect of the Priestly Writing, in spite of the fact that it is the most clearly defined source and comprises over half the Pentateuch.[1] A major reason for this is a negative evaluation of its theological worth, expressed explicitly and forcefully in many of the older standard introductions and critical investigations. It is worthwhile identifying some of the reasons for this distaste.

a. The roots of critical biblical study in German Protestant thought have had a profound impact on the way in which the cult has been described. A negative evaluation of the cult was reinforced by the alignment of the Priestly material with Roman Catholicism, Pharisaism and legalism,[2] and theological study of P has been relatively neglected by Protestant scholars.[3] In contrast, a number of

---

1.   Noted by Koch (1958: 36), Saebø (1980: 358), Hayes and Prussner (1985: 274).

2.   Hayes and Prussner (1985: 140, 274); cf. Fuchs-Kreimer (1981). On the negative attitude of Wellhausen, see the articles in *Semeia* 25 (1982); Saebø 1980; Weinfeld 1979: 2-15. The anachronistic suspicion of the 'legalism' of the Priestly cult (cf. Janowski 1982: 6-8) is similar to that directed at Pharisaic and rabbinic Judaism (Sanders 1977: 33-59; Neusner 1981: 19-33; cf. Heschel 1955: 320-35).

3.   This is less and less the case.

Jewish scholars have made detailed studies of P,[1] and the traditional authority of the Torah has encouraged a positive attitude. Although the modern critical approach to the Bible was adopted whole-heartedly in Roman Catholic circles only recently, the positive appreciation of ritual in this tradition has perhaps contributed to the appearance of several sympathetic reflections on Priestly material by Roman Catholic scholars.[2]

b. A second factor which encouraged a negative evaluation of the cult (or certain aspects of it) is to be found in the Bible itself, above all in the prophetic criticism of the cult. This, when coupled with the high value placed by Protestant scholars upon other aspects of prophetic thought, such as its individualism and moral appeal, naturally led to a tendency to undervalue priesthood and ritual in the Old Testament. The preference for the prophets over the law was expressed by means of a 'canon within the canon', in which the cultic texts were evaluated from the perspective of the prophetic books.

Today it is acknowledged that the contrast is overdrawn, and the prophets manifest considerable continuity with the earlier legal and cultic traditions.[3] Indeed, it has even been stated that 'the priests, not the prophets, were the real custodians of the care of souls in ancient Israel, and priestly theology created a universe of meaning which could deal with the totality of life in its many dimensions and exigencies'.[4]

c. The Priestly Writing has a distinctive style, and this has been described as 'boring', 'pedantic', or 'repetitive'.[5] McEvenue has

1. However, their contributions tend to provide the materials for a synthesis rather than the synthesis itself (cf. §3.1). A theology may have to transcend the categories in the text and communicate in terms relevant to the modern reader. For evaluations of Jewish biblical scholarship and the debate about the possibility of a Jewish theology of the Hebrew Bible, see Haran (1970), Goshen-Gottstein (1975), Levine (1979), Levenson (1987).

2. E.g. de Vaux (1961), McEvenue (1970), Blenkinsopp (1976), Lohfink (1982: 167-238).

3. Both the relative chronology (Zimmerli 1965) and the theological opposition (Barton 1986: 110-15) are now viewed more cautiously.

4. Hayes and Prussner (1985: 275).

5. A number of examples are noted by McEvenue (1971: 1-9). The attitude may be illustrated by Hillers (1969: 158): '[P] contains much material written by priests

suggested an alternative 'new approach' by comparing Priestly texts
with children's rhymes and tales, which have a similar love of repetition.[1] While his positive attitude is refreshing, the new approach is far
from convincing, particularly when extended to the cultic texts.[2]

There are more plausible explanations for the particular style of the
Priestly writings. It is likely that they were meant to be esoteric,
technical and informative, and they should not be compared directly
with writings that intend to communicate with a wide audience
immediately and memorably (e.g. the prophets or wisdom literature).
The specialized nature of the literature also accounts for the absence
of interpretation and explanation of the rituals, as has often been noted.
P reflects rather than actively communicates a world of meaning. To
some extent, it could be said that its form is inappropriate for its
status as a sacred scripture claiming to be relevant and authoritative.
The interpretation of P for the ordinary reader has normally required
indirect methods of exegesis, such as allegory and typology.[3]

d. In the last century the study of the Old Testament cult was often
carried out in dialogue with the discipline of anthropology. This phase
of study can be represented by the two great Victorian scholars, James
Frazer and William Robertson Smith. For them, the Priestly cult
shared many features with 'primitive' societies. However, this view was
closely allied with a judgment that the level of intellectual and cultural
attainment in such societies was grossly inferior to that of the Victorian
age. Aspects of Israelite religion were seen as a divine accommodation

---

for priests, details of sanctuary furnishings, and the niceties of ancient rituals of such
a monumental dullness as to test severely the endurance of the most dedicated Bible-
reader'.

1.   McEvenue (1971: 1-18). Similarly Scheehan (1977).

2.   The major part of McEvenue's book is a fine stylistic analysis of three
Priestly narratives. Even if a category of children's literature existed (doubted by
Lohfink 1978: 196 n. 25), it is unlikely that cultic law can be so described. The
occurrence of repetition in both genres is notable, but it is a complex and widespread
phenomenon and can serve many different functions (cf. §4.3.3).

3.   Allegorical and ethical exegesis of the cult goes back at least to Philo. This
need not be evaluated negatively, as some recent treatments of Leviticus Rabbah have
shown (e.g. Heinemann 1971; Neusner 1985). Recent 'typological' interpretations
of the Tabernacle from a non-critical perspective are summarized by Nixon (1984).
However, these writings are often more informative about the theology of their
authors than about the Priestly Writing (Childs 1974: 537-43, 547-50).

to primitive superstitions and errors, an accommodation destined in the course of time to be superseded by the true and 'spiritual' form. In recent times anthropologists have emphasized the ethnocentrism of this perspective (cf. §3.3).

e. The difficulty Victorian anthropologists had in interpreting other cultures remains today, though in a modified form. The social and religious world reflected in P is vastly different from that of a modern industrial society. Bridging the gulf between conceptual worlds has been a major concern of anthropologists. Unfortunately, there is little agreement as to how this should be done, but an awareness of the problem should alert us to the inappropriate value judgments evident in the writings of many past interpreters.

Whether acknowledged or not, these factors have led to a predominantly negative evaluation of the Priestly texts until comparatively recently. One goal of this study will be to further the rehabilitation and reassessment of the Priestly cultic texts through elucidating the Priestly conception of the world. In part, this stems from a conviction that these texts belong to Holy Scripture, and may be studied with profit. Yet even apart from this, there is a place for studies that strive to give another world-view a sympathetic interpretation.[1] While such an enterprise may not necessarily lead to the solution of long-standing problems of interpretation, it may supply a conceptual framework within which the texts may be read with an enhanced understanding.

1.3 *Historical-Critical Investigation of P*

1.3.1 *Introduction*
The last section has emphasized the importance of the cultural and theological context in which the Priestly writings are interpreted. The interests, beliefs and historical context of those *reading* the text influences the questions asked and the methods used to answer them.[2] This

---

1. An increasing number of positive statements about the Priestly perspective can be found, such as by Anderson (1988: 454): 'To enter sympathetically into this part of the Pentateuch is like standing in an ancient cathedral, whose symmetrical design and religious symbolism, hallowed by centuries of worship, produce a solemn sense of the holiness and majesty of God' (cf. Ackroyd 1968: 99-100; Saebø 1980: 373-74; Hayes and Prussner 1985: 275; Milgrom 1985: 304).

2. See the histories of OT interpretation, such as Clements (1976) and Rogerson (1984).

awareness can be an important corrective to the objective historical goal assumed by much technical biblical scholarship. This has been primarily interested in the authorship and origins of the complex texts found in the Pentateuch. In a number of recent studies, other questions have attracted interest and stimulated alternative approaches.

John Barton has suggested a helpful scheme for integrating the different kinds of question that can be asked. At the centre of biblical (and literary) study is the *text*, which may become the focus of a literary or structural investigation. However, the interpreter may have a special interest in the external *reference* to which the text refers, whether historical or theological. Finally, the way in which the text reveals its *author* may be of interest.[1] All of these facets are generally present, but an interpreter's principal interest will be reflected in the critical methods chosen, with their corresponding weaknesses and strengths.

This may be helpfully applied to research into P. For example, the architecture of the Tabernacle may be discussed as the reference of the texts in Exodus 25–40 without regard to issues of authorship. Traditional historical-critical study has had a special concern for discovering the original *author* or *authors* responsible for these chapters. Another important approach to the theology of P has concentrated on the way it was intended to move its original *readers* by means of its message or kerygma. Finally, under the impact of methodologies such as structuralism (cf. §3.2), the focus of interest has shifted to the *text* itself.

It will be argued that the Priestly cultic texts are particularly appropriate ones for this final approach. Of course, the adoption of a particular method has dangers. Some relevant studies of Priestly material by structural anthropologists have been rightly criticized for being imprecise, inaccurate and out-of-date. Yet these infelicities are not necessarily fatal, and insights from other disciplines have proved most fruitful when explored with an awareness of the gains of traditional scholarship.[2]

---

1.   Barton has a helpful diagrammatic representation of his scheme (1984a: 201; 1984b: 23, 24), which is derived from the literary critic M.H. Abrams (1953). Similar diagrams may be found elsewhere (e.g. Barr 1973: 61).

2.   'Explorations of the social dimensions of the Old Testament world are most useful when employed in conjunction with more traditional interpretative tools' (Wilson 1984: 82). The need for caution is stressed by Emerton (1976) and

It is not surprising that non-specialists usually work with the 'final form' of the text. However, the received text has also become the starting point of an increasing number of specialist studies, even when there is an awareness of historical-critical issues.[1] Since the position taken on a number of controversial critical issues has serious implications for the theological investigation of P, additional comment is required. A full review of these matters is unnecessary here, but the next two sections clarify and defend the assumptions made in the rest of the book.

1.3.2 *The Unity of P*

The isolation of a distinctive and independent 'source' with a special interest in the cult was an early achievement of the historical-critical method.[2] Eventually P was identified as the latest of the four sources that had contributed to the Pentateuch.[3] However, it was also clear that P was not a unitary composition, but displayed an unevenness in style, vocabulary and subject matter. There has been a constant tendency to graft onto the skeleton of the documentary hypothesis features of the 'supplementary hypothesis', which postulates that a core body of material has been supplemented by additional material in the course of time.[4] The character of these additions has been understood in various ways, such as the juxtaposition of literary strata, the successive productions of a school, or a collection of distinct traditions.

There continues to be a tension between the atomistic and unitary approaches to P, since no detailed analysis of Priestly strata has proved persuasive,[5] and the position adopted crucially affects the theological

Rogerson (1980), but errors in detail need not affect basic insights.

1. E.g. Milgrom (1970a: 1-2), Wright (1987a: 3-5), Kiuchi (1987: 17); contrast Janowski (1982).

2. For the early debate about P, see now Graham (1990: 117-51).

3. The Graf–Wellhausen documentary hypothesis is reviewed in the standard introductions. According to Loader (1984), it should perhaps be called the 'Kuenen hypothesis'.

4. Eissfeldt (1965: 158-70).

5. Soggin (1980: 136). North (1951: 56) describes Baentsch's commentary on Leviticus, with its array of suffixes distinguishing strata within P, as a *reductio ad absurdum* of the atomistic tendency. Unitary theories are equally unlikely. For a criticism of some of Radday and Shore's (1985) statistical arguments on the Genesis texts, see now Portnoy and Petersen (1991).

treatment of P. If rigorous criteria are applied in the effort to separate out Priestly strata, each subdivision is substantially reduced in size and scope. This makes it exceedingly difficult to construct a full-scale theology for that stratum, or of P as a whole. Moreover, while analysis may increase the uniformity of the strata identified, it also undermines the comprehensiveness, persuasiveness and theological value of the documentary hypothesis as a whole.[1]

One analysis of P has, however, proved extremely popular, not least because of its simplicity and theological potential (§1.4). Early on it was realized that P contained two types of material: narrative (beginning at Gen. 1) and cult (from Exod. 25).[2] In 1948 Noth proposed that the Pentateuch was dominated by a basic Priestly narrative (*Grunderzählung*, P_g), to which was later added supplementary material (*sekundäre Erweiterungen*, P_s) that primarily concerned the cult.[3] This fundamental distinction has been adapted, refined and extended by many of Noth's successors.[4]

However, his position has not gone unchallenged. The distinction used by Noth may well be a somewhat artificial criterion imposed on a complex and many-sided text. The delicacy of the criteria is illustrated by the recurrent disagreement about how far P_g extends and how unified a source it is. Both narrative and cult probably reflect fundamental aspects of the Priestly perspective, and the distinction should not be used as a criterion for chronological priority.[5] There is also a greater unity between the cultic laws and the narrative than Noth's theory implies. Overlapping vocabulary and common concerns link various priestly narratives and laws,[6] and the narrative framework of

1. Thompson (1970: 115).
2. Wellhausen traced a narrative source based on four covenants (Q) in his earlier work (1876–77), but discussed the cultic-legal parts (P, *Priesterkodex*) in the first part of the *Prolegomena* (1885).
3. Noth (1948: 7-19). Von Rad's (1934) twofold division of P is generally rejected (Humbert 1940; Noth 1948: 9).
4. The most important definitions of the extent of P_g (Noth, Elliger, Lohfink, Weimar) are given in Appendix 1 (together with an earlier analysis by Holtzmann). Other lists may be found in Borchert (1956: 6-7) (cf. also Campbell 1989: 87-91).
5. Levine (1976: 686) even argues that 'the actual cult served as a basis for the Priestly narrative'.
6. Fohrer (1970: 183), Rendtorff (1977: 112), Saebø (1980). Soggin (1975) points out that the links between narrative and cult are closer for P than the links between narrative and inserted legal material in JE.

the law is important theologically for relating the divine role in Israel's beginning to Israel's continuing experience of God through the cult.[1] Noth's analysis also faces the same problem as the atomistic analyses of P. A theology of the cult based on the narrative alone is severely limited by the fragmentary nature of P_g in sections of great cultic interest.[2] The difficulty is increased if it is not P_g itself, but the way it has transformed earlier material or added new perspectives that is significant.[3]

Other considerations support the position of those who prefer to assume a substantial unity in the final form of the Priestly text. 'Inconsistencies' in the canonical text may reflect a complex theology rather than a complex process of literary growth and redaction.[4] Or minor inconsistencies may have been regarded as relatively unimportant by later redactors. The diversity and inconsistencies of style found in many religious buildings and liturgies suggest that this is particularly true of the cultic sphere.[5] Past societies were even more tolerant.[6] The presence of a considerable quantity of older material in P suggests that the theology of P was not affected by historical change as much as has been sometimes suggested.

Another aspect of Noth's work with theological implications is his insistence that the Priestly Writing does not continue into Joshua. Traditional source criticism identified a number of passages that bear a Priestly stamp,[7] but sustained Priestly narrative ceases in Joshua. Noth argued that P-like passages should be discounted. Recent works

---

1. Ackroyd (1965: 95-96).

2. Note the implications of Weimar's sceptical analysis (Appendix 1).

3. Noth (1948: 262), Koch (1959: 101), Elliger (1952: 122). Compare the criterion of dissimilarity familiar in New Testament criticism. The unique is highlighted at the expense of the typical if this principle is applied rigorously.

4. Weinfeld (1983: 105). The complexity of defining 'contradiction' is stressed by Goldingay (1987: 15-28).

5. Sandmel (1961: 119) writes of the resiliency of the religious mind which is able to accept 'contradictions, discrepancies, anomalies and the like'. Koch (1959: 104) writes of 'einige wenige Leitgedanken, denen die bunte Welt kultischen Brauchtums unterworfen wird'. Zevit (1976: 196 n. 17) comments 'Pr [the Priestly redactor-compiler] read his composition [Ex 7–12] for consistency on the level of meaning and not on the level of plot'.

6. De Vaux (1971: 38), Tsevat (1974).

7. E.g. Carpenter and Harford (1902: 368-76).

have emphasized the difficulty of distinguishing Priestly sources from Priestly influence.[1]

1.3.3 *The Holiness Code*

Leviticus 17–26 raises the problem of P's unity in an acute fashion, since it exhibits many unique features. Since the last century, its special emphasis on holiness has been noted and enshrined in the standard abbreviation 'H' (*Heiligkeit*). Not only may P be distinguished from H, but several studies have traced a complex redaction history in H itself. Its chapters include at least three kinds of material: old laws and customs, collections of these older laws, and a Priestly redaction.[2]

However, the same question arises for H as for P: is it necessary to distinguish these levels if the interest is in the overall perspective rather than the detailed tradition history of the texts?[3] Despite its complex origin and character, and its distinctive vocabulary, idiom and subject matter, there is good reason to include H as a witness to the theology of P.[4] Notwithstanding differences between them, H is closer to P than to any other part of the Old Testament.[5] The content, language and theology overlap to a considerable degree, even if these

1. Blenkinsopp (1976: 286-89) argues that the land is presupposed by several Priestly institutions, and there may be Priestly contributions in Joshua, even if P did not play a decisive role (cf. Rendtorff 1977: 26-27; Lohfink 1978: 198 n. 30; Seebass 1985). Auld (1980: 93-98) provides a sophisticated defence of Noth's contention that there is no significant *influence* by P on Joshua even though there are passages reminiscent of P. He argues that the end of Numbers depends on Joshua, and that analysis of the Pentateuch should start at the end rather than at the beginning (p. 117).

2. Driver (1913: 47), Cazelles (1966: 825), Kilian (1963; 1967: 254-60), Thiel (1969: 44-45). More complex analyses have been made (e.g. Elliger 1966: 14-20 distinguishes four layers Ph_1 to Ph_4). Cholewinski (1976: 138-41) concludes that the main redactor wished to correct P, but that there is also a minor final P redaction. Knohl (1987), on the other hand, argues that the 'Holiness School' edited the 'Priestly Torah'.

3. E.g. Zimmerli (1980) investigates the meaning of holiness in the whole of H.

4. Haran (1981a: 329 n. 12). Wenham (1979b: 6-8) and Wagner (1974) minimize the differences between H and P. Patrick (1986: 152) perceives 'the final form of the text as exhibiting intellectual and artistic design, within which even the Priestly layer can be included'.

5. Similarities between H, Deuteronomy and Ezekiel are of less significance (cf. Haran 1979).

also display differences. A sharp distinction between H and P cannot be maintained, as is witnessed by various passages outside Leviticus 17–26 that are reminiscent of H. It is normally held that the Priestly redaction of H is patchy, some sections being taken over unchanged and others subjected to extensive revision. This suggests that the editors perceived no basic incompatibility with the Priestly perspective.

Although much of H deals with ethical matters only indirectly related to the cult, there are important exceptions which help fill out the Priestly theology. The laws in H frequently complement and supplement themes found in P. The detailed investigation of this study seeks to demonstrate that it is theologically fruitful to treat H with P, even if H's distinctive terminology and viewpoint must be taken into account when necessary (e.g. §2.2).

1.3.4 *The Independence of P*

F.M. Cross is perhaps the best known exponent of the view that P should be treated not as an independent source but as the decisive redaction of the Pentateuch. In his view, P systematically expands JE, according to its own periodization of history, while using older documents available to it. It is not a narrative work, and often merely provides the chronological and structural framework into which the other sources, including writings from priestly circles, were synthesized into a more or less coherent whole.[1] Others have followed or modified Cross' position,[2] although it has not received universal approval.[3]

Rendtorff has recently argued a sophisticated and controversial form of the supplementary hypothesis. The sources are not continuous narratives that were later combined, but are rather redactional levels which build upon earlier strata. The major complexes of material should be treated separately if their key themes are to be properly

---

1.   Cross (1973: 294-322).

2.   Friedman (1981c: 80) draws on Cross but distinguishes a pre-exilic collection of material (P_1) from an exilic tradent (P_2) who both edited and composed. P_1, which is not a narrative and includes much more than the normal P_g texts, is parallel to a pre-exilic Deuteronomistic stratum (Dtr_1). See the critical review by G.I. Davies (1983b).

3.   E.g. by Lohfink (1978: 199 n. 31), who argues that a dependence on JE does not exclude the possibility that P is a separate source, and that its priority in the Pentateuch is due to the way it was made the basic document for the decisive redaction.

discerned.[1] The Priestly contribution is best thought of as a final reworking (*Bearbeitung*) rather than as a source that can be traced consistently through the Pentateuch. While Rendtorff's approach suggests an indefinite number of stages in the redaction,[2] the stress on continuity encourages the search for theological coherence.

1.3.5 *Summary*

This brief survey has demonstrated the lack of consensus concerning basic critical questions about P.[3] The independence, extent and unity of the Priestly material has been vigorously contested and no consensus is in sight. However, a number of reasons have been given for adopting an approach which assumes a large degree of unity in the Priestly cultic texts (including H). There is sufficient continuity and unity of outlook to continue calling this body of diverse texts the 'Priestly Writing', and to make it the subject of a theological treatment.[4]

1.4 *Kerygmatic Theologies of P*

1.4.1 *The Kerygmatic Approach*

There have been surprisingly few full-scale theological studies of P, in spite of the fact that it is the most clearly definable source. Although many aspects of the cult have received detailed treatment, much of the challenge and difficulty of the Priestly material is how so many disparate concepts and institutions can be held together as a more or less coherent whole. Two kinds of response to this challenge have emerged, which may be designated the kerygmatic (§1.4) and the systematic (§1.5) approaches to the theology of P.

The former associates P (usually it is P_g) with a particular historical period and social background, which provides a key to P's overall

---

1. Rendtorff (1990b). Various responses were collected in *JSOT* 3 (1977).

2. Van Seters (1979: 666-67).

3. This reflects the uncertainty pervading Pentateuchal studies about the existence and nature of the sources. See the recent review by Whybray (1987).

4. Wellhausen recognized that tracing earlier and later strata required a finer source analysis, but could also state (1885: 385), 'The similarity in matter and in form, the perfect agreement in tendencies and ideas, in expressions and ways of putting things, all compel us to think that the whole, if not a literary, is yet a historical unity'.

message or *kerygma*.[1] Assuming a particular setting, it is possible to note parallels or contrasts between the historical and religious background of that time and the Priestly institutions and perspective. The text is therefore read in the light of a historical context quite different from the overt setting of the narrative, with the result that there emerges a much more definite and specific message than that based on a traditional reading. Thus 'what is narrated corresponds to situations, possibilities, experiences and problems of the readership for which it is intended. In the garments of the past they are offered help in living and possible courses of action.'[2]

There are a number of ways in which the possible message is related to the presumed historical context. The goal of P could be the *legitimation* of contemporary cultic institutions. Or it could be *programmatic* for the future, meant to guide and encourage, or to correct what was seen to be defective. If programmatic, the descriptions could be more or less subject to historical constraints. The tabernacle chapters could be the building instructions for a viable historical institution, a paradigmatic pattern to be adapted to a later era, or an idealistic blueprint for a utopian future.[3]

The content of the presumed Priestly kerygma depends largely on the dating of P. For Wellhausen, the Priestly system was primarily a product of the theoretical zeal of the Babylonian priests in postexilic times.[4] P sought to conform the past order of worship with that of postexilic orthodoxy, thus legitimating Israel's divine worship. The existence of a central sanctuary, the distinction between priests and Levites, sacrifices for sin, and the full liturgical calendar, all belong to the postexilic perspective and practice, but are retrojected by P into the wilderness period. Rather than legitimation of the early postexilic

1.   The term 'kerygma' is central to von Rad's conception of OT theology, and was used by Brueggemann and Wolff (1976) in their influential essays on the kerygma of the sources (cf. Jones 1981; Groves 1987: 78-83).

2.   Lohfink (1978: 211; my translation).

3.   Haran (1978: 122; cf. 1983) describes P as 'Between Utopia and Historical Reality' (cf. Pfeiffer 1948: 191; Uffenheimer 1979). Similar ambiguities beset the interpretation of other priestly texts, such as Ezek. 40–48 (Eichrodt 1970: 531), the Temple Scroll (Maier 1985: 110), and the rabbinic purity laws (Neusner 1973: 16). Some institutions are probably more utopian than others (e.g. the Jubilee and Sabbatical law).

4.   Note Wellhausen's conclusions to various sections of the *Prolegomena* (e.g. 1885: 38, 82).

cult, Vink has suggested that the Priestly Code is a programmatic
work, produced in the late Persian era (around 400 BC).[1] The Priestly
stories are sophisticated aetiological and programmatic statements,
serving practical goals associated with Ezra's mission. P manifests a
number of concerns characteristic of contemporary sources, such as
an authoritative law, precise genealogies, a priestly (rather than a
royal) hierarchy, and a concern for separation and purity.

Most recent scholars have set the decisive formulation of P in the
exilic period, and related its theology to the historical circumstances
of the exiles. They point to a number of important institutions in the
Priestly narrative (e.g. circumcision, Sabbath) which could remain in
force even when the centralized cult no longer existed.[2] The concern
with external boundaries, evident in the concern for purity and holiness, is to encourage the exiled Israelite community to remain united
and faithful to their God.[3] The texts assuming a central cult (e.g. the
Tabernacle and sacrificial texts) may be understood programmatically
to refer to the future restoration.[4] The kerygmatic interpretation is
strengthened if Noth's view that P did not continue into Joshua
is adopted (§1.3.2). The sure note of future, but delayed, possession
of the land is thereby aligned with the position of the exiles awaiting
the return from exile.[5] This kerygma of the Priestly narrative
is intended to convey a message of hope through its treatment of
key theological words or themes such as blessing,[6] memory,[7] covenant,[8] atonement[9] and presence (§4.6.2).

---

1. Vink (1969: 12-18). For example, the census demands are to encourage
generous giving by wealthy Dispersion Jews (p. 103).
2. Elliger (1952: 141), Kilian (1966: 39-41).
3. Douglas (1975: 307), Houston (forthcoming).
4. Clements (1965: 122), Koch (1958: 40), Lohfink (1978: 21), Fretheim
(1977: 315).
5. Elliger (1952: 143), Kilian (1966: 41-45), Cross (1973: 295-96).
6. Brueggemann (1976a) focuses exclusively on the P narrative, although he
does not exclude other approaches.
7. Klein (1981: 66) thinks that this theme is able to demonstrate 'the theological
continuity between the earlier and later part of this Pentateuchal stratum'. Von Rad
(1962: 241-42) suggests that ליהוה (for Yahweh), and זכר, זכרון (remembrance) sum
up the key themes of P.
8. Since in P the Sinai revelation is not called a covenant, Zimmerli (1960) has
suggested that this was to reaffirm the priority of the eternally valid Abrahamic
covenant of grace. But see Hillers (1969: 158-66).

A number of scholars, particularly Jewish scholars, have expended considerable effort in attempting to prove that the whole of P is a pre-exilic work.[1] Some recent linguistic studies have cast doubt on the lateness of Priestly language.[2] Haran relates P to several features of Hezekiah's reign, particularly the impulse towards centralization. He is able to maintain a link between P and Ezra's reading of the law by considering this as the occasion of P's publication rather than its composition.[3] The lack of P's influence on other pre-exilic texts is traced to a sociological rather than a chronological factor, in that these texts were intended strictly for the priests.[4] It is even possible that a number of cultic rituals and institutions go back to the earliest period of Israel's history, however greatly elaborated in the course of transmission. Possible ancient institutions include the portable tent shrine,[5] the scapegoat ritual and the Levitical function of guarding the Tabernacle.[6]

1.4.2 *The Limitations of Kerygmatic Theologies*
While kerygmatic theologies of P are invariably full of theological interest, they are subject to a number of difficulties. The survey above has demonstrated that there is no longer a scholarly consensus on any of the critical questions which a kerygmatic theology must presuppose. The dating of P, its unity, its extension into Joshua, and its relation to other sources are all disputed. The external background is equally unsure, and aspects of the Priestly cult have been compared with Canaanite, Mesopotamian or Persian religious practices.

9. Koch (1966).

1. For example, Kaufmann, Milgrom, Haran and Weinfeld (see the review by Zevit 1982). Jewish scholars do not normally distinguish pre-exilic and exilic strata, either in P or in the texts with which it is compared.

2. The linguistic studies of Hurvitz (1974, 1982, 1983) and Rendsburg (1980) have so far lacked an adequate comparison with a sophisticated supplementary hypothesis. Hurvitz (1982) argues that Ezekiel depends on P, but he accepts both P and Ezekiel as single units (cf. Lohfink 1978: 201 n. 33 and the reviews of Hurvitz's book by Becker 1983 and Davies 1987). Haran (1979) argues that Ezekiel and P represent independent traditions.

3. Haran (1978: 132-48). But see Milgrom's review (1981c).

4. For the private character of priestly rituals in the ancient Near East, see Cohen (1969) and Weinfeld (1972: 183).

5. Cross (1947).

6. Milgrom (1970b: 208).

Divergent critical positions have led to the same texts being interpreted plausibly against several different contexts.[1] It is difficult to prove that parallels or contrasts derive from a conscious polemic or dependence, since the arguments are necessarily indirect. The ease with which a good theological 'fit' for several different historical periods is attained may indicate the inherent richness of the material as much as a redactional shaping.[2]

Thus a theology depending upon definite answers to introductory matters is inherently fragile.[3] Indeed, it appears likely that no one date or historical period is decisive in the composition of a work of such magnitude and complexity. The final text is probably due to a steady growth and elaboration over a considerable period.[4] In general, cultic rituals and liturgy develop slowly and their form is maintained over long periods of time, although the interpretation may change more rapidly.[5] A gradual growth is likely to modify the influence of any particular period in the crystallization of the Priestly theology.[6] All of these considerations make it less likely that extensive sections of P

---

1. Whybray (1987: 111). Elliger (1952: 135) optimistically expounds the text's *Transparenz* according to his particular interpretation.

2. For example, Damrosch (1987: 71-72) considers that Lev. 10.1-3 reflects patriarchal, Sinaitic, monarchic and exilic layers of history.

3. Brett (1991) distinguishes helpfully between what a text says and why it says it (the motive). The latter is far more difficult to determine, since it is only indirectly deduced and is sensitive to the presumed *Sitz im Leben*. Brueggemann writes concerning his own essay, 'If the dating is shifted, then much of the argument indicated above concerning theological intentionality will need to be drastically revised' (Brueggemann 1982: 131). Similarly, if P continues into Joshua, then a kerygmatic interpretation stressing the parallel between the exile and the wilderness experience loses much of its force.

4. Driver (1913: 142), von Rad (1962: 231), Ackroyd (1967: 101), Rendtorff (1990a: 7). It is increasingly realized that large parts of P are early, and the disputes focus on the dating of its framing and the extent of later redactions and additions. Rendtorff (1963) and Koch (1959) have attempted to trace the development of the Priestly laws using form-critical analyses.

5. Driver (1913: 154). Cross (1973: 322-23) finds an 'archaizing language' in P.

6. Ackroyd (1969: 1) suggests that older material is subordinated and neutralized by the exilic setting, but this could be a much more regular pattern, which may indeed start from Sinai. A similar process may be detected in the Psalms (e.g. Childs 1981: 520-22) and the later redactions of the prophets (e.g. Clements 1977).

reflect a particular historical situation, or that they were written as part of a propaganda exercise.

There is a further fundamental question which is sharply disputed by different presentations. It is unclear how the Priestly presentation is related to the historical realities of the cult, past, present and future.[1] None of the proposed categories (correspondence, legitimation, program, ideal, fiction) have proved fully persuasive.[2] In view of our ignorance of the history of the cult and the role of the Priestly traditions, it is difficult to relate P to the development of Israelite religion.

It is instructive to compare von Rad's approach, since he is able to discuss the theology of the cult only by setting aside the kerygmatic approach and emphasizing the continuity of the priestly tradition:[3]

> It is obvious that a body of varied cultic material (P[s]) has been secondarily inserted into P. It has been rightly said that only what is organically connected with the account of the history proper is to be attributed to the original P. But the actual volume of secondary matter can hardly ever be precisely isolated from the original. We are dealing here with specifically priestly literature, about whose laws of growth we as yet know very little. Since this literature, in contrast with JE, had never left the sacral sphere, we have probably to reckon with a much steadier process of elaboration; and we ought not to make too wide a gap between the finished form as it was planned and achieved and the secondary accretions.

1.5 *Systematic Theologies of the Cult*

1.5.1 *Kerygmatic and Systematic Theologies*

A systematic theology of the cult which starts from the final form of the text is able, at least initially, to avoid the problems of dating and reduction which beset the kerygmatic approach. The challenge is to classify and understand the different aspects of the cult in a satisfying and comprehensive way, rather than to trace its literary and historical development.

---

1. For example, the Tabernacle may be a realistic anti-Temple blueprint for the future cult (Fretheim 1968), an idealized retrojection of the Jerusalem temple (Wellhausen 1885: 37-38), 'a theological reconstruction of the temple as distinct from its purely material refurbishing' (Clements 1965: 111), or a utopian vision far removed from realistic fulfilment (Haran 1978: 149, 189-204).

2. Cf. Noth (1948: 267), Vink (1969: 12-14), Schmidt (1984: 100-101).

3. Von Rad (1962: 233).

There is considerable evidence that this is an appropriate way in which to approach the cultic material. Many of the cultic laws and institutions are not tied to a specific historical period (e.g. the sacrifices and the purity laws). Rather, they are fundamental to a stable national religion, and as such they have much in common with the cults of neighbouring countries. Although the cult may have been instituted at a specific point (Sinai in P), the detailed laws need not reflect that history except in a general way. They may be related more closely to the structure of the created world and society.[1]

Of course, a systematic approach also has its limitations, and its weaknesses tend to be the strengths of kerygmatic theologies. Kerygmatic theologies have difficulty coping adequately with the quantity of cultic texts,[2] and systematic descriptions of the cult frequently underestimate historical, literary and redactional influences. Ideally, the two approaches should complement one another, and it is recognized that a systematic study such as this inevitably runs the risk of one-sidedness.

The tension explored here has a reflex in the two important approaches to Old Testament theology.[3] The kerygmatic theologies may be aligned with von Rad's emphasis on the history of traditions, which depends on a reconstruction of the history of Israel's sacred texts and religion. The 'cross-sectional' approach, classically illustrated by Eichrodt's theology, is more concerned with systematic description of a common world-view, and with exploring more stable theological structures. Both theologies in practice borrow from the alternative approach. Von Rad treats much of the Priestly material systematically, and Eichrodt seeks to trace the history of the development of the cult.[4]

---

1. Childs (1962a: 68) describes the Priestly concept of memory (as conveyed by זכר) in these terms: 'The concern of the priestly theology is not to relate recent Israel to a past event. There is no tension between past and present because the past mediated an eternal order. Rather the concern is to maintain the sacred order and relate Israel to it.' Similarly Lohfink (1978: 214) speaks of 'paradigmatische Weltkon - stellationen' in P_g.

2. One 'advantage' of adopting a P_g /P_s distinction is that the extent of cultic material that needs to be dealt with is much reduced.

3. See Hasel (1982: 50-58, 69-75).

4. E.g. von Rad (1962: 232-79), Eichrodt (1961: 98-177, 392-436, etc.).

1.5.2 *The Dimensions of the Cult*

The difficulty of writing a satisfactory theology of the Priestly texts[1] has not prevented general accounts of Israelite religion being written, and these have to be organized in some way. Some of these are less unsatisfactory than others in presenting a theology of P. The distinctive perspective of the Priestly material can be distorted if categories foreign to the Priestly outlook are employed, or if it is assimilated to a broader discussion of the history of Israelite religion. Other problems arise if the discussion is based upon a particular aspect. In accounts devoted to the Priestly cult, a common approach is to search for a key word or concept (preferably also found in the Priestly narrative), by which the Priestly theology can be encapsulated.[2] However, these are usually able to subsume only a small proportion of the available material. A recurring problem in the study of P, and in Old Testament theology in general, is the need to find categories in which the unity of large sections of the Bible can be appropriately expressed. An awareness of the disunity of a text often stifles the search for deeper unities which remain relatively constant while other factors change. A systematic theology should be based on categories more comprehensive than isolated words or individual themes, yet these must be related to a wide range of Priestly vocabulary and concepts.

It is worthwhile to re-examine the traditional ways in which the diverse content of the Mosaic cult was suitably summarized and explained. Bähr's *Symbolik des mosaischen Cultus*, first published in 1837, illustrates well the fourfold classification of spheres of cultic life which proved a suitable framework for many detailed studies:[3]

Structure	Title	Dimension
Book 1	Stätte—Stiftshütte	Spatial
Book 2	Personal—Priester	Personal
Book 3	Handlungen—Opfer und Reinigungen	Ritual
Book 4	Zeit—Feste	Temporal

---

1. Remarks such as the following are common: 'The document in no sense develops anything like an even reasonably complete theology of the cult' (von Rad 1962: 243).

2. Examples of this are noted above in §1.4.1.

3. Bähr (1837). On some of its weaknesses, see Keil (1887: 125-52) and Childs (1974: 538-39, 548-49).

Each of Bähr's books corresponds to a broad dimension[1] of cultic experience. They refer to basic aspects of humanity and are useful categories by which to organize a wide diversity of cultic acts and institutions.

The advantage of such an approach is that it transcends the limited scope available if a theology is organized by word, formula or theme. For example, a number of recent theologies have focused on the theme of *Presence*, which can embrace several aspects of the Priestly theology (cf. §4.6.2). However, despite the importance of this theme, it cannot embrace the totality of the Priestly world-view. P is also concerned with matters which have no direct connection with God's presence, and indeed, impurity and death are better related to God's absence. Admittedly, absence can be regarded as the opposite of presence, and it therefore belongs to the same field of discussion. But this raises the possibility that there are other concepts which show the same polarity, and that there are larger unities. Presence can, in fact, be closely related to the spatial dimension, and the polarity of presence and absence can be related to the graded character of that dimension.

Older works that discussed the cult in this way were often called 'Archaeologies', and employed a similar arrangement of material. Keil described the goal of the genre in this way: 'Commonly... Archaeology is regarded... as a setting forth, not so much of the *movement* and *progress* of the development, as rather of the *position* which the history has obtained in the *course* of its development'.[2] The older Archaeologies were primarily descriptive, but Wellhausen employed the same schema for answering comparative and historical questions.[3]

The same structure, more or less disguised or elaborated, controls

---

1. The term 'dimension' will be used in a semi-technical way to describe these four facets of cultic existence.

2. Keil (1888: 2)—author's italics. Benzinger (1927: 5-9) gives a brief history of the genre. See also Nowack (1894).

3. In the first section of the *Prolegomena* the chapter titles are, 'The Place of Worship', 'Sacrifice', 'The Sacred Feasts', 'The Priests and Levites' (Wellhausen 1885). The fifth chapter ('The Endowment of the Clergy') is an aspect of the fourth. Haran (1978: 1 n. 1) comments, 'Wellhausen, with his feeling for perfection, is still the only one to have come close to an all-embracing description of the biblical cult in its four dimensions'.

practically every discussion of the cult in the standard theologies.[1] Haran observes, '[The possible dimensions] are at most four in number: place (or institution), time (or occasion), act (or ceremony) performed, person (or personnel) performing it—and no description of cult is complete unless it embraces them all'.[2] The order of presentation varies from scholar to scholar, but I have followed the order illustrated by Bähr, which is the most popular for good reasons. It approximately follows the canonical order:

Dimension	*Priestly texts*
A The Spatial Dimension	Exod. 25–27; 30–31; 35–37; 40; Num. 1–4
B The Personal Dimension	Exod. 28–29; 38–39; Lev. 8–10; Num. 5–6
C The Ritual Dimension	Lev. 1–7; 11–15; Num. 7–10; 19
D The Dimension of Time	Lev. 16; 23; Num. 28–29

There is a certain narrative logic. The presence of God, manifested at Mount Sinai, can accompany his people by being mediated through the Tabernacle. The inauguration and maintenance of this holy shrine requires a specialized class of people—the priests. Their primary function in the Tabernacle is the offering of sacrifices, but sacrifices are also required for the ordination of the priests. A section on sacrifices is therefore inserted before the fulfilment of the command to ordain Aaron and his sons.[3] The determination of the yearly cycle of festivals and offerings is not of immediate urgency, so its systematic presentation comes later.

The order also has a theoretical appropriateness. A building has a permanent plan which alters little with time and provides a stable and clear structure which can 'ground' further, more abstract, reflection. A higher level of complexity is apparent in the description of people, who move, grow and sometimes change in cultic status. Nevertheless,

1.   Additional chapters may describe general themes, such as holiness and purity, but these occur in association with one dimension or another. To my knowledge, in recent years only Haran (1978) and de Vaux (1961) have attempted large-scale syntheses of the cult.

2.   Haran (1978: 1). This major study is now foundational for any work in the field, including this one. However, its scope is much wider than the present study, since it is a collection and adaptation of articles written on a wide variety of topics that often range far beyond the Priestly texts. It concentrates on historical and exegetical issues with a limited, though valuable, degree of synthesis.

3.   Although this is usually regarded as a later insertion, it is an appropriate one (Noth 1965: 18). On the redaction of Exod. 25–40 see now Gorman (1990: 45-52).

any society requires some stable organization if it is to maintain its corporate life throughout the generations. In contrast, it is the essence of rituals that things change and new states are brought about. Ritual generally involves a complex prescription about how various classes of people are to move and behave in space and time. Yet ritual is also customary, and traditional patterns of action are repeated at regular intervals. The spacing and duration of these intervals is the role of the final dimension, the dimension of time. It sets out the kind of rituals and actions fitting for a particular occasion. It is therefore appropriate for the study to begin with the simplest and most easily visualized structures (the spatial dimension), and proceed to the more complex.

1.5.3 *The Principle of Grading*
If the systematic method is chosen, there is the difficulty that texts or institutions may involve several dimensions at once. Further, while it may be useful to distinguish the dimensions initially, how is it possible to do justice to the ways in which the dimensions overlap and connect? A solution to this problem requires a principle or a pattern sufficiently abstract and general so as to be common to all four dimensions. Such a structure or theme can transcend individual dimensions and apply in diverse contexts, thus embodying the unity and order which is the presupposition and goal of the Priestly world-view.

The nature of this common structure has already been intimated in the title of this study: graded holiness. Holiness, or rather the holiness word group (see Chapter 2), is employed in all four dimensions, and reflects a graded conception of the world. In various contexts, it is possible to detect levels of holiness ranging from extreme sanctity to extreme uncleanness. However, this grading is not limited to the lexical indicators, but pervades the material institutions and laws of the cult as they are worked out in the four dimensions. The dimensions may be correlated according to their gradings, and this may be represented graphically in what will be called the Holiness Spectrum:

	I	II	III	IV	V
	Very Holy	*Holy*	*Clean*	*Unclean*	*Very unclean*
	קדש קדשים	קדש	טהור	טמא	טמא
Spatial	holy of holies	holy place	court	camp	outside
Personal	high priest	priest	Levites, clean Israelites	clean, minor impurities	major impurities, the dead
	(sacrificial animals)	(sacrificial animals)	(clean animals)	(unclean animals)	(carcasses)
Ritual	sacrificial (not eaten)	sacrificial (priests eat)	sacrificial (non-priests eat)	purification (1 day)	purification (7 days)
Temporal	Day of Atonement	festivals, Sabbath	common days		

Various forms of the Holiness Spectrum have been suggested, though not with the same precision. For example, Wenham has suggested:[1]

Life		*increasingly* →			*Death*
Normality		*abnormal*			*Total Disorder*
holy of holies	altar	Tabernacle court	camp	outside camp	Sheol
God	priests	deformed priests	Israelites	unclean	dead
	perfect sacrificial	blemished sacrificial	edible (clean)	inedible	carcasses (unclean)

The elucidation and exploration of the Holiness Spectrum will be the major task of the following chapters, but it should be regarded as an ideal representation. It is most clearly represented by the spatial dimension, which will be used as the main index by which to identify the other categories. However, all the laws and institutions of the cult are much more complex than is indicated by the diagram, and close attention will be paid to its inadequacies and inaccuracies. Yet despite its approximate character, the scheme is arguably the best systematic approach to the Priestly cultic texts so far proposed. Although it needs to be complemented by other methods and insights, it holds out the

1.   Wenham (1979b: 177 n. 34; similarly, Wenham 1982: 123).

promise of summarizing a great deal of Priestly material with a considerable degree of flexibility and theological interest. The approach thus seeks to fulfil an important task of Old Testament theology—that is, to set out the thought-world and the underlying assumptions of the texts being studied. Barton has commented:[1]

> The role of Old Testament theology is. . . nearer to the role of (say) a guide to the Elizabethan thought-world in helping us to an understanding of Shakespeare, than it is to the function of a handbook of Christian doctrine.

The inhabitants of the Elizabethan or Priestly world did not need a guide to the conceptual topography of their world. But to someone from another era, it is helpful to relate the concepts of the texts to those of the contemporary world. Concepts such as grading and dimension may be artificial, but they can be helpful. I have constantly tried to relate them to the detailed language and content of the Priestly texts.

1.6 *Summary*

A number of factors have hindered theological study of P, including a negative subjective evaluation (§1.2), and scepticism about its unity and coherence (§1.3). I have suggested that the degree of disunity in P has been over-emphasized, and that a theology of the Priestly cultic texts is possible. Two approaches to the theology of P have emerged, the kerygmatic (§1.4) and the systematic (§1.5). Reasons were given why the second type is more appropriate for the Priestly cultic texts, and a framework for the systematic description of the Priestly cult was briefly described, embodied in the *Holiness Spectrum*. This is a diagrammatic representation of a fourfold division of cultic matters (the dimensions) and a common structural principle (grading).

Chapter 2 discusses the lexical level of the Holiness Spectrum. Four common words in the Priestly vocabulary (holy, profane, clean, unclean) witness to P's graded conception of the world. This provides a good introduction to the discussion of the full Holiness Spectrum (Chapters 4–7). But before this, Chapter 3 discusses anthropological perspectives on concepts that occur frequently in discussions of the cult. Comments by structural anthropologists about classification,

---

1.   Barton (1983: 106).

grading and ritual have proved useful in putting the discussion in a wider context.

The body of the study consists of a detailed exploration of grading as it applies to the four dimensions of space (Chapter 4), person (Chapter 5), ritual (Chapter 6) and time (Chapter 7). Attention is paid to the overlap of the dimensions, and to the limitations and strengths of the Holiness Spectrum. The concluding chapter (Chapter 8) briefly discusses implications arising from the study for the the theology of the Priestly cultic texts within the larger discipline of Old Testament theology.

Chapter 2

CONCEPTS OF HOLINESS AND PURITY

2.1 Introduction

2.1.1 In biblical Scholarship

At the lexical level, the Holiness Spectrum is principally represented by four Hebrew words: holy (qdš, קדש), profane (ḥl, חל), clean (ṭhr, טהר) and unclean (ṭm', טמא).[1] By means of these (henceforth called the holiness word group), P is able to classify certain aspects of the world in a graded manner. The Holiness Spectrum makes possible a number of important observations about the Priestly understanding of holiness and purity. However, the Holiness Spectrum is also an artificial construct, with only an indirect relation to specific texts. So it is to be expected that a study of these words will demonstrate its limitations as well as its usefulness.[2]

While such a broad approach has weaknesses, it avoids some of the limitations which beset other approaches. The entries in the dictionaries and lexicons (and similar word studies) are usually restricted to an analysis of individual words, which are isolated from their context. This remains true even when there is an awareness of the wider semantic field. Moreover, the lexical approach generally becomes more widely relevant only when it goes beyond a mere list of occurrences. Another danger in this approach is the search for a common

---

1. Compare Dussaud (1921: 35): 'In a general way, the texts allow us to note four main values of states and objects: impure (ṭame), pure (ṭahor), sacred (qodesh) and most holy [sacro-saint] (qodesh qodashim)'. A full treatment would include less frequently used words such as šeqeṣ (שקץ), piggûl (פגול), niddâ (נדה), tô'ēbâ (תועבה), and the verbs kpr (כפר piel), ḥṭ' (חטא piel and hithpael; see §6.2.2), and ḥnp (חנף qal). For discussions of the lexical field of clean and unclean, see Paschen (1970: 19-30), Cazelles (1975), Zatelli (1978: 30), Amorim (1985: 237-70).

2. For example, Dussaud's (1921: 30-42) systematic presentation over-simplifies.

essence or meaning to a word, drawing on texts from the whole of the Bible (and elsewhere).[1] While a word's general meaning may be relatively constant throughout the Old Testament,[2] the Priestly writings have given holiness and purity a range of meaning and significance which deserves an independent and integrated treatment.[3]

For a better grasp of the meaning of a term, a group of related words, including synonyms and antonyms, should be investigated.[4] One problem is how to define the limits of an investigation. A study of related words (a lexical field) shades into the study of an idea or concept (a semantic field), which may be represented by several words occurring in the same context.[5] The external idea which is chosen can be broad or narrow, and inevitably there is a choice to be made between rigour and scope.[6]

An even more comprehensive approach is suggested by some of the recent discussion of metaphor and analogy (cf. §3.2). The starting point for theological concepts is basic physical and social experiences

1. Synthetic surveys of holiness are illustrated by Baudissin (1878). P is treated separately by Gilbert (1978), but his scope is limited. Others (e.g. Lagrange 1903; Dussaud 1921; Henninger 1975) treat more of the related terms. See also Fridrichsen (1916), Leenhardt (1929), Cazelles (1985) and Levine (1987).

2. Ringgren (1948: 30) remarks, 'The notion of holiness seems to have been surprisingly constant'.

3. Commentaries on the relevant books tend also to be restricted by their scope (one book rather than the Priestly corpus) and method (analytic rather than synthetic). The major commentaries on Leviticus by Noth and Elliger are primarily interested in literary-critical rather than theological questions. Those by Wenham and Rendtorff are more concerned with theological issues.

4. These groups have been called semantic (Barr 1961: 235) or lexical fields (Silva 1983: 161-63). Sawyer (1972) studies words for salvation, but the results are somewhat disappointing.

5. Silva (1981: 26-27); Lyons (1977: 250-69). Sawyer (1972: 30) distinguishes between an associative field, which includes all sense relations, and the lexical group, in which the terms are more closely related as synonyms. Levine (1987: 241) argues that 'the language of holiness will lead us to a consideration of the *idea* of the holy'. Gammie (1989: 5) starts with the idea of the holy, but then carries out a lexical investigation of holiness in the Pentateuch.

6. Zatelli (1978), for example, includes 16 words for purity and impurity in a study that surveys the whole Bible, but he restricts himself to the adjectives. Vivian (1978) includes Qumranic and Mishnaic texts in his study of separation. The Old Testament theologies tend to choose broad organizing categories, while word studies are more restricted.

of life. In the cult, these are integrated and related to the character of
God and his demands on Israel. Some of the structural parallels which
allow this analogical process to take place are represented by the
Holiness Spectrum.

The broad approach faces the problem of superficiality, especially if
the theme is followed through the whole Bible. Even though this study
is restricted to the Priestly corpus, the discussion of relevant words,
texts and institutions is selective and superficial. Nevertheless, I hope
to demonstrate that the broader perspective introduced by the Holiness
Spectrum is able to shed light on the meaning of words and texts in P.

2.1.2 *In the History of Religion*

Holiness has been of great interest to historians of religion. In particular, the contrast between the sacred and the profane has played a central role in the writings of Rudolf Otto and Mircea Eliade in their
comparative studies of religion. Their language and the concepts they
employ have influenced many studies of holiness in the Bible. For
example, Muilenburg, in an article on holiness, not only alludes to
Otto's characteristic language (e.g. 'numinous'), but also organizes his
discussion along broad lines sketched out in Otto's *The Idea of the
Holy*.[1] Eliade's strong dualism between 'The Sacred and the Profane'[2]
reflects significant ideas that are reflected in the translation and
understanding of cultic vocabulary.[3]

Despite their popularity, is that it has proved difficult to relate
satisfactorily the theoretical ideas set out by Otto and Eliade on the
one hand, and the lexicon of holiness in P on the other.[4] It is note-
worthy that Otto does not discuss holiness in P, despite the frequency

---

1.   Compare Muilenburg (1962: 616) and Otto (1926: 101-102). The meaning of
the word is widened into a concept that goes beyond strict lexical control. See the
critical comments by Bianchi (1975: 171-75) and Gammie (1989: 7-8).

2.   The title of an influential volume (Eliade 1961).

3.   This may be illustrated by the translation of Leviticus 10.10 (see §2.2.1).
Eliade's language is sometimes followed (e.g. 'sacred and profane', NJPSV, NEB,
REB, NASB, JB, NJB, NJPSV), while older or more traditional works have tended to
use the usual biblical translations (e.g. 'holy and common', RV, RSV, NRSV, GNB;
NIV 'holy and profane' is a mixed form). Morphologically related terms are preferred
by the AV ('holy and unholy') and Luther ('heilig und unheilig').

4.   Costecalde (1985: 1354). 'Numinous' is a particularly vague term, but
nonetheless remains fashionable (e.g. Terrien 1978: 372; Terrien 1982; Müller 1978:
589; Amorim 1985: 146, 154).

with which the *qdš* root appears there. A major difficulty is that the subjective and psychological aspects of holiness stressed by Otto are of secondary interest to the Priestly writers.[1] For them, it is rather that holiness is located in the God-ordained ordering of the sanctuary, as reflected and safeguarded in the laws and institutions of the cult. God's holiness may be ultimately hidden and inviolable in the Holy of Holies, but the primary emphasis is on the visible and realized holiness of the sanctuary, mediating his nearness and accessibility ('before Yahweh'). Only at certain times is the whole sanctuary out of bounds (e.g. Exod. 40.35; Lev. 16.17). The holiness and glory of God may be unique, but they are expressed not so much in terms of human reactions of dread, vitality and fascination, but through a developed system of cultic laws and prohibitions.

Similarly, while many of Eliade's observations about sacred space and time are fruitful and thought-provoking, his analysis seems too blunt and general to apply to P. The Priestly laws and institutions deal with a subtler grading of space than a simple dualism of sacred and profane. Further, the Priestly presentation of the cult is generally free from mythological motifs.[2] In general, the central ideas of Eliade and Otto have not proved as useful as was once thought.[3]

2.2 *The Semantic Field of Holiness*

2.2.1 *Holy and Profane, Clean and Unclean*

The terms in the holiness word group may be related to one another in several ways.[4] Lev. 10.10 is a key text in many of the discussions.

ולהבדיל בין הקדש ובין החל	to distinguish between the holy and the profane
ובין הטמא ובין הטהור	and between the unclean and the clean

From other texts, it is clear that holy and profane, clean and unclean are opposed pairs. If strict parallelism exists, this could suggest that the pairs holy/unclean, profane/clean are equivalent in some respect.[5]

1. Caird (1980: 176-77), Comstock (1981).
2. Shiner (1972).
3. On Eliade, see Smith (1972), Bianchi (1975: 184-91), Alliband (1980), Allen (1978). Otto is criticized by Bianchi (1975), Needham (1981: 62) and Leach (1985: 223, 251, 255).
4. See Söderblom (1911: 376-78), Henninger (1975: 400-14), Amorim (1985: 13-20).
5. The translation of the AV ('holy and unholy') indicates a symmetrical binary

Scholars have drawn attention to various phenomena where holiness
and impurity share a common character, both in P and in other religions. However, this is not necessarily due to an original identity
(§3.3), and it is inconsistent with the strong contrast in the Priestly texts
between holiness and impurity. It is preferable to assume a chiastic
structure to the parallelism, i.e., that holy and clean, profane and
unclean are aligned, though not identified.[1] Holiness is akin to cleanness
and strongly opposed to uncleanness. In Barr's representation:[2]

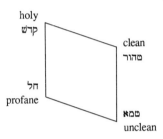

The relation between the pairs related vertically is more strictly
defined than those related horizontally.

The lexical aspect of the Holiness Spectrum represents both opposition and similarity.[3]

קדש קדשים	—	קדש	—	טהור	—	טמא	—	טמא
very holy	—	holy	—	clean	—	unclean	—	very unclean

The terms widely separated are at opposite poles, while those which
are adjacent are more closely related, although there is a break
between clean and unclean. One disadvantage is that the scheme
excludes the profane, though the rarity of the noun excuses this to

structural opposition, but it does not show the special linguistic marking of holiness.
קדש often has a linguistic and theological stress that is lacking in חל, but which it
shares with טמא. Similarly, the word 'purity' in English has a positive content
lacking in the Priestly טהור.

1.   The parallel structure of the verse should not be stressed, since it is an
abstract and general summary of the priestly task, and the formulation here may
depend on pragmatic, stylistic or rhythmical considerations (Zatelli 1978: 95).
Chiasmus is an important feature of Priestly style, both on a larger and smaller scale
(Lund 1929; McEvenue 1971—referred to as palistrophe; Paran 1989: 163-74).

2.   Barr (1972: 15).

3.   For a discussion of semantic opposition and polarity, see Lyons (1977:
270-90).

some extent.[1] On the other hand, it represents additional grades of holiness and impurity which are of great importance in P, even though they are not clearly reflected in the lexicon.

Only on the basis of the context is it possible to make the distinction between grades of holiness and impurity.[2] Thus while *qodeš q°dašim* (קדש קדשים) is frequently found, it is not yet a technical term with a fixed meaning or reference (§4.2.1). Impurity could arise from many different sources, and exists in various degrees according to its power of contagion and the purification required for it.[3] Although in P the particular nature of an impurity takes precedence over a consistent systematization, the texts allow some generalizations to be made.

Jewish interpreters distinguished three principal degrees of impurity. Although P is less systematic, they are a useful starting point and are summarized below.[4]

Cause	*Technical Term*	*Translation*
corpse impurity	אב אבות הטומאה	father of fathers of impurity
major impurity	אב הטומאה	father of impurity
minor impurity	טומאה	impurity
rendered impure by a major impurity	ולד טומאה	child (or offspring) of impurity

The most severe impurity results from contact with a corpse, which is called the 'father of fathers of impurity', since one who has touched a

---

1.   In P, חל is used only in Lev. 10.10, although the context implies that it was an important priestly task (cf. Ezek. 22.26; 44.23). Lyons (1977: 275) describes words with negative polarity as those which are regarded as lacking in some quality (e.g., small indicates lack of size). חל may well imply a lack of holiness.

2.   A large number of synonyms for impurity exist in English, aside from the possible adverbial and adjectival qualifications of clean and unclean. 'Unclean' is the weakest and usually indicates minor impurity, whereas 'impurity', 'defilement' and 'pollution' have stronger overtones and are more appropriate for major impurity. For Meiggs (1978: 314-15), mess, dirt and pollution are distinguished by the increasing threat they pose.

3.   Amorim (1985: 287 n. 2) suggests that the degree of impurity is indicated by (1) the time required for its purification, (2) the importance of the sacrifices for its purification, (3) the power of contagion. He relates a fourth factor (degree of isolation) to hygienic factors.

4.   See also Appendix 2; §§5.4.2, 6.3. The complex rabbinic rules are summarized by Elijah of Vilnah (trans. in Danby 1933: 800-804), Meyer (1965), *EncJud*, XIII, 1405-14. Rashi appears to be the first to have used the technical term for corpse impurity (e.g., *b. Bab. Qam. 2b*).

corpse becomes a 'father of impurity'. A 'father of impurity' can communicate an impurity to persons and objects in various ways. Such a major impurity (as it will be called) is distinct from a minor impurity, which cannot be communicated. That which is rendered unclean by a major impurity (called a 'child' or 'offspring' of impurity) could also render other objects unclean by various degrees, though after a certain point the chain ceases.

While in detail this scheme is more systematic than that of P, it points to the significant double grading which is incorporated into the Holiness Spectrum.[1] Minor impurity is non-communicable (e.g. it is a permanent attribute of unclean animals), and a person is easily purified from it. Major impurity is more serious, usually communicates minor impurity, and requires stronger measures for its purification. Corpse impurity, though in some ways unique, may be regarded as belonging to the class of major impurities (§6.3.2).

2.2.2 *The Dynamics of the Holiness Spectrum*
The holiness word group can refer not only to a status, but also to the transitions between states. The nouns and adjectives correspond to a particular grade in the Holiness Spectrum, whereas the associated verbs describe moves between grades. G.J. Wenham has proposed a simple scheme that provides a useful basis for discussion.[2]

---

1. The terminology is unclear, both in the Hebrew (where there are few lexical distinctions), and in English (where there are many). The two grades have been described in various ways: (a) contagious and non-contagious uncleanness, (b) major and minor pollutions (Frymer-Kensky 1983), (c) communicable and non-communicable impurities (Wright 1987: 163-64), (d) 'primarily, i.e. inherently unclean. . . and secondarily unclean, i.e. things unclean after and because of contact with the inherently unclean' (Durham 1963: 81), (e) dynamic or contagious uncleanness (Vos 1968: 62). 'Unclean' and 'very unclean' have been used in the Holiness Spectrum to emphasize the structural contrast with the 'holy' and 'very holy' pole, but a strict terminology has not been maintained.

2. Adapted from Wenham 1979b: 26. Curiously, Wenham refers to sin and infirmity rather than sin and impurity.

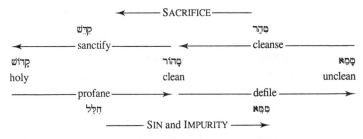

The following remarks refer primarily to the first two dimensions of the Holiness Spectrum, which are concerned with places and persons (or objects).[1] The temporal dimension can only be partly fitted into the scheme, since time cannot be clean or unclean, and although the Sabbath is holy and may be sanctified or profaned (§7.3), there is no mention in P of profane time.

Wenham's scheme could also give the impression that the steps between unclean, clean and holy are regular and uniform, but this is an oversimplification. Much more attention is directed to the identification of the impure and the holy than what is clean or profane. Furthermore, the language of purity and impurity does not necessarily overlap with the language of holy and profane. Although Wenham introduces a 'profane' step for the move from a holy to a clean state, this is primarily to maintain the symmetry of the diagram rather than to reflect Priestly vocabulary. Both Wenham's diagram and the Holiness Spectrum are too limited if taken by themselves, and need to be complemented by more specific analysis of Priestly vocabulary and texts.

A better suggestion is that holiness (and its opposite, the profane) represents the divine relation to the ordered world, and the clean (with its opposite, the unclean) embraces the normal state of human existence in the earthly realm. The holy–profane pair represents (positively and negatively) the divine sphere, and this may be distinguished from the human sphere (which is marked by the opposition between clean and unclean).[2] The presence of a holy God and a holy

1. Less attention is paid to these, but vessels, clothing, seed and beds may become unclean (Lev. 11.32-38; 15) and must then be purified or destroyed.

2. Cf. Baudissin (1878: 46), von Rad (1962: 272). Paschen (1970: 60) considers that purity has primarily a social rather than a cultic function (contrast Gispen 1948: 190; Amorim 1985: 250). God is never called pure (Levine 1987: 243-44). A similar distinction between divine and earthly spheres has proved useful in an

sanctuary in the midst of Israel ensures that these two points of view overlap in a complex way.

2.2.3 *The Divine Sphere: Holy and Profane*

If the 'holy' is defined as that which belongs to the sphere of God's being or activity, then this might correspond to a claim of ownership, a statement of close association, or proximity to his cultic presence.[1] It is a strongly personal term, first of all associated with Yahweh.[2] But since the normal state of earthly things is purity, it requires a special act of God to make a thing or person holy. God ultimately consecrates or sanctifies (*piel* or *hiphil* of קדשׁ),[3] although he may make use of persons and material means. Moses anoints both the sanctuary and the priests with the holy anointing oil (Exod. 40.9-11, 12-15), but this is in strict accord with the divine instruction, and the infilling by the glory of God at the consecration emphasizes the limitation of the purely human construction. The consecration consists of a double movement, since the initiation of a new relationship with the divine realm entails a corresponding separation from the earthly sphere.[4]

Indian context (Dumont and Pocock 1959: 30-31). An alternative view is that there is an 'energy', 'force' or 'power' in the holy which is lacking in the realm of the clean and the unclean. But holiness is a stable state for what belongs to the divine realm: holy cultic vessels are as inactive and harmless as any others in the absence of interference. Furthermore, impurity shares some of the same energy (see §3.3.3).

    1.   Compare the meaning of the root in Akkadian (*qadāšu*), Ugaritic (*qdš*), and other Semitic languages (Costecalde 1985: 1372, 1381, 1391-93; Levine 1987: 242-44).

    2.   In contrast to some earlier theories, the religious and personal character of the word is fundamental in P. For a careful discussion of a non-religious meaning of *qdš* (e.g. 'pure' or 'bright' in Lam. 4.1), and the difficulties of deducing an original meaning of the word, see Emerton (1967).

    3.   Jenni (1968: 59-60) suggests that the *piel* expressed a more temporary consecration that the *hiphil*. Waltke and O'Connor (1990: 438) suggest that the *piel* focuses on the results and the *hiphil* the process. 'Consecration' is generally preferred here, since it evokes the ritual context, and is less easily confused with 'sanctification', with its personal and ethical overtones.

    4.   Baudissin (1878: 47). Separateness is often thought to be the basic meaning of holiness, but it is more its necessary consequence. Consecration is a separation to God rather than a separation from the world (Snaith 1944: 30), and holiness has a positive content (Costecalde 1985: 1392-93). The theory that the original etymology was separation (cf. Costecalde 1985: 1356-61) is now abandoned (e.g. Bunzel 1914: 22-26; Gilbert 1978: 257; Müller 1978: 590).

There is a crucial distinction between holy objects and holy persons. The holiness of objects is permanent, and they can never again enter the profane sphere.[1] Although there may be attempts made to defile or profane them, it is never stated that these are successful. Although the Tabernacle had to be purified periodically, associated impurity did not immediately compromise its holiness, which is a further hint that there are two spheres which overlap in a complex way. The dedicated holiness of objects also allowed a special measure of God's presence to be manifest on important occasions. At the consecration of the sanctuary, the glory of Yahweh fills the Tabernacle, but not even Moses can enter (Exod. 40.34-35).

Priests, on the other hand, live both in the profane and holy spheres, though at different times. In order to minister in the holy sanctuary, the priests had to be holy themselves, and to this end were consecrated at Sinai (Lev. 8–10; §5.2.1). But in contrast to holy objects, their holiness was only active in the holy area, and there was no penalty if a priest became unclean outside the sanctuary. Yet priestly holiness was more than a mere potential, and it affected certain kinds of behaviour outside the sanctuary (§5.2).

The restriction of holiness to the priests and the sanctuary is in tension with other occurrences of the root where it has a much broader scope.[2] Holiness can describe God's demands on the whole of Israel, which is called to imitate God's own holiness (Lev. 19.2).[3] This meaning often occurs when the passage is referring to matters other than the cult in the narrower sense. Thus holiness should characterize Israel in its distinctiveness in relation to the nations with regard to purity laws (Lev. 11.44-45) or moral behaviour (Lev. 19). On special cultic occasions, when all Israel was involved (cf. §7.2), they attained the broader holiness, which was not permanent and ceased as a natural consequence of time.

---

1. Thus the bronze censers of the sons of Korah become part of the permanent furniture of the cult (Num. 16.37-40 [H 17.2-5]).

2. Cf. Zimmerli (1980: 495). The wider meaning is particularly characteristic of H (Lev. 20.7), but it is implied elsewhere (Lev. 11.44; cf. outside P, Exod. 19.6, 10, 14; Deut. 7.6; cf. §3.5.2). Houston (forthcoming) considers that this national aspect reflects a 'Holiness Redaction' of an earlier Priestly text characterized by a restricted understanding of holiness (cf. Knohl 1987). The interpretation in the text takes a contextual understanding.

3. Zimmerli (1980: 502).

A ritual which relates the potential holiness of all Israelites to the specific cultic holiness of the priests is found in Numbers 6. The Nazirite vow was open to all Israelites, male or female, priest or lay. The vow entailed restrictions similar to those which the high priest had to observe.[1]

	Nazirite	*High Priest*
Status	holy to Yahweh	holy to God
	קדש הוא ליהוה (Num. 6.8)	קדש הוא לאלהיו (Lev. 21.7)
Dedication	head is dedicated	head is anointed (§5.2.1)
נזר root	נזר אלהיו על ראשו	נזר משחת אלהיו עליו
	(Num. 6.7)	(Lev. 21.12; cf. Exod. 29.7; Lev. 8.12)
		wears dedicated rosette
		ציץ נזר־הקדש
		(Exod. 39.30; cf. 29.6; Lev. 8.9)
Purity	not to touch a corpse[2]	not to touch a corpse
	(Num. 6.6-7)	(Lev. 21.12; §5.2.4)
	begins the vow again if defiled	(unable to minister if defiled)
	(Num. 6.9-12)	
Drink	abstains from wine during	abstains from wine during
	vow (Num. 6.4)	ministry (Lev. 10.8)

The holiness of the Nazirite was only temporary and non-communicable and so not confined to the sanctuary or to the priesthood (cf. §§2.2.3, 7.2). Nevertheless, he was subject to restrictions during his vow which put him on a par with a ministering high priest.[3] While the vow determined behaviour in ordinary life, it was closely tied to the cult by the sacrifices necessary when he was accidentally defiled

1. 'His [Nazirite] taboos raise him to the level of the high priest', Milgrom (1976a: 67 n. 240).

2. The mourning restrictions for the high priest were complete (Lev. 21.11). The list of those for whom the Nazirite may not defile himself (father, mother, brother, sister: Num. 6.7) may be compared with those forbidden to the high priest (father, mother: Lev. 21.11) and contrasted with those for whom a priest could defile himself (mother, father, son, daughter, brother, virgin sister: Lev. 21.2).

3. Or indeed above him, since, presumably, even the high priest could drink wine when he was not ministering (§5.2.4). A priest's hair also had to be trimmed (Ezek. 44.20; cf. Lev. 10.6), whereas the Nazirite was to let it grow.

(Num. 6.11-12) and when he completed his vow. After the specified time the Nazirite had to go to the door of the tent of meeting, where the priest performed a full selection of sacrifices ('ōlâ ḥaṭṭāt šᵉlāmîm, vv. 14-17; cf. tᵉnûphâ vv. 19-20).

This last ritual was probably a desanctification, a *rite de passage* (§3.2.4) which effected the Nazirite's move from a holy to a normal clean status. Amorim has helpfully distinguished between negative desecration (or desanctification) and positive desecration (or profanation). The former is a voluntary and necessary aspect of moving from the holy to the profane sphere.[1] This concept can explain a number of minor rituals: (1) the high priest changes his clothes and washes on the Day of Atonement (Lev. 16.23-24),[2] (2) the vessels used to cook holy sacrificial meat are scoured (metal or stone vessels, Lev. 6.28 [H 21]; Num. 31.23) or destroyed (earthen vessels, Lev. 6.28 [H 21]; 15.12), (3) the Nazirite shaves his head and offers sacrifices at the end of his dedication period (Num. 6.13-20),[3] (4) the fruit of a vine cannot be eaten in the fourth year, for it is holy to Yahweh (Lev. 19.24), but may be eaten thereafter.[4] The ḥll root is not generally used to describe desanctification,[5] but it is often indicated by a ritual similar to that of a purification.

In contrast to this, there can be a deliberate attempt to treat the holy as profane, a serious transgression of cultic law and an act of rebellion against God. It is described by the piel of ḥll, and results in the extreme penalty (death, according to Exod. 31.14; Lev. 22.9; Num. 18.32).

---

1. These spheres are implied by Lev. 10.10 (§2.2.1), where ḥōl is opposed to qādôs in a very general statement. It indicates that the profane is in some way incompatible with the holy, but not essentially sinful.

2. Baentsch (1903: 385-86), Porter (1976: 131), Kiuchi (1987: 136-37).

3. De Vaux (1961: 466), Kiuchi (1987: 55), Milgrom (1990b: 48), Rodriguez (1979: 121).

4. Amorim (1985: 163-84). In the last case, the Samaritan Pentateuch reads חלולים (MT קֹרֶשׁ הִלּוּלִים לִיהוה), and this could be correct (NEB: 'and this releases it for use'; cf. Porter 1976: 158). Other cases of desanctification are less certain. The person who burns the remains of the ḥaṭṭāt outside the camp has to wash his clothes and bathe (Lev. 16.27-28), but as with other rituals outside the camp this is probably a purification (Amorim 1985: 175; Kiuchi 1987: 137). According to one interpretation, the king in Ugarit had to undergo a ritual of desanctification (ḥll ydm, KTU 1.115 line 6; Xella 1981: 106-107, 367).

5. However, the holiness of the item being desanctified is mentioned in all four cases.

The various occurrences seem to be in contexts where God's holiness is in some way compromised (it is opposed to the *qdš* root in Lev. 22.31-2).[1] Profanation, like holiness, is possible in any of the four dimensions, place (the sanctuary, Lev. 21.12, 23), people (the priests, 21.4), sacrifice (the holy portions, 19.8, 22.15) and time (the Sabbath, Exod. 31.14).

Amorim has described the distinction between desecration and defilement in the following way.[2]

> While holy tangible realities may be desecrated and defiled, intangible realities such as the Sabbath, the Name, and Yahweh are not affected by defilement. . . ḥll action deprives something or someone of holiness, while ṭm' acts have no effect on Him.

Defilement is a more concrete act, one closely tied to the purity laws. It is a serious cultic sin to bring the the unclean into contact with the holy.[3] Such an action produces a dangerous mismatch of levels in the Holiness Spectrum, since the holy and the unclean are at least two degrees removed and at opposite poles. Many of the laws and institutions of P are designed to reduce this possibility, especially in the region of the Tabernacle.[4]

In one case there is an overlap between defilement and profanation, in the laws determining when a priest may defile himself by contact with the corpse of a close relative (Lev. 21.1-4). From the point of view of clean and unclean, he defiles himself (יטמא, vv. 1, 3, 4), but the priest's consecration also means that a deliberate defilement will lead to profaning his holiness (להחלו, v. 4).

---

1.   The *piel* of *ḥll* is found predominantly in H. Men can profane Yahweh's holy name (שם קדשי, Lev. 18.21; 19.12; 20.3; 21.6; 22.2, 32). Milgrom argues that *m'l* (מעל) is the equivalent in P to *ḥll* in H (Milgrom 1976a: 86). In H, *ḥll* characterizes sins such as human sacrifices to Molech (Lev. 18.21) and prostitution by the daughter of a priest (Lev. 21.9).

2.   Amorim (1985: 3).

3.   The sinful character of defilement is sometimes prominent. Frymer-Kensky (1983: 404) suggests that there is a set of 'danger beliefs' concerning sinful acts, in addition to 'pollution beliefs'. H asserts that certain sexual offences defile (Lev. 18.24; 20.21; 21.25; also Num. 35.34), and these are subject to the death penalty.

4.   After Korah's rebellion (Num. 16–17), the priests and the Levites are commanded to guard the holy things and the Tent of Meeting (Num. 18.1-5; Milgrom 1970a: 19-33).

2.2.4 *The Human Sphere: Clean and Unclean*

The other pair of terms (clean–unclean) is at home in the life of Israel outside the cult. Normal life is characterized by being in a state of purity, a concept that is neutral relative to the holy and the unclean. It is of significance primarily in that it is a presupposition for approaching the holy. Minor impurity is a common state of affairs to which no blame is attached, and which is dangerous only in proximity to the holy.[1] Purity is a necessary but not sufficient condition for consecration.[2] For example, potential priests must first of all be legitimate heirs of Aaron. The realm of the clean and unclean therefore has a certain independence from the divine realm. It was necessary to be clean before approaching the holy, not so much from any special virtue in being clean, but because the antipathy between holiness and impurity was absolute.[3]

The vocabulary of purity and impurity may be illustrated by two important texts in the purity laws, the food laws (Lev. 11) and the rules about skin disease (Lev. 13–14; see §§5.4.2, 6.3.3). Creatures may be permanently clean or unclean (cf. Lev. 11.47), but the interest is primarily in the identification of unclean animals (vv. 4, 5, 6, 7, 26, 27, 28, 29, 31, 35). Someone who touches a corpse becomes unclean (יטמא, vv. 24, 27, 31, 39) and remains in a state of uncleanness until evening (וטמא עד־הערב, vv. 25, 28, 40, 40), when he becomes clean (וטהר, cf. v. 32). An ethical factor is introduced when someone deliberately defiles oneself (*hithpael* ותִּטַּמְּאוּ, vv. 24, 43). The *piel* is used to indicate a deliberate act of disobedience (ולא תטמאו את־נפשתיכם, v. 44).

The *piel* ('defile') is also used to explain why the person with skin disease has to be expelled so as not to defile the Israelite camp (ולא יטמאו את־מחניהם, Lev. 13.44). However, Leviticus 13–14 also employs a declarative *piel*[4] to indicate the cultic-legal nature of the decision which the priest makes about whether someone has the disease or not (e.g. Lev. 13.59 לטהרו או לטמאו; טמא 12×, טהר 9×). The

---

1. Procksch (1933: 88).

2. Explanations of holiness in terms of purity (e.g. Bunzel 1914: 24-25) are therefore inadequate.

3. Lay Israelites must be clean to eat the peace offerings (Lev. 7.19-21), or the Passover (Num. 9.13), since these possess a minor grade of holiness (§6.4.5).

4. Or perhaps more accurately, delocutive *piel* (Hillers 1967: 322-23; Waltke and O'Connor 1990: 402).

specific form of the declaration was probably טהור הוא (6× Lev. 13) and טמא הוא (8× Lev. 13–14). The *piel* (הִמְטַהֵר, Lev. 14.11) also describes the role of the priest in the purification of the sufferer, who is himself signified by the *hithpael* (הִמַּטֵּהר 12× in Lev. 14).

Just as purification is a conscious act rather than an automatic cleansing, so defilement usually describes a deliberate act. Although it may occasionally be a legitimate, though serious, event (Num. 6.9; Lev. 11.24), it is generally an act of conscious disobedience to God's laws (e.g. Lev. 18.24). This is one way in which sin and impurity are closely associated (Lev. 16.16; cf. §§6.2, 7.4). The danger of impurity, the extent of the required purification, and the penalties for disobedience are correlated with the grade of impurity. The most extreme form must be carefully purified, even though contracted in an accidental or inevitable way. Someone who suffers corpse impurity and refuses to make use of the proper means, defiles the sanctuary, and is cut off (Num. 19.13, 20; cf. §6.3.2).

The exceptions to this pattern (usually in H) point to important Priestly ethical values. Defilement could characterise practices which were completely forbidden, such as sexual transgressions (e.g. Lev. 18.24; 21.1-4), an appropriate use, since sexuality in general was strictly controlled by purity laws. On the other hand, accidental defilement of a Nazirite defiled his consecrated status (וטמא ראש נזרו, Num. 6.9). The use of the *piel* could have been due to the degree of holiness inherent in the Nazirite status (v. 5).

The Priestly interest is naturally in the way matters of purity and impurity affect the cult, but the significance of the laws is much wider than this. It is likely that the Priests were also experts in the wider implications of the purity laws. This may have encouraged the transfer of cultic language to the legal and theological spheres, as in texts which refer to the defilement of the land as a result of sinful acts (e.g. Lev. 18.24-5; 20.22-6; Num. 35.33-4).

2.3 Conclusion

The Holiness Spectrum provides a good starting point for an analysis of the Priestly concepts of holy, clean and unclean. The texts bear witness to many of the transitions between these states, but the limitations of the model are seen in the way that it does not clearly represent the significant differences between the closely linked pairs of holy–profane and clean–unclean. For this reason another perspective was explored. It was suggested that the holy and the profane could be characterized by the subjects' presence in or absence from the divine sphere, while the purity laws were primarily concerned with non-cultic matters. However, the two spheres overlap, and the laws and language of the cult reflect a complex interaction.

Purity was necessary for consecration or any approach to the holy, and it was important that no impurity came into contact with the holy. On the other hand, re-entering the profane realm was a natural event, one sometimes marked by rituals. But any attempt to profane the permanently holy was a major offence. In certain contexts, people other than priests are regarded as holy, but this exists alongside the special cultic holiness. Defilement and profanation can also describe activities that were not strictly associated with the sanctuary, but which had serious effects on the relationship between God and his people that stood at the heart of the cult.

Chapter 3

The Holiness Spectrum

3.1 *The Challenge from Anthropology*

Anthropology[1] has frequently supplied the concepts and models for understanding aspects of Israel's religion that seem strange and puzzling, since records of similar customs could be found in the distant tribes and societies that were of great interest to anthropologists. The investigation of Israelite religion from an anthropological perspective is associated particularly with the names of William Robertson Smith[2] and James Frazer.[3] In this early phase of study, the key explanatory categories were closely tied to evolutionary presuppositions about the development of humankind (§3.3), and an important goal of anthropological study was to trace the development of religion from its earliest stages.

More recently there has been a shift in anthropology from historical and comparative questions to contextual and structural ones, as has also been true in the case of biblical studies. Structuralism is a general movement of thought which has had a profound impact on many disciplines, but in biblical studies has influenced the analysis of narrative

---

1.   'Anthropology' in this context does not mean the doctrine of man as a branch of Christian systematic theology (Rogerson 1978: 9). The relation of anthropology and biblical studies has been reviewed by Hahn (1966: 44-82), Rogerson (1978; 1983), Culley (1981), Evens (1982), Lang (1983; 1985), Leach (1983; 1985: 1-20) and Eilberg-Schwartz (1990: 1-21). Anthropological insights are particularly evident in the commentaries on Leviticus by Porter and Wenham.

2.   His major work was *The Religion of the Semites* (1889; 3rd rev. edn with further notes by S.A. Cook in 1927). His life and work have been reviewed by Peters (1968), Beidelman (1974) and Rogerson (1979).

3.   His *The Golden Bough* (1890; 3rd edn, 1911–15) is generally used in the abridged version (1922).

rather than the cult.[1] Nevertheless, social or structural anthropologists[2] have adapted structuralist ideas to their own questions and have thereby illuminated aspects of the way societies interpret the world in which they live.

Despite the fact that the Bible is a text and not a living culture,[3] there is a growing consensus that anthropological insights can help to clarify important Priestly ideas. So far, biblical scholars have not used anthropological studies extensively in the investigation of Priestly texts, and several essays written by anthropologists have met with criticism.[4] However, the challenge to understand the texts remains, and any approach which deals with central questions of meaning and interpretation deserves careful consideration. With reference to Leviticus, Childs remarks:[5]

> Many of the large questions once posed so forcefully by W.R. Smith have not again been addressed, but the more modest, limited concern with specific terminology will certainly provide a solid foundation for dealing with the broader issues.

And Blenkinsopp sets out a comprehensive challenge at the end of an important article on P:[6]

> P is not, of course, a fieldworker's transcript of ancient ritual and myth but the product of priestly and scribal piety and learning. A study of its structure suggests, nonetheless, that beneath the surface one can still make out the contours of an encompassing mythic pattern. It is also possible to interpret the ritualism of P as embodying a concern for man's concrete existence in relation to the cosmos, his corporeality, the significance of

---

1. Wilson (1984: 22). Surveys of structural interpretations of OT texts include Barton (1984a: 104-207), Culley (1985), and Mayes (1989).

2. The different branches of anthropology are distinguished by Leach (1982: 13-54) and Honigmann (1973). Structural anthropology is often linked closely to the writings of Claude Lévi-Strauss.

3. Lévi-Strauss does not consider that the Bible contains the sort of material which an anthropologist can appropriately study, but others disagree (Leach 1983: 21-22; Mayes 1989: 1-3).

4. Leach's studies of biblical texts and themes (e.g. Leach 1970; Leach and Aycock 1983a) have attracted much criticism (e.g. Emerton 1976).

5. Childs (1979: 183). He also supports the social-anthropological view of the purity laws as part of a total symbol system (Childs 1985: 87).

6. Blenkinsopp (1976: 291-92). His article is limited to literary structures in P, but does not exclude other perspectives. Others note the same deficiency in Old Testament study (e.g. Worgul 1979: 4-5, 12).

> bodily states, his entire existence on the temporal and spatial axis. . . It goes without saying that a theology of P incorporating such insights still remains to be written.

This study is in part a response to this challenge. It remains rooted in the field of Old Testament studies, and it is readily acknowledged that the anthropological perspective is based on the secondary literature. Its value has been found not to lie in specific methods and explanations, since there is generally as wide a divergence of opinions on these in anthropological study as in Old Testament study.[1] Rather, the insights of anthropologists have provided inspiration for new questions and new ways of looking at familiar material.

In this chapter, some of the concepts and models which have proved useful in recent anthropology are introduced and used to illuminate the holiness spectrum (§3.2). Some older anthropological terms are critically examined in the light of newer perspectives and, where possible, reinterpreted positively from a structural perspective (§3.3). The value of structural insights is then tested by a closer look at the concepts of purity and impurity (§3.4), and the rules of mourning and mixtures (§3.5).

3.2 *New Perspectives from Anthropology*

3.2.1 *Some Recent Perspectives*
Modern studies of religion from an anthropological perspective are often marked by an interest in the way in which a culture orders and structures the world. Every culture has a history, but this is often unknown and may be of little significance in unlocking the puzzle of how a society perceives the world and lives in it. The structural anthropologist is concerned above all with the way an organized world-view links the individual, the community, and the natural world. This world-view is generally reflected and sustained by the ritual and social life of the group.

'World-view' suggests a relatively stable set of categories and values through which experience is filtered and ordered conceptually.[2] It is

---

1. Despite their stature, Lévi-Strauss, Geertz, Douglas, Turner and Leach have not been without their critics, some of whom are referred to in the notes.

2. This may be variously called a world-view, a symbol-system, a root-metaphor, or a classification system.

helpful to distinguish between states and transitions,[1] and also whether these transitions are regular and repeated ones, or bring about permanent changes (§3.2.4). In particular, the character of purity, impurity and holiness in P can be clarified by a discussion of the underlying world-view that gives them significance. P is very similar to other societies, both ancient and modern, in which investigations into ideas of purity and impurity have considerably increased our understanding.[2]

3.2.2 *Classification and Symbolism*

The Holiness Spectrum represents a certain classification of the world. Structural anthropologists have found that the classification system of a culture often sheds light on its particular conception of the world.[3] An experience is defined and understood by being assigned to its proper place in the known order of things.[4] A socially agreed classification of experience provides the necessary stability and limits for human identity, social discourse and constructive thought.

The specific character of the classification varies from group to group. If the criteria for a classification are based upon clear-cut boundaries in the natural world, they are likely to be common to many societies. Other classifications vary widely from society to society, since there is freedom to construe and construct the world in

---

1. Turner (1967: 93-94). This duality has been expressed in many ways: religious thought and action, or belief and ritual (Dumont and Pocock 1959: 12-13); models of and for reality (Geertz 1979: 81); root-metaphors and key scenarios (Ortner 1973a); the 'statics of social systems' and its dynamics (Leach 1982: 224). This distinction is not the same as that between the synchronic and diachronic, or history and myth (which is at the heart of Lévi-Strauss' concern, e.g. 1966: 245-69).

2. These range from sophisticated large scale societies, to small scale traditional cultures (e.g. Tambiah 1969; Burton 1974; Ferro-Luzzi 1974; Ngubane 1976; Meiggs 1978; Hage and Hurary 1981). Specialists have employed anthropological insights in studying ancient Greece (e.g. Parker 1983), the New Testament (e.g. Newton 1985), the rabbinic writings (e.g. Neusner 1973; 1979), and the Early Church (e.g. Brown 1971).

3. For anthropological treatments of classification see above all the various writings of Needham (e.g. 1973; 1979) and Goody (1977). A seminal essay on the subject is by Durkheim and Mauss (1963).

4. This has been noted by philosophers (e.g. Langer 1957: 266-94), art historians (e.g. Gombrich 1977: 76), and sociologists (e.g. Berger 1977: 18-19), as well as anthropologists.

an agreeable way which is specific to a certain group at a particular time.[1] The classes can then point to significant aspects of social organization or religious belief. The classes and associated customs may seem peculiar and bizarre to the outside observer,[2] but the wider cultural context often makes sense of what is being expressed.[3] This larger context also serves to control interpretations of symbols and customs which are ambiguous, and often performed rather than explained.

The degree to which a bundle of beliefs reflects a coherent and systematic conception of the world varies from culture to culture, and even within a culture.[4] Some societies perceive the world in a more ordered and systematic way than others, and some groups or individuals may have an unusually unified view of things.[5] Specialist classes in a society develop a highly refined classification system in the sphere of their particular interests. However, old and new beliefs can also mingle inconsistently, thus making it difficult to set out an absolutely unified world-view.

The Priestly Writing displays an interest in classification (e.g. lists of clean and unclean animals, various types of sacrifices) that is found nowhere else in the Old Testament to the same extent.[6] The precision with which certain classes are defined has long indicated to scholars that P represents a specialist priestly class with sufficient leisure and

---

1.   Hunn (1977: 60-62). Similarly, Lyons (1977: 247-48) describes how language can be biologically or culturally salient for expressing an environment. Materialists stress the former, and idealists the latter (p. 240).

2.   One problem with the older style of anthropology (such as is associated with the name of Frazer) is that it brought together superficially similar customs which should have been related to the cultural context which gave them meaning.

3.   See for example the essay by Smith (1972a).

4.   Douglas (e.g. 1973; 1975; 1978a) has attempted to classify different societies according to the strength of their external boundaries ('group') and their internal coherence ('grid'). However, her theory is based on a linguistic model which concentrates on the individual speaker, and it is doubtful whether 'grid' is a very useful social concept (Wuthnow *et al.* 1984: 122-28). Although her system has influenced a number of biblical studies (e.g. Pilch 1981; Malina 1986), her typology has not found general acceptance among anthropologists and will not be employed further here.

5.   Note Turner's dependence on one special informant (1967: 131-50).

6.   In the ancient Near East there was an extensive priestly literary tradition with a sophisticated knowledge of lists and tables (cf. Kingsbury 1963; Levine and Hallo 1967; Goody 1977: 82-103).

incentive to reflect intensively on the world.[1] Von Rad stresses the importance of this wider perspective:[2]

> Our understanding of all the cultic activities so far mentioned would, however, be left hanging in the air, unless we were to see them in relationship to ideas which are much more comprehensive. They have their place and significance in and for a world which in God's sight was divided into clean and unclean, holy and secular, blessing and curse. For Israel this tension and polarity was a basic datum of all life—it was so universally valid that it had to be assumed as present and taken for granted even where it is not mentioned *expressis verbis*, as for instance in the prophets.

Since treatments of the cult often refer to its symbolism, I should explain my view of the relation of symbolism to some of the themes introduced so far.[3] A symbol will typically refer to more than one area of experience, and provides a focus for these different frames of reference to interact and illuminate one another. Simple symbols (sometimes called signs) have a one to one correspondence between the symbol and what is symbolized. The most interesting symbols, however, succeed in 'condensing' several areas of life into a symbolic unity, and the symbol outside a context (and often in it) is ambiguous.[4]

Metaphors, which may be regarded as linguistic symbols, also relate two or more areas of experience. One of these areas is the more concrete and basic, and 'grounds' the more obscure area in human

1. Levine (1963) discusses the refined priestly classification of sacrificial animals. Elsewhere there is no need for such accurate classification, and consequently the same words have a broader semantic field. Similarly, G.A. Anderson (1987) points out that the same Hebrew word may have markedly different meanings in a priestly sacrificial context and a non-priestly context.

2. Von Rad (1962: 272).

3. This discussion of symbol is necessarily very limited. See further Firth (1973), Sperber (1975) and Ricoeur (1967; 1976).

4. This is the language of Turner (1967: 19-47). He introduces the notion of a multivalent or multi-referential symbol, since it refers to several areas of experience. In a ritual the most important and recurring symbols may be called 'dominant ritual symbols'. Ortner's (1973a) interesting classification distinguishes 'summarizing symbols' (which synthesize a complex system of ideas, e.g. the American flag) from 'elaborating symbols', which include root metaphors and key scenarios and help to sort out ideas and translate them into action. Holiness in its broader meaning perhaps comes closest to being a summarizing symbol, pointing to all that God requires of Israel.

experience.[1] It is often the case that several symbols or metaphors are
linked together within a larger system. A powerful 'root metaphor'
can provide the basis for a great number of derivative perspectives. If
several symbols are manipulated in a ritual by analogy to a natural
process (e.g. washing), then it can be useful to speak of an extended
metaphor or model (e.g. washing is a model for ritual purification). It
is a reminder that symbol are usually not isolated or static, but form
part of a complex symbol-system.[2]

In the Priestly cult, the purification model is particularly important.
Purity and impurity are powerful symbols for social and religious
values, based on the presence and absence of the ritual equivalent of
dirt. The process of purification from defilement provides a valuable
model for the offering of a sacrifice. Blood corresponds to water, and
purifies from impurity in the ritual context of sacrifice.

A sophisticated understanding of metaphor and symbol promises to
provide a basis for the critical evaluation of traditional studies of
symbolism. Modern treatments of cultic symbolism are generally very
cautious, partly due to a reaction against the simplistic interpretations
of pre-critical exegetes.[3] A symbol or ritual action is open to a number of interpretations, and it is often difficult to choose just one.
However, structural anthropology and linguistics encourage us to look
at the overall context for a guide to an interpretation. Symbols, like
words, should be interpreted together in a symbol-system rather than
as isolated units of meaning. This should help to eliminate arbitrary,
anachronistic or unlikely explanations.

3.2.3 *Grading*

When an object (or person) is classified according to a particular trait,
it is assigned to one of several classes or levels, and these are often
ordered in a certain hierarchy or priority. At the simplest level, there

---

1. Lakoff and Johnson (1980: 118) list some of these basic experiences as
follows: 'physical orientations, objects, substances, seeing, journeys, war, madness,
food, buildings, etc.'. Most of these take on central symbolic significance in the
Priestly cult.

2. Black (1962). The interrelation can be static or dynamic. Ortner (1973a:
1340) distinguishes an orientation (cf. root metaphor) from a strategy (cf. model).
Strategies are 'programs for orderly social action in relation to culturally defined
goals'.

3. See Childs on the problem of determining the symbolism of the Tabernacle
(1974: 537-39).

are only two alternatives, comprising a binary opposition.[1] For example, in certain contexts, a male is valued more highly than a female (e.g. Lev. 27.1-8). If an object can belong to one of several binary classes, then a more complex classification is possible. For example, the cultic value of an animal depended both upon its sex (male/female) and its size (large/small cattle).

However, other dimensions of experience are more nuanced, and there may be several classes.[2] As well as a black/white dichotomy, there can be a continuum or spectrum with several serially ranked elements.[3] The complete spectrum will have two extreme poles, but there can be other levels in between. In certain cases, a nuanced grading may be unnecessary, in which case a simple binary class is formed. The Tabernacle exhibits several grades of holiness, but defilement threatened any or all grades of holiness.

Both kinds of grading may be illustrated from a chart drawn up by Douglas Davies.[4]

Sacred ———————————————————— Profane			
God	Priesthood	People	Gentiles
Temple		Camp	Wilderness
Life			Death
Being	Transient	Existence	Nothingness
Order ——————————— Ritual ——————————— Chaos			

However, some of these categories are general and not directly related to the Priestly texts. The following table lists some of the more evident binary oppositions in P, some of which are developed more fully than others.[5]

1. Binary classification has been exploited to an extraordinary degree by Lévi-Strauss (e.g. 1966). See also Evans-Pritchard (1956: 231-38). Lists of binary oppositions pertaining to different cultures are given in Needham (1973).

2. Leach (1979: 166), Lyons (1977: 281-90).

3. 'Spectrum' is an appropriate description, since it is a metaphor taken from the behaviour of light. From the human perspective, the visible spectrum can be split into a range of colours (the various classes or grades). These may be related to one another in various ways (cf. Lyons 1977: 283, 290).

4. Davies (1977: 394).

5. Few biblical scholars have explored polarity in the Bible, though see Bertholet (1948) and Goldingay (1984; 1987: 191-99). Wenham (1982: 123) writes of 'two poles of existence' (positive/negative) in the OT: God/Chaos, Life/Death, Order/Disorder, Normality/Deformity, Cleanness/Uncleanness.

Dimension	Dominant Category	Subordinate Category
Spatial	centre	periphery
	east	south, west, north
	visible	invisible
	untouchable	touchable
Personal	priest	non-priest
	leader	ordinary Israelite
	clean	unclean
	male	female
Sacrificial	male	female
	large	small
	normal	blemished
	clean	unclean
Festival	feast-day	fast-day
	festival Day	ordinary day
	Sabbath	ordinary day

Holiness is often characterized by several of the features in the dominant category, while impurity is often associated with the subordinate classes. The complex and nuanced ideas of holiness and impurity that this leads to are explored in the rest of the study. Items of particular significance can possess multiple-holiness or multiple-pollution (cf. §3.3.4).[1] Holiness and uncleanness are not in themselves fixed properties; an object or person is holy or unclean by being associated with one pole or other of the Holiness Spectrum.

It is possible to take a second look at the Holiness Spectrum from this perspective. A dimension (§1.5.2) consists of a number of objects of the same class. These manifest graded values, with the 'holy' pole being regarded more positively than the 'unclean' pole. The normal state of affairs is in the middle, where clean, lay Israelites go about their everyday work inside or outside the camp. The four dimensions can be related to one another by their similar grading in the vertical axis. For example, the extreme holiness which the high priest embodies (the personal dimension) is matched by the extreme holiness of the innermost sanctum (the spatial dimension). As a result, it is often possible to draw up a grid, which sets out the gradings along the

---

1.   Needham (1975; 1979: 65-67; 1980: 51-60) develops the idea of 'polythetic classification', in which several factors contribute to the definition of an object or quality, but none of them are conclusive.

various dimensions (the horizontal axis), and the correlations between them (the vertical axis). Of course, the table that results (§1.5.3) must not be interpreted rigidly (§3.3.1).

3.2.4 *Ritual and* Rites de Passage

A person's or community's life includes important changes, and these are often affirmed, brought about, corrected and evaluated in ritual. In P, various rituals mark the transitions between a number of the states in the Holiness Spectrum, particularly the clean and the unclean (purification) and the clean and the holy (consecration). The rituals in P have a wide variety of forms and functions, but many of them share the same structured pattern. Given the rarity of explanations in P, it is valuable to seek whether anthropological literature on similar rituals can shed light.[1]

A promising theoretical framework has been provided by van Gennep, who early this century described a large number of rites marking the transition from one stage of life to another.[2] He proposed that these *rites de passage* generally have three phases (the separation from the initial state, the transition state, and the final adoption of the new state), which together effect the transition:

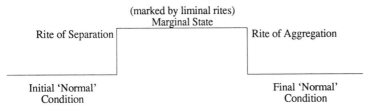

Specific rites occur at certain times, and special prohibitions and restrictions (or taboos §3.3.4) have to be obeyed in the marginal state (cf. the ordination of priests, §5.2.1). *Rites de passage* satisfy the psychological needs of the individual undergoing a life crisis, as well as the needs of the community for creating and maintaining throughout the generations an agreed set of values and ways of life. Of particular interest is the observation that what is appropriate for the marginal

---

1. For bibliography on ritual see Grimes (1985). Important studies include Zuesse (1975, 1979, 1987), Grimes (1982), Jennings (1982). The writings of Turner (e.g. 1967, 1969, 1974) have been especially influential.

2. Van Gennep (1960: 11). Turner (1967: 93-111) in particular has developed his insights. See also Leach (1976: 78).

state is often in opposition to what is the rule in everyday life. In P, this is apparent in various laws (e.g. concerning clothes and food).

The same scheme can elucidate the structure of other rituals, such as purifications and sacrifices (cf. Chapter 6). However, the purpose of a simple purification rite is not a permanent transition to another state, but the restoration of an original state of affairs.[1] The length of time spent in the marginal state may vary from one day to the rest of life.

3.3 *Older Concepts*

3.3.1 *Primitive Societies*
Certain customs and ideas found in P are commonly traced to an earlier stage of the Israelite or Canaanite cult. While this is a valid enterprise, it can be dangerous when bound to an evolutionary theory of development that presumes that an earlier 'primitive' stage of thought preceded a later 'religious' understanding.[2] The quest for the origins of religion was a favourite exercise of the earlier anthropologists. Frazer, for example, supposed that people originally thought magically (§3.3.2), and only later did this become personal religion and, in the fulness of time, rational scientific thought.[3] Today, his confident reconstruction has been thoroughly demolished, but his ideas still lie behind many treatments of the cult in the Old Testament and the ancient Near East.[4] Although discussion of magic and taboo based upon these old notions has diminished in recent years, the inadequacies of the whole framework of thought still do not seem to have been established.

There are, to be sure, significant differences between 'primitive' or 'traditional' societies, and modern ones, but the character of these differences needs to be formulated carefully. The features associated

1. Gorman (1989: 52-55) distinguishes between rites of passage, founding rituals, maintenance rituals and restoration rituals.

2. Frazer has been criticized on a large number of points by anthropologists (e.g. Evans-Pritchard 1965: 27-29; Blythin 1970; Douglas 1966: 22-28; 1982), philosophers (Wittgenstein 1979), and scholars of comparative religion (Smith 1973; Gaster 1959).

3 E.g. from the conclusion to the abridged *Golden Bough*, 'the movement of the higher thought, so far as we can trace it, has on the whole been from magic through religion to science' (Frazer 1922: 711).

4. E.g. the writings of Mowinckel, Eichrodt, Snaith and Elliger.

with so-called 'primitive'[1] societies may often be found in the modern world—albeit severely attenuated—and *vice versa*.[2] The differences between ancient and modern society should be related to economic, social and educational factors, rather than a different kind of thinking or belief. Humanity is a unity, and this is assumed by anthropologists as they attempt to make sense of peculiarities (puzzling to us, not to the 'natives'!) by paying close attention to the complete cultural context.[3]

Confusion and misunderstanding can arise when the classification system of an interpreter differs from that of the text or culture under interpretation (§3.2.2). It is often difficult to understand another culture's language and symbols because it represents a different classification of the world. An explanation in one set of categories (anthropologists speak of the 'native' point of view) can easily mislead someone working with another set (the 'observer's' point of view).[4] For example, a modern interpreter will be familiar with the distinction between fish and birds, but not between clean and unclean animals, except in a hygienic sense. The hygienic classification of clean and unclean may be familiar to us, but is misleading when interpreting a society that uses purity concepts as part of a sophisticated symbol-system.

However, an outside perception is not necessarily a disadvantage. Indeed, it is often the anthropologist from another culture who is able to work out the logic of a world-view. For the 'natives', the underlying logic of the culture's beliefs and rituals may well be implicit and unrecognized.[5] It is a valid goal to formulate explanations in a systematic

---

1. 'Traditional' is perhaps a less prejudicial term, which stresses that small-scale societies of today are not necessarily identical to the 'primitive' cultures which existed before the rise of civilization. See now the comprehensive discussion in Eilberg-Schwartz (1990).

2. See the amusing satire of Miner (1956). Also Douglas (1970: 28-39).

3. Leach (1982: 15). The problem of the rationality of primitive cultures has attracted extensive debate (cf. Wilson 1970; Finnegan and Horton 1973; Douglas 1975).

4. A distinction is sometimes made between emics (the study of the native point of view) and etics (the observer's point of view). But see the comments by Runciman (1983: 119) and Feleppa (1986).

5. Turner (1967: 26-27). An analogy is often drawn with language: a person may be linguistically competent without being able to analyse grammar (Needham 1973: xx).

form which would meet approval from a native. However, it is also important not to impute too much system and precision to a culture.[1] Needham rightly emphasizes that a structuralist analysis is mneumonic and suggestive, and that it refers to a collective representation rather than to individual perceptions. Contextual interpretation remains of first importance.[2]

3.3.2 *Magic*

There are a number of Priestly rituals, or elements of them, which are often described as 'magical'. The concepts of magic and religion which lie behind this imposed classification are complex, and they have been the cause of a great deal of confusion.[3] Many different criteria have been suggested to identify the presence of authentic magical rather than religious acts,[4] but the effort has not proved very fruitful. The consensus opinion amongst biblical scholars concerning the meaning of the term seems to be that magic is marked by a belief in an automatic efficacy, and is found where there are attempts to manipulate or coerce God by certain means.[5] This represents an extremely materialistic and mechanical interpretation of ritual, and is in danger of abstracting the symbol or rite from a complex multi-stranded setting. Social, religious and psychological truths embodied in symbol and ritual cannot really be reduced to a simple interest in

---

1.	Goody (1977) points out that lists, tables and written structures are a feature of literary, rather than less developed cultures, and there is a temptation to fill in all the blanks in a system that is not fully worked out in a culture. For example, Wenham (1979b: 177 n. 34), extends the spatial dimension to include Sheol. But this does not appear to be a significant concept in P (on Num. 16.30, 33 see Budd 1984: 184).

2.	Needham (1973: xxiv-xxx).

3.	The difficulty in distinguishing magic and religion has brought about the use of terms such as 'magico-religious'. Thus van Gennep (1960: 13-14) considers the magico-religious to consist of theory (religion) and technique (magic), though these two aspects are inseparable. 'Magic' employed as an explanatory category often indicates more about the beliefs of the commentator than the culture being described, and there is rarely significant correspondence between the observer's magical categories of explanation and the native vocabulary. Leach (1982: 133) considers that 'the word has no meaning whatever'.

4.	Goode (1949) argues that these show some sort of divergence, but even this may be to claim too much. See also the survey in Rogerson (1978: 46-53).

5.	E.g. Levine (1974: 77-91) and Yamauchi (1983: 174-77).

manipulating the world, although effective achievement of goal may be one of the concerns.[1]

The roots of this conception may be traced back to Frazer, who distinguished two classes of magic. Homeopathic magic was marked by a 'law of similarity', and contagious magic depended on a 'law of contact'.[2] Rituals and symbols are thus understood in a narrowly mechanistic way (by analogy with the 'laws of nature'), so that a feature or action is intended to bring about a result in the same way that a cause brings about an effect. Despite the criticisms made above, it may be possible to align the two types with the static and dynamic aspects of a cultural system (§3.2.1). Homeopathic magic points to the symbolic correlations between the dimensions of a classification system, whereas contagious magic refers to the symbolic character of ritual action, in particular touch (§3.3.3).[3]

Hence sin, impurity and holiness can be represented in material and physical ways, but this does not mean that they were 'literally' considered as things. All conceptual language can be related to basic experiences of the world, and metaphors can lose their conscious association with the original experience so that they become conventional.[4] But this does not make them 'literal', and in their own terms they are adequate to represent and direct participation in the social and religious aspects of life.[5]

1. Geertz (1980) discusses the shift from mechanical cause-and-effect models to those which draw their explanatory categories from other fields (e.g. life as a play, a game, a text). The latter increasingly characterizes the interpretative methods of the social sciences and anthropologists often draw upon other disciplines, such as linguistics (Lévi-Strauss), drama (Victor Turner), or sociology (Mary Douglas).

2. Frazer (1922: 11-12). On the background see Fraser (1990: 17-32, 119-35).

3. 'An authentic symbol strives for approximation to that which it symbolizes' (Blythin 1970: 54). 'When he had finished investigating magic, Frazer had done no more than to name the conditions under which one thing may symbolize another' (Douglas 1966: 23). Symbolic actions are based on 'persuasive analogies' (Tambiah 1973).

4. Lakoff and Johnson (1980). The difficulties anthropologists have in determining the extent of conventional language is discussed by Keesing (1985).

5. It is also possible that the Frazer school overestimated the effectiveness of the mechanics of the ritual. It has been pointed out that in traditional societies, the security and reliability of people is basic, and it is the physical world which is unknown, dangerous and arbitrary. In our technological and pluralist society, this order has been reversed.

Even at the level of causal action, the agnostic and objective ideals of historical research can be in danger of excluding *a priori* the divine and spirit world.[1] There is a fine line between impersonal magical manipulation and the assurance of a response based on a reliable knowledge of God's character.[2] Contemporary rituals and prayers can seem equally automatic and divorced from personal devotion. But it is doubtful whether an authentic individual response to God is the chief concern of the Priestly authors. If the main concern is conformity to the social order of things, it is not necessary to distinguish between the personal and the impersonal.

This perspective clarifies the Old Testament concern in its references to sorcery, divination, and other 'magical' practices. In this context, 'magic' is a reported reality rather than a pre-emptive explanation.[3] The denial of such practices is not a condemnation of a different mode of efficacy, but a judgment about the illegitimate character of the power behind the ritual.[4] A 'magical' symbol is perfectly acceptable, if the source of its power is Israel's God, if it is consistent with his character, and if its purpose is integrated into his will.[5]

3.3.3 *Contagion*

The transmission of holiness and impurity by touch was particularly puzzling to early investigators, and was explained by means of various analogies. Frazer's classification of contagious magic, defined by the Law of Contact or Contagion, is based on physical models.[6] This could be a medical metaphor (impurity as a contagious disease),[7] or a

---

1. Steiner (1956: 145-46). Leach's neglect of the supernatural dimension is a fatal flaw in his discussion of symbolism, magic and religion (e.g. Leach 1976: 29-32; 1985: 224-27).

2. Gaster (1959: 171, 176) and Rowley (1967: 140-41). Douglas (1966: 59) suggests 'for Magic let us read Miracle', and draws attention to the efficacy of the sacraments (Douglas 1973: 26-27).

3. This is the language of Runciman (1983: 65, 81-85), whose work is discussed by Rogerson (1985).

4. Fishbane (1971).

5. The pejorative use of 'magic' has also affected studies of non-Israelite religion (Anderson 1987: 1-19, 123-26; Hillers 1985).

6. Frazer's (1922: 38) choice of material medium ('like the ether of modern physics') has been advisedly abandoned!

7. Indicated by the very word 'contagion'. The impurity of certain 'contagious' diseases (especially leprosy) encouraged this conception.

physical one (holiness as electricity),[1] and others have been added in recent years.[2] However, these common analogies encourage the reduction of a highly symbolic action to a simple physical event. Holiness and impurity are conceived as substantial forces or substances, which can be manipulated according to impersonal and automatic rules.[3]

It is necessary to stress that the proper context for understanding the symbolism of touch is social and theological,[4] not psychological ('primitive thought') or physical (efficacious magic). The effective role of touch for the individual and the community depends upon a common understanding of the social and divine order of things. The difficulty in understanding communicable holiness and impurity from our perspective is that the cultural context that makes sense of these concepts no longer exists with the same force. Our realities are more abstract or more physical, but the Holiness Spectrum can provide a guide to the proper cultural context of the Priestly world-view.

One special gesture involving touch is the laying on of hands (*smk*, סמך). The meaning of the action is disputed, particularly in the sacrificial act (§6.1.2), but in the light of its significant social and religious role (Lev. 24.14; Num. 27.23) it should not be understood mechanically. Similarly, 'magical' belief in the efficacy of a word (especially a blessing or a curse) is better described as faith in the

---

1.   Robertson Smith (1927: 151). The analogy has been considered particularly appropriate for the ark's holiness (Proksch 1933: 91-92). Harrison (1980: 168-69) mentions a theory that the ark was electrically charged! The influence of the analogy on anthropologists is discussed by Needham (1977: 82-84) and Keesing (1985: 205).

2.   In the context of explaining the mechanism of atonement, impurity has been interpreted as dirt which may be removed by blood acting as detergent (Milgrom 1983a: 87; Wright 1987: 34-38, 77), as a magnetic force attracted to the sanctuary (Milgrom 1983a: 79-80), or as a hostile demonic force attacking the sanctuary (Levine 1974: 77-78). The analogies are often mixed, adding to the confusion.

3.   The positive character of a person who possesses the power of contagious holiness is sometimes called *mana*, in contrast with the negative force of pollution. The term is still occasionally found in biblical studies (e.g. Füglister 1977: 157, 162; Müller 1978: 594), but is given short shrift by most anthropologists (e.g. Steiner 1956: 106-15; Evans-Pritchard 1965: 33, 110; Philsooph 1971; Keesing 1984; Boyer 1986).

4.   Thus it is not surprising that the scope of contagion changes with time. In an important article Milgrom (1981c) traces how changes through time tend to keep in step with the beliefs and behaviour of the people.

working of the supernatural being who is invoked.[1] In the context of the Priestly world-view, both divine and human parties are agreed that certain things happen after contact, and the effectiveness and reality of this action is on a par with that of other spheres of life.[2]

With regard to the Holiness Spectrum, contagion is one way in which the special character of the extreme poles of experience is marked, whether of the holy or the unclean. The similarities between holiness and impurity arise not from an original identity or a common essence,[3] but because they are potent opposites with enormous social and theological significance. Meeting God and meeting death are both momentous events that profoundly touch a person's life. The laws of contagion are a means by which this truth is expressed and regulated.

3.3.4 *Taboo*

The concept of taboo shares the same problems of definition and interpretation as magic and contagion. For Robertson Smith, taboos comprised rules about contagion which stemmed from an earlier and inferior stage of superstition.[4] He explained the similarities between holiness and pollution by the assumption that they were originally the same thing. Frazer defined taboo as 'negative magic', and in line with his physical analogy, compared a taboo to an electrical insulator, which could prevent a dangerous discharge of power from taking place.[5] The psychological bent of the early anthropologists also led to

1. Thiselton (1974), Tambiah (1968, 1973). The material and objective character of words can be understood in terms of the similar way that words and things can affect those whom they touch. The social dimension of speech is acknowledged in law (e.g. Lev. 24.10-23).

2. The effectiveness of performative words and rituals in a particular social and religious context of meaning is stressed by anthropologists, and in linguistics has been developed by speech-act theory (Lyons 1977: 725-38).

3. As thought by Robertson Smith (1927: 446) and Frazer (1922: 223). Feldman (1977: 63-72, 99-104) points out 'patterns of paradox' between holiness and impurity, but this is not the same as original identification.

4. See especially Robertson Smith (1927: 152-64), whose view is discussed by Steiner (1956: 50-58). Biblical scholars have written of 'primitive' or 'ancient' or 'vestigial' taboos.

5. Frazer (1922: 19-20, 223). Compare Levine (1987: 244), who understands taboo as 'the negative dimension of holiness—its dangers, its restrictiveness, and its insulation from the profane'.

the source of taboo being traced to fear, often of spirits.[1]

A wide range of cultic rules were subsumed under the concept of taboo by these earlier scholars, and this interpretative tradition continues today.[2] However, the theoretical basis for its use is rarely explicit, and it often means little more than 'cultic prohibition'.[3] The difficulty arises when certain prohibitions are separated out from the rest in accordance with some prior notion of taboo. In these cases, the classification may well say more about the investigator than about that which is being investigated.[4]

Despite the negative and evolutionary overtones of the word, it is possible to reinterpret taboo in a similar way to magic and contagion. To call something taboo is not to explain it, but to point to the larger structure of rules and social boundaries in which that prohibition finds its home. Zuesse writes, 'Taboo is the structural behaviour of culture, and all cultures are sustained by taboos'.[5] It points to a system of prohibitions and sanctions by which the social and religious structure of a society is maintained. The full cultural context of a taboo is involved, 'In that full context taboos are rational, or perhaps rather supra-rational, since they involve not merely the cognitive but also the physical, moral, and spiritual levels of experience'.[6] In P, rules of taboo keep the various classes of the Holiness Spectrum distinct from one another, and reinforce the normative classification system which it

1.   Webster (1942) writes, 'Who shall interpret the fancies, tricks and childish guesses of the primitive mind'. This theory is found particularly apposite for mourning customs (reviewed and rejected by Feldman 1977: 3-16).

2.   Snaith in his writings (1944, 1967), following Frazer (1903: 17), applies the term to the Nazirite, Sabbath rules, impurity from corpses and childbirth, and unclean animals. Blood is often so described (e.g. Snaith 1967: 84). Milgrom (1981a: 285) mentions the taboos of mixtures, and observes that 'a garment of mixed fabrics is also taboo because it is contagiously sacred'.

3.   E.g. Haran (1978: 175, 183, 186, etc.).

4.   Compare Gottwald's (1979: 545-46, 550) characteristic socio-economic interpretation of taboo (cf. Rogerson 1985: 254-55).

5.   Zuesse (1974: 493). He also relates taboo to sacrifice: 'The structure of sacrifice *is* taboo. . . Sacrifice in one or another of its forms is necessary everywhere to restore harmony destroyed by a breach of taboo' (p. 498).

6.   Zuesse (1974: 494-95). Leach (1964) in an influential essay proposes a more idealist position by treating experience as a continuum upon which the human mind imposes classes separated by taboos (see the criticisms by Halverson 1976 and Howe 1981). But writers have pointed to the importance of natural boundaries (§3.2.2), and a shared prelinguistic knowledge (Hallpike 1979: 69-71).

embodies. For P, the taboos could apply to all Israel (e.g. the dietary rules), or be status-specific (e.g. the high priest may not marry a widow).

Conformity to the rules is largely a matter of habit, but explicit sanctions reinforce obedience. It is dangerous to cross boundaries,[1] since the transgression of a norm can provoke a reaction from whoever or whatever is associated with the preservation of the order, whether demons,[2] God (or the gods), nature or society. The identification of the agent in this reaction is often ambiguous or undefined,[3] and more than one sanction can operate.[4] The primary concern is often the preservation of order through the appropriate retribution or ritual (§3.2.4), rather than the consequences incurred by overstepping the bounds.

3.3.5 *Summary*
The older paradigm, which has in the past dominated the interpretation of cult and religion in both anthropology and biblical studies, is inadequate in many respects. It was based on mistaken or one-sided views of primitive mentality, efficacious magic, material contagion and superstitious taboo. Its principal categories of explanation were therefore confused and confusing.

A structural approach, on the other hand, is often able to reread the evidence fruitfully in ways that do not assume an evolutionary scheme or a peculiar mode of thinking. The Priestly texts reflect a world-view delineated by taboos and rules of contagion and maintained by sanctions and corrective rituals. The static and dynamic aspects are unified by means of a symbol-system specific to the particular social and religious character of the priestly circle responsible for these texts.

---

1. 'One might say that taboo deals with the sociology of danger itself' (Steiner 1956: 20-21, cf. 146-47; Douglas 1966: 4; 1975: 288).

2. Taboos are sometimes traced to demonic sources, as in the commentary by Snaith (e.g. 1967: 69, 103). However, in P the demonic world occurs very rarely, and the world order depends unequivocably upon God.

3. The personal or impersonal character of 'retribution' in the Old Testament has been extensively discussed (Koch 1972). This objective and impersonal aspect may also be reflected in the passive or general words which describe the consequences of transgression (e.g. נשא את עונו, נכרת). See also §6.2.

4. Milgrom (1970a: 5-8) points out that death for an encroacher may come from God or man.

3.4 *Purity and Impurity*

3.4.1 *Theories of Purity and Impurity*

The general points made above may be illustrated by reference to three particular areas, each of which will have a part to play in the subsequent discussion. Purity and impurity are central terms in the Holiness Spectrum, and they require a more detailed consideration (§3.4). A number of laws concerning mourning customs (§3.5.1) and mixtures (§3.5.2) also bear upon the discussion.

The concept of purity and impurity in P is a difficult one, and has proved of great interest to anthropologists as well as biblical scholars. The laws which define who or what is clean or unclean (primarily Lev. 11–15)[1] have long puzzled commentators. Many different solutions have been proposed,[2] but the discussion in the previous section has indicated why many of these theories are inappropriate, as well as being insufficiently flexible to account for the range of the material.[3]

For example, the *hygienic theory* asserts that impurity should be closely related to disease or the danger of coming to bodily harm.[4] The diseases which may be caught from a pig (Lev. 11.7-8) can be described in great detail,[5] as can the medical advantages of washing (Lev. 15), quarantining a leper (Lev. 13), and even the doubled time of purification for a mother after the birth of a girl compared to a boy (Lev. 12).[6] But despite the exercise of considerable ingenuity, such 'medical materialism'[7] is hard pressed to span the range of

---

1.   Sometimes this section is known as the laws of cleanness (*Reinheitsgesetze*; Baentsch 1903: 353; Elliger 1966: 12-13). The 'laws of impurity' would perhaps be a better description.

2.   Surveyed by Döller (1917), Gispen (1948), Douglas (1966: 29-32) and Henninger (1975: 476-82).

3.   Comprehensiveness is Douglas's goal (1966: vii). The need for external controls to limit symbolic and allegorical fancy is stressed by Wenham (1979b: 168-69, 171) and Childs (1974: 538-39).

4.   Earlier authors of this opinion are reviewed by Döller (1917: 231-35).

5.   E.g. Cansdale (1970: 99), Harrison (1980: 124-26).

6.   Macht (1933). Harrison, in particular, expounds the 'hygienic legislation' (1980: 142) at every opportunity.

7.   The phrase is William James's (Douglas 1966: 32). Compare the economic materialism of Harris (1971: 31-48; 1986: 67-87), who argues that it was economically disadvantageous for Israel to breed the pig (or other unclean animals), rather than sheep, goats and cattle.

prohibitions or to find explicit support in the text.[1] It tends to impose modern rational and pragmatic concerns onto a complex cultural symbolism with quite different concerns.[2]

Another inadequate alternative is the *cultic theory*, according to which objects or actions of importance in pagan cults were declared unclean or defiling.[3] There are several references to the necessity for Israel to reject the religious practices of other nations, but these forbidden practices are not purity laws, and the defilement that they bring is of a different kind from that found in Leviticus 11–15.[4] In addition, the number of cases which may be explained in this way is small, and the evidence suggests that Israel shared most of its purity laws with other cultures, with which it shared much of this cultural symbolism. There is even less evidence that the source of impurity lies in demonic forces.[5]

3.4.2 *Structural Theories of Impurity*
Dissatisfied with these traditional theories, several authors have sought an understanding of purity and impurity inspired by concepts of classification and order. The stimulation for this line of investigation came largely from Mary Douglas's seminal volume *Purity and Danger*, which is influenced by the structural anthropological perspective. In one chapter she discusses the food laws of Leviticus 11 in relation to her broader understanding of anomaly and defilement.[6] Every culture

---

1. For incisive criticisms, see Wenham (1979b: 167-68).

2. When illness or disease was experienced, it was either accepted as an inevitable fact of life, or traced to God's judgment on disobedience (Lev. 26.25; Num. 12.10; outside P, Num. 11.33).

3. Milgrom (1963: 294-96). This perspective is found frequently in Noth's writings.

4. These are called 'danger beliefs' by Frymer-Kensky (1983: 404). In Lev. 20.25 the structure, not the content, of the food laws distinguishes Israel from the nations.

5. E.g. Döller (1917: 242-47), Snaith (1967: 69) and Levine (1974: 77-78). Lev. 16 should be considered exceptional, not typical (§7.4).

6. Douglas (1966: 41-57). The chapter contains several minor inaccuracies. For corrections see Carroll (1978: 341), Firmage (1990: 179-81), Milgrom (1990: 176-83). Houston (forthcoming) argues that שׁרץ (*šereṣ*) refers to number ('swarm', 'teem'), rather than mode of movement. This weakens Douglas's proposal that there is a normative form of movement for the three classes of fish, flesh and fowl.

has a particular classification of the world, which is necessary for social coherence and conceptual well-being. Unclean animals are those which offend in some way the proper mode of locomotion for the medium in which they exist (land, sea and air), and are thus anomalous in the Priestly classification system.

Extending her ideas to the opposite concept of holiness, Douglas defined this as wholeness and completeness. The external physical expression of holiness is a body perceived ideally as a perfect container. For the body with its boundaries and functions can stand for society. That which blurs the boundaries of the body (impurity or pollution) is anomalous, dangerous to the ordered society, and to be avoided (or at any rate purified). Bodily discharges are defiling because they break the perfect unity of the body, and hence orifices and bodily boundaries are focuses of intense anxiety, particularly in the presence of the holy.[1] Emissions and blemishes that spoil the perfection of the body therefore disqualify a person from approaching God.

A similar view was formulated independently in an essay by Jean Soler originally titled 'Sémiotique de la nourriture dans la bible'.[2] The norm for diet is vegetarianism, and only herbivores are clean. Carnivores and those which do not conform to the norm are unclean, including animals and people with blemishes. The dynamics of defilement are accounted for by extending this category, so that 'to the blemish must be added alteration, which is a temporary blemish'.[3] Death is the major pollution, because it is the most extreme alteration possible.

A modification of Douglas's view is proposed by Michael Carroll, who suggests that the unclean is characterized by 'those things anomalous with respect to the *Nature/Culture* distinction'.[4] Just as the body separates self from the world, so culture distinguishes humanity

---

1. Her emphasis on boundaries has been criticized, on the basis that they are often fuzzy (Murray 1983), or that anomalies are often innocuous (Needham 1979: 44-47). There are numerous exceptions to her rules, such as the snake (Feldman 1977: 51) and (with regard to the later development of Kashrut) the chicken (Alter 1979: 49).

2. Soler (1973). For another wide ranging, but rather unconvincing, structuralist treatment, see Kristeva (1982: 90-112).

3. Soler (1979: 133).

4. Carroll (1978: 345).

from the beasts. From Genesis, Carroll deduces that meat-eating is a cultural preserve of humans, so carnivores are unclean because they invade this category. He then applies the theory to other unclean things: vermin invade the home, sharks have no scales and leprosy distorts the human appearance, thereby blurring the boundaries between nature and culture.

Despite their freshness and originality, these essays have not escaped criticism, aimed both at their detail and at their theoretical basis.[1] Above all, Douglas does not distinguish clearly the Priestly concepts of holiness, purity and the various grades of impurity. She defines holiness and impurity abstractly,[2] but then seeks to relate them to texts that have a very concrete understanding of holiness and its transmission by contact.[3] The blemishes in priests and sacrifices do not make them unclean or even unholy (since they may eat of the most holy portions), but they do disqualify from participation in the cultic ritual. This could suggest a more rigorous application of the idea of normality for a serving priest, but it may be an *ad hoc* practical measure and insignificant in terms of the general picture.

Dan Sperber has examined carefully Douglas's views on classification and anomaly.[4] He concludes that anomalies are not necessary in the flexible process of developing a classification system.[5] Rather than focusing on the negative phenomenon of anomaly, he suggests that there is also a positive evaluation of exemplary animals, which embody the norm[6] and may be sacrificed. Animals that are particularly anomalous

1. Various criticisms of Douglas's approach are made by Leach (1971) and Edwards (1970). Other discussions include Isenberg and Owen (1977), Wuthnow *et al.* (1984: 77-132) and Morris (1987: 203-18).

2. E.g. 'Holiness means keeping distinct the categories of creation' (p. 53). 'To be holy is to be whole, to be one; holiness is unity, integrity, perfection of the individual and of the kind' (p. 53). The intellectual and conscious character of her idea of holiness is challenged by Alter (1979: 48).

3. For example, unclean animals do not transmit uncleanness and disqualify from temple worship. Only carcasses do this, and it did not matter whether they were of clean or unclean animals (Feldman 1977: 50 on Douglas 1966: 55).

4. Sperber (1975).

5. Meiggs (1978: 310) suggests that Douglas's anomalies are often examples of dirt and mess, rather than impurity.

6. This aspect is already present in Douglas's work, since she points out that 'Cloven-hoofed, cud-chewing ungulates are the model of the proper kind of food for a pastoralist' (1966: 54).

in comparison with them are labelled unclean.

Another major criticism of Douglas' work is that it assumes the priority of structural and classificatory notions, which are then worked out in social distinctions and laws. The order might well be the reverse: the categories are specifically designed to bring out distinctions significant on other grounds.[1] Folk classification systems are flexible enough so that anomalies are, strictly speaking, unnecessary.[2]

3.4.3 *Death and Impurity*

A second theory that has attracted widespread support by both anthropologists and biblical scholars is that impurity is linked to death in some way, whether directly or symbolically.[3] Many of the unclean animals and birds are carnivores, scavengers or omnivores.[4] The pig's omnivorous and scavenging habits may explain its special cultic association. It was sacrificed not because it was a sacred animal,[5] but because its uncleanness made it an appropriate offering to chthonic deities, or as a funerary sacrifice.[6]

This coheres with a Priestly concern to avoid death and all associated with it, a trait which is reflected in many texts in a great variety of ways.[7] Above all, corpse impurity has a special power and virulence (§§5.4.2, 6.3.2). Other sources of major impurity can be related to death, particularly the appearance of blood during menstruation and

---

1.   Bulmer (1967: 21), Carmichael (1976: 5 n. 15), Houston (forthcoming). Her view on the priority of criteria is supported by Milgrom (1990: 183-86).

2.   Sperber (1975).

3.   E.g. Dillmann (1886: 479), Paschen (1970: 63-64), Feldman (1977: 34-35), Füglister (1977: 157-60), Amorim (1985: 285) and Kiuchi (1987: 63-65). Von Rad (1962: 277) comments, 'every uncleanness was to some extent already a precursor of the thing that was uncleanness out and out, death'.

4.   Kornfeld (1965). Hunn (1979: 111) thinks that 18 or 19 out of 20 birds are carnivores or scavengers.

5.   As Robertson Smith (1927: 290-91) suggested.

6.   De Vaux (1971: 252-69), Houston (forthcoming). The ritual function of unclean items is noted by Douglas (1966: 159-61).

7.   An unusual text is Num. 35.29-34. Here the blood shed (cf. Gen. 9.5-6) by a murderer pollutes (חנף *hiph.*, v. 33) the land, and must be executed. The people must not allow atonement to be made (יכפר *pual*, v. 33) for the blood, for otherwise they would defile the land (v. 34, reading the plural תטמאו with the versions; cf. *BHS*). The language in this passage (e.g. כֹּפֶר v. 31) is legal and theological rather than cultic in the stricter sense (Janowski 1982: 159-62).

other discharges.[1] The symbolic equivalence between blood and death can be made in various ways, but it is clear that there is a close association of ideas.[2] Wasted semen not only decayed but, like menstruation, indicated the loss of a possible new life, and so could be counted as doubly decaying (Lev. 15.16-17).

The same stress is found if the opposite thesis is considered: that holiness and the cult have to do with life and the living God. God is the God of the living and not the dead, and promises life for the obedient, but death for those who disregard his laws. A number of the cultic symbols and rituals express the theme of life (§§4.6.1; 6.3).

3.4.4 *Modifications of the Structuralist Approach*

Neither the structuralist nor the death theory has proved completely persuasive. Many structuralist explanations use general concepts only indirectly related to the language and content of crucial texts.[3] Their abstract character also enables them to be manipulated almost at will. Death, on the other hand, is a central biblical concern and sufficiently concrete, yet it is uncertain that it can be a complete explanation or that it does justice to the classificatory interest evident in the Priestly material.

In many cases we simply do not know enough to be sure about the correct explanation of a purity law, or whether a single explanation is sufficient.[4] Life is often too complex and disorganized to be subordinated to a single intellectual structure,[5] or reduced to a dominant

1. According to the Mishnah, discharges from women are characterized by a continuing flow of blood (for men the equivalent is semen, *m. Zab.* 1–2).

2. Death can result from violent bloodshed, or the loss of blood in illness. Blood can also be tied to life, since life is lost when it is shed. Such multivalence is a frequent characteristic of powerful symbols (§3.2.2). Wenham (1983: 434), for example, calls both semen and blood 'life liquids', although it is likely that the symbolism is more ambivalent.

3. For example, Soler is able to unify disparate laws with the help of broad categories, such as 'cut' or 'blemish'. The excessive flexibility of explanatory categories is a familiar criticism of Lévi-Strauss, who has influenced Soler (Alter 1979: 48-49). Similarly 'nature' and 'culture' are notoriously hard to distinguish (though see below).

4. E.g. Driver (1902: 164), Hunn (1979: 112), Kirk (1981: 44-46).

5. 'Any cultural system is likely to exhibit anomalies, inconsistencies, haphazardly determined elements—to be governed, in other words, by a predominant syntax but not by an inviolable grammar' (Alter 1979: 49).

morbid perspective. In response to criticisms of her earlier work, Douglas suggested that various criteria could overlap and lead to multiple pollution (e.g. for the pig).[1] Hunn has helpfully pointed out two complementary aspects of symbolic anthropology: the idealist (e.g. a structuralist approach) and the materialist (e.g. 'death' explanations).[2]

Examples of these two types of explanation are often found for puzzling aspects of the Priestly purity system. Those creatures which are not immediately associated with death can be linked, with sufficient ingenuity.[3] The uncleanness arising from sexual intercourse is another puzzle (Lev. 15.18),[4] since the potential generation of a child might be considered life-enhancing and non-polluting.[5] Both structuralist and 'death' explanations have been given for this.

Thus an impurity could have an idealist, a materialist or a mixed rationale.[6] On the structuralist side, the bat is an anomalous mixture of what an animal is expected to be like (it has fur) and what a bird is (it flies).[7] The camel, the rock-badger, the hare and the pig, the unclean animals of Leviticus 11, are all sole representatives of their

---

1. Douglas (1975: 272). In another work she stresses the political-religious context of the Maccabean revolt during which this particular symbolism was reinforced (1970: 60-63). Botterweck (1977: 846) lists three factors: (1) the decline of the pig's natural habitat, (2) its exclusion on classificatory grounds, (3) Israelite avoidance of its cultic associations.

2. Hunn (1979: 112).

3. E.g. the bat, the camel or unclean fish. Kornfeld (1965: 136) traces the uncleanness of the camel to the death connotations of the wilderness it traverses. Carroll (1978: 344) proposes that the shark must be the paradigmatic unclean fish, although he admits that he has no evidence.

4. Sexual intercourse is defiling in many cultures (Döller 1917: 64-76).

5. Structuralist explanations include: (1) any bodily discharge destroys the wholeness of holiness (Douglas 1966: 51), (2) the function of the penis is ambiguous, producing both semen and waste (Whitekettle 1991: 43-44). 'Death' explanations are: (1) semen, as a 'life liquid', is lost (Wenham 1983: 433-34), (2) some semen is wasted in intercourse and will decay (Meiggs 1978: 312-13; Porter 1976: 120).

6. Wenham (1983: 433) subsumes normality/abnormality to the life/death contrast, but these may be complementary criteria for purity/impurity.

7. Professor J.R. Porter (personal communication) has pointed out that it is classified as a bird in Lev. 11. Its impurity could be due to its dirtiness, its distasteful flesh (Driver 1955: 7, 18) or its unclean dwelling places (Kornfeld 1965: 143). However, its position at the end of the list suggests some anomaly (Driver 1955: 18).

taxonomic orders or sub-orders in Palestine.[1] We should not necessarily regard the matter statistically. The classification system in Leviticus 11 could be a structuralist way of affirming 'life' values and could have developed over time to reflect different cultural situations, new perceptions and recent discoveries.[2] While the situation for any particular purity law or unclean animals can be disputed, the evidence is sufficient to suggest that we need to be open to a range of explanations.

Meiggs noted that not all bodily emissions were defiling and suggested that there was an additional 'death' factor, in that polluting substances should also decay.[3] Eilberg-Schwartz adds a criterion of uncontrollability.[4] This helps to explain why some emissions are taken up into the larger symbol system, and given a special significance through the purity laws.

To some extent, these two approaches reflect the traditional anthropological distinction between nature and culture.[5] Houston has sought to give due weight to both aspects.[6] Structural features which he notes are that the distribution of clean and unclean animals illustrate a grading in both horizontal and vertical dimensions. The ideal sacrificial and edible animals are located not too near and not too far.[7] Vertically, creatures in the sky (most birds) are more acceptable for sacrifice in the Canaanite world than creatures of the sea. The more material aspects of the food laws are found in the exceptions to this rule of grading. Birds of prey are unclean (the death factor). The monotheistic outlook prohibits sacrifice of ambiguous animals especially associated with death. Houston points out animals associated with the immediate living environment (e.g. dog, vermin) are inedible and

---

1. Hunn (1979: 112-14).

2. Hübner (1989) argues that the prohibition of eating pigs was an exilic innovation. Milgrom (1990: 189) suggests that the rules for animals were developed on discovering anomalies.

3. Meiggs (1978: 313). Furthermore, they must threaten to gain access to the body in some undesirable way. See also Henninger (1975: 430), Ellen (1979: 15), Frymer-Kensky (1983: 401), Murray (1983: 396), Needham (1979: 47).

4. Eilberg-Schwartz (1990: 186-88) notes that controllable bodily fluids tend to be less polluting than uncontrollable ones (e.g. menstrual blood, discharges).

5. E.g. Carroll (1978).

6. Houston (forthcoming).

7. The same pattern is found in the social domain with regard to marriage partners and the allowed degrees of consanguinity (see §5.2.4).

unclean; domestic animals are clean and fit for sacrifice (e.g. ox, sheep, goat), and wild animals may be clean or unclean, edible or inedible.[1]

3.5 *Two Examples*

3.5.1 *Mourning Customs*
The two polarities of life/death and normality/abnormality are closely related. The same God who orders the universe sets life in its midst, and a conformity to the world-order is necessary for life to flourish.[2] Life in society, cult and the world is the normal state of affairs, but death invades the world and destroys the proper order at every level. The uncleanness of the dead person indicates the incompatibility between the sphere of death and the living God.

The death of a person has fundamental social significance, affecting the close relatives. So it is understandable that they too can hardly avoid becoming unclean through contact with the corpse. This applies even to the priests, although the extent of the allowed impurity is limited (§5.2.4). The close connection between death and disorder is shown clearly by the mourning customs.[3] These assimilate the mourner to the dead in various ways, but this has positive as well as negative aspects. Mourning customs show with particular clarity the close association between death and disorder. The customs are symbolic expressions of death and the way it disrupts the normal order of things.

Limitation in time characterizes mourning customs, just as limitation in space and time characterizes the social effects of impurity. It allows an expression of grief as limited as the effects of death should be. Time serves to deal with corpse uncleanness, just as it serves to overcome the loss of the dead person to the community and individual. Mourning in other ways may be more extended, but it too is limited and eventually comes to an end. The purity laws and mourning rituals each in their own way contribute to the reconstruction of the

---

1. Correlations between food, purity and marriage laws are noted by Tambiah (1969) and Leach (1979: 165).

2. The Priestly theme of the blessing consequent upon conformity to the divine order is prominent in Gen. 1 and Lev. 26 (see Westermann 1968).

3. Spronk (1986) stresses the emotional and psychological rather than the social aspects (e.g. 'an act of sympathy of the living with the deceased, an expression of communion of the living with the dead', p. 245).

social and emotional order that death has disturbed. They provide a controlled framework for the powerful forces (such as death, menstruation and childbirth) which inevitably and unavoidably come upon a person, to be acknowledged and brought within the realm of cultural order and control.[1]

One of these customs, which is mentioned several times in P, is the untidying of hair. The symbolism of hair is rich, culturally variable and complex.[2] However, general considerations and the other mentions in P and the Bible provide a framework for interpretation. Hair is an appropriate symbol for several reasons, particularly because it grows continuously and it has to be groomed and cared for. The first feature implies that it can symbolize life,[3] and the second suggests a structural contrast between the ordered and groomed hair of everyday life and its disordered character in death, since the living concern for its care is no longer present.[4]

This symbolism is extended to include a person with a skin disorder (the $m^e\bar{s}\bar{o}ra'$, מצרע; cf. §5.4.2). The $m^e\bar{s}\bar{o}ra'$ experienced a kind of living death by being excluded from society and the cult (§5.4.2), and had to carry out mourning customs such as dishevelling the hair (וראשו יהיה פרוע, Lev. 13.45) and tearing the clothes (ובגדיו יהיו פרמים, v. 45). From the structural point of view, there is a contrast between the $m^e\bar{s}\bar{o}ra'$ and those bound up with the source of life (the ministering priests). The priests are forbidden to dishevel their hair in mourning while serving at the sanctuary (Lev. 10.6), but may do so on leaving (except for the high priest, who is forbidden to do this at any time, Lev. 21.10; §5.2.4).

If the $m^e\bar{s}\bar{o}ra'$ is healed, his or her hair is shaved (Lev. 14.8, 9). This probably represents a new start, the cessation of the period when the hair was dishevelled, and the beginning of a new life in the community (§6.3.3). Refraining from cutting the hair was a mark of taking a Nazirite vow (Num. 6.5), and probably marked the duration of one's vow. Cutting the hair indicated either the start of a renewed vow (Num. 6.9) or the resumption of normal life (Num. 6.18-19).

---

1. Henninger (1975: 473-74).
2. For an anthropological perspective see Firth (1973: 262-98).
3. Milgrom (1971b: 908), Pedersen (1940: 265). Hallpike (1969: 257) further suggests that the quantity of hair, its appearance in quantity at puberty and its disappearance in old age also reinforce the association with life.
4. Feldman (1977: 94).

The other common mourning customs can be analysed in similar ways, and appear in the same contexts. The wearing of torn clothes by the mourner (Lev. 10.6) and the *mᵉṣōraʿ* (13.45) expresses the way in which death destroys human dignity and rank, of which clothes are the supreme cultural medium. Priests are forbidden to do this while ministering in the sanctuary, and the special priestly garments are preserved throughout the generations (Exod. 29.29-30), and in this way they are appropriately associated with the God who lives for ever.

3.5.2 *Mixtures*

The laws about mixtures give substantial support to the importance of structural elements, but again, there are other factors to be taken into account. Lev. 19.19 sets out laws prohibiting the mixing of two kinds of animals, seeds and clothes. It has a close parallel in Deut. 22.9-11 (different seeds not to be sown together, ox and ass not to plough together, wool and linen not to be used in the same garment). If these laws are linked with others, then an intriguing pattern begins to emerge. There is a structural contrast between what is forbidden in the profane sphere and what is allowed in the realm of the cult (cf. Deut. 22.9, 'the crop and the yield will become holy'.[1] It is possible to set up a table of four kinds of mixtures, each of which exhibits two different kinds of behaviour:

Mixtures	Profane	Holy	Texts
seed/seed	forbidden	allowed	Lev. 19.19; Deut. 22.9
wool/linen	forbidden	allowed	Lev. 19.19; Deut. 22.11
animal/animal	forbidden	[forbidden]	Lev. 19.19; Deut. 22.10
human/animal	forbidden	[forbidden]	Exod. 22.19; Lev. 18.23; 20.15; Deut. 27.21

There are further hints that this structural contrast is valid for the Priestly conception. The priests wore clothes with mixed wool and

---

1. The most probable interpretation is that the crop will become the property of the sanctuary and the priests. Driver (1902: 252) notes that the verb (וקדש) is synonymous with היה קדש (e.g. Lev. 27.10, 21—a similar agricultural context). The allegorical interpretation by Carmichael (1982: 397-402) of the mixture laws in the light of the patriarchal narratives is unpersuasive. In line with the point of view adopted here, Houtman (1984) suggests that the laws reflect the desire to maintain the separate classes which make up the world-order.

linen weave (§5.2.3), but this is forbidden in the laws of mixtures, which are addressed to the general Israelite population. Num. 15.37-41 appears to be an exception, but it probably confirms the general rule that mixtures are associated with holiness. The blue threads were almost certainly wool, since it is colour-fast, unlike linen, the normal wear. Although mixed wool and linen is forbidden for standard clothing used in the profane world, the tassels can symbolically represent the holiness of an obedient people (v. 40).[1] However, the wide scope of this holiness matches its lesser quality relative to that of the high priest. He has a higher degree of holiness, corresponding to the far greater quantity of mixed materials in his special garments.

The second pair of mixtures in the table exhibits a different character, since it concerns sexual union. A sexual mixture of two animals is forbidden in Lev. 19.19. This text uses a rare word (רבע *hiphil*) to describe illegitimate sexual intercourse,[2] a word which is only found in two other places and describes bestiality (Lev. 18.23; 20.16), a human/animal mixture that is also strongly prohibited.[3]

The different rules can be related to the order in creation, which ascends from plants to animals to men.[4] In mixing seeds and clothing materials, there is mere juxtaposition of the lesser forms of being; but animals and people are at the apex of life, and the laws prohibit conjunction of a sexual nature. Mixing for the first pair is a relatively harmless structural feature, which has been given a cultural relevance and has been used to symbolize holiness, since mixtures of this kind are prohibited for common use. The second pair is prohibited under any circumstance, because it is a real danger to the normative order of

---

1. Milgrom (1983c: 65).

2. This can be aligned with Deut. 22.10 if 'ploughing' (חרש) with an ox and an ass is given a sexual force (e.g. Carmichael 1982: 403-404; Mayes 1979: 308), but this meaning is not attested elsewhere in the Bible.

3. Bestiality is also described as תבל (Lev. 18.23), from the בלל root, used in P to describe the mixing of cakes or flour with oil (Exod. 29.40; Lev. 2.5). תבל is defined (BDB, p. 117) as 'confusion, violation of nature, or the divine order'. The only other occurrence (Lev. 20.12) describes incest, another forbidden mixture of sexual roles.

4. This order corresponds to that of the creation in Gen. 1, both in terms of creation (plants: fifth day; animals and human beings: sixth day), and dominion expressed in terms of food (animals and people eat plants, vv. 29-30; the human being has dominion over the animals, v. 28).

creation.[1] It is bound up with the power and danger of sexuality, a sphere of life carefully regulated in P (cf. §5.2.4).

In Lev. 19.19 (all three rules) and Deut. 22.9 (seeds) there is a lexical correlation through the same rare word: *kil'ayim* (כלאים), of two kinds. These mixtures were not significant in themselves, but reflected other important concerns: the distinction between the profane and the holy, and illicit and legitimate sexuality.[2] Dyed wool and fine linen were expensive items, because of the skill they demanded and the cost of the materials. The degree of elaboration of embroidery depended on the importance of the individual,[3] and they were therefore appropriate garments for a priest to wear in God's service. This mixture was taken up into a larger symbol system through a structural contrast with behaviour in the profane realm, but other mixtures were left alone. Some, but not all, mixtures can acquire symbolic significance within the world-view of P.[4]

3.6 *Conclusion*

Recent anthropological studies have encouraged us to view the Priestly texts in a more sympathetic light. While the world we live in is a very different one from that of the Israelite priesthood that stands behind P, an approach which concentrates on questions of order and structure is a useful starting point for understanding. An exploration of classifi-

---

1.   The prohibitions of Lev. 19.19 have a positive reflex in the command that seeds (v. 11-12) and cattle (v. 24) should reproduce after their own kind (למינו, v. 12; cf. v. 24; Ramban on Lev. 19.19). The special distinction between human beings and cattle, which are also created on the sixth day, is signified by humanity's creation in God's image (v. 26-27), so that mixing between these kinds should be of particular concern. The positive reflex of this is that men and women are intended for one another sexually (v. 27).

2.   Houtman (1984: 227-28) also mentions the dire results of the sexual mixing of the divine/human spheres in Gen. 6.1-4.

3.   Milgrom (1983c: 61-62). Kennedy (1899: 69) associated the special sanctity of the four tassels with the same number of horns on the altar (Exod. 27.1-2), but there is no evidence that the coincidence of number was seen to be significant.

4.   A classification can take on a theoretical character and be developed independently of a social setting, particularly if it is imbued with scriptural authority and prestige. This may be what has happened in the later systematization of the purity laws and the laws of mixtures in the Mishnah. In *m. Kil.* 8.2, the 'two kinds' are extended to include combinations of clean and unclean animals (see further Mandelbaum 1982: 1-24).

cation and grading in P promises deeper insights than those based on the older styles of anthropology, which are now seen to be inadequate in various ways.

The Holiness Spectrum is a flexible way to explore these issues of classification, structure and grading, and it provides a framework for treating the various theories of holiness and purity. Two theories stand out by virtue of their comprehensive scope and explanatory power. One is idealist, focusing on the human ability to classify the world, and to fuse together cultural, social and theological meanings. From this perspective holiness is wholeness and freedom from imperfection and anomaly, while impurity is defect and mixture. The other theory is realist, concentrating on the inescapable realities of death and life, and impurity points to death and expresses the negative side of the Priestly concern with life before the living God.

The first theory is more suited to a structuralist approach, since it assumes stable, fixed structures or processes in terms of which deviations are significant. The second has a clearer referential content, and is concerned with irreversible events, events less amenable to a static structural analysis. However, these two approaches are often found to complement one another, and both may be related to the idea of order. Anomaly is as much an offence against an ordered world as is the destructive power of death. The Holiness Spectrum is one way to integrate the two theories through their common polar structure: normality–anomaly for one, and death–life for the other. Both are required to make sense of the full range of the Priestly world-view.

Chapter 4

THE SPATIAL DIMENSION

4.1 *Introduction*

The spatial dimension is the clearest expression of the Holiness
Spectrum in its grading and its polarities. The architecture of the
Tabernacle and the camp comprises a stable classification of space
with the various zones separated by distinct boundaries (§4.2.1).
Although the spatial dimension is intimately related to the personal
dimension, this chapter draws primarily from Exodus 25–31, 35–40,
and treats only the simpler aspects of that interrelationship. A discussion of the architecture of the camp is postponed until later (§5.4.1).

The graded holiness of the Tabernacle has been discussed in detail
by Menahem Haran in a series of studies summarized in his book,
Temples and Temple Service in Ancient Israel.[1] A large part of this
chapter is concerned with relating Haran's observations to the framework of the Holiness Spectrum. Many of the details are summarized in
tabular form so that the extent to which the spatial grading is worked
out can be clearly perceived.

4.2 *The Tabernacle*

4.2.1 *The Zones of Holiness*
The Tabernacle and the camp define a number of distinct zones or
spheres, separated usually by clearly defined boundaries.[2]

---

1. Haran (1978). Discussion of the numerous technical terms is left to the standard monographs and dictionaries. In most cases the structural observations made
here are not affected.

2. The traditional reconstruction of the architecture of the Tabernacle has been
assumed in the following discussion (cf. Kennedy 1902: 657; Henton Davies 1962:
499; Haran 1978: 152; Janowski 1982: 223).

```
┌─────────────────────────────────────────────────────────┐
│                                                           │
│              inner          outer                         │
│   Boundaries  curtain       curtain            entrance   │
│                 ┌────┬──────────────┐                 ▌   │
│   Grade    │ I  │     II           │    III        │  IV  │
│                 └────┴──────────────┘                 ▌   │
│   Zone     Holy of  Holy Place          Court        Camp │
│            Holies                                         │
│                                                           │
└─────────────────────────────────────────────────────────┘
```

The zones have different shapes (§4.2.2), and are not necessarily of a uniform degree of holiness or purity. It is possible to correlate the holiness word group with the spatial dimension through the terms applied to the various zones.[1]

Zone	Description	Translation	References
I	קדש הקדשים	Holy of Holies	Exod. 26.33; Num. 4.4,19
II	הקדש	The Holy Place	Exod. 26.33; 29.30; Lev. 6.30 [H 23]; Num. 3.28; 28.7
III	החצר	The Court	Exod. 27.9-19; Num. 4.26, 32
A	מקום קדוש*	A holy place[2]	Exod. 29.31; Lev. 6.16, 26, 27 [H 9, 19, 20]; 7.6; 10.13; 24.9
B	פתח אהל מועד*	Entrance of the Tent of Meeting	Exod. 29.4, 32, 42; Lev. 1.3; 3.2; 12.6; 16.7
I–III	המקדש	The Sanctuary	Exod. 25.8; Lev. 12.4; 19.30; 20.3; Num. 3.28
IV	מקום טהור*	A clean place[3]	Lev. 4.12; 6.11 [H 4]; 10.14; Num. 19.9
V	מקום טמא*	An unclean place	Lev. 14.40, 41, 45

* only part of the area

1. Durham (1987: 351) writes of 'three interlocked circles of symbol and function' (this corresponds approximately to zones I, II, III). Wright (1987: 231-47) describes in detail the Priestly 'cultic topography'.

2. This probably refers to the holy quality of the place, rather than a specific locale (Wright 1987: 232-35). 'In a holy place, in the court of the tent of meeting' (במקום קדש בחצר אהל־מועד, Lev. 6.16 [H 9]; cf. v. 19; Exod. 29.31/Lev. 8.31) thus refers to holy areas in the court rather than indicating that the court is holy (Haran 1978: 185 n. 20; Wright 1987: 233 n. 2a). מקום הקדש (the area of the holy place, Lev. 10.17; 14.13) also occurs.

3. This could be outside the camp (zone V: Lev. 4.12; 6.11 [H 4]; Num. 19.9) or inside (zone IV: Lev. 10.14, describing where the family of the priest eats the peace offerings in a clean place; LXX has ἐν τόπῳ ἁγίῳ).

It is likely that the terms used had not yet acquired a fixed meaning, so that the vocabulary could vary according to the context. קדש הקדשים, for example, probably had a comparative or a qualitative force, rather than a local one. It refers primarily to the innermost shrine (I) in contrast to the holy place[1] (II, Exod. 26.33), but it can also describe the altar (in III, Exod. 29.37 and 40.10), or the whole Tabernacle[2] (I–III, Exod. 30.29). These last uses would have been appropriate to describe the special degree of holiness pertaining to an act of consecration or sacrifice. The incense altar (II) is termed קדש הקדשים on the Day of Atonement (Exod. 30.10).

The standard grade of holy space is the area where ordinary sacrifices and rituals were performed by the the priests. The greater holiness of the inner sanctuary relative to this was expressed in various ways, whether linguistically (e.g. the article in הקדש, or the superlative form קדש הקדשים), by the material gradation (§4.4), or by the special laws which governed dealings with the inner sanctuary (§4.5).

It is likely that the court comprised several areas, but it is difficult to determine their character and location. The altar of burnt offering is holy,[3] and the priests are required to perform other cultic acts in a holy place (מקום קדוש).[4] On the other hand, lay persons are allowed into the court to participate in such acts as the slaughter of the sacrifices, which took place to the north of the altar (Lev. 1.11).[5] The area on which they stand could be regarded as possessing a lesser degree of holiness, or the people there could be regarded as being raised to a certain degree of holiness. The court is a transition area where such ambiguities are to be expected.

---

1. הקדש could also refer to the Holy of Holies (I: Lev. 10.4; 16.2-3, 16, 20, 23); or to the forecourt (III: Exod. 28.43, Lev. 10.18). מקדש הקדש also refers to the innermost shrine (Lev. 16.33). See Haran (1978: 172 n. 50) and Milgrom (1976a: 35-37). The more nuanced distinction between the Holy of Holies and the Holy Place is only relevant in certain contexts.

2. Milgrom (1970a: 23 n. 78) has shown that המקדש refers to the whole of the holy area (i.e. I–III; similarly Haran 1978: 14-15). The 'Tabernacle' (משכן) is interchangeable with the 'Tent of Meeting' (אהל מועד, Haran 1978: 272), and usually refers to the central building (i.e. I + II) rather than an area.

3. It is anointed with the holy anointing oil (Exod. 30.26), and only priests were allowed access to it (Num. 4.13-20).

4. E.g. where the priests eat the most holy sacrificial flesh (Lev. 6.26 [H 19]).

5. Milgrom (1970a: 17-18, 43 n. 166) quotes rabbinic sources which propose two different grades of holiness in the court (cf. Baudissin 1878: 41 n. 1).

Haran has argued for two grades of holiness in the court. The area between the altar and the sanctuary manifests a communicable holiness and is only accessible to the priests, and the space between the altar and the entrance to the court (known as the פתח אהל מועד, the 'entrance to the Tent of Meeting') has a minor degree of holiness and lay people are allowed to gather there (Lev. 8.3-4; Num. 10.3; 16.19).[1] Against this, Milgrom asserts that it was the objects in the court, not the ground or the enclosure, that were considered holy, and that the laity were, in principle, allowed anywhere in the court.[2]

If holiness is a quality as much as a place, it is possible that the grade of holiness depends partly upon the ritual context. On holy days, all Israelites attain a certain degree of holiness (§7.2.1), and the same could be true when a lay person participated in a sacrifice or other ritual. In accordance with this, great care is taken to ensure that no Israelite intrudes or encroaches upon the sanctuary. This would make sense of the tendency to stress the holiness of the whole sanctuary (implied by such terms as מקדש).[3] The Levitical guard at the entrance would prevent an unauthorized entrance by those who were unclean or who were not going to present a sacrifice (§5.3.1).

The different areas of the sanctuary were separated by the walls of the central building and by the court enclosure. The three entrances were described by several phrases, indicating that they too had not yet received standard names. Only the first, the *pārōket* ('veil') is called holy (פרכת הקדש, Lev. 4.6).[4] The other two are called *māsak* ('screen') and are defined from the outside in terms of the area or building that a person would enter.[5] The entrances had a higher grade of holiness

---

1. Haran (1978: 184). He also suggests that there is a Priestly tendency to make the whole court holy and the reserve of the priests. פתח אהל מועד could also be translated 'the opening of the Tent of Appointed Meeting' (Durham 1987: 390). פתח refers, strictly speaking, to a 'doorway' or 'opening', but by metonymy could refer to the area near to it. The meaning may have changed in the course of history (Durham 1987: 396).

2. The area 'belongs to the lower category of the "sacred"' (Milgrom 1970b: 207 n. 25). Haran reaffirms his position (1978: 186 n. 24).

3. Haran (1978: 185-87).

4. Exod. 26.31 = 36.35; 40.26; Lev. 4.17; 16.2, 12, 15; 21.23; Num. 18.7. Also פרכת העדת (Lev. 24.3), פרכת המסך (Exod. 35.12; 39.34; 40.21; Num. 4.5), מסך (Num. 3.31).

5. Terms for this screen between zones II and III include מסך פתח אהל מועד (Num. 3.25), מסך לפתח המשכן (Exod. 26.36 = 36.37), מסך הפתח לפתח המשכן(Exod.

than the walls, as suggested by the special weave of their fabric
(§4.4.2).

4.2.2 *The Consecration of the Tabernacle*

The Priestly texts describe the Tabernacle as a stable structure, but
not an eternal one.[1] At Sinai, God commands Moses to construct the
Tabernacle, thus setting the central institution of Israel's worship
within a narrative framework. The Tabernacle's holiness is not eternal
or essential, and the 'ground state' of its materials in the earthly realm
is purity, so it has to be consecrated. Only then will God be able to meet
with the people of Israel and preserve his holiness (Exod. 29.44). This
takes place by anointing with holy oil (Exod. 40.9-11; Lev. 8.10-11),
and the success of the ritual is made clear by the appearance of the
cloud over the Tent of Meeting and its filling with the divine glory
(Exod. 40.34).[2]

The consecration of the Tabernacle had numerous implications for
Israel's life and organization. It meant that a dedicated priesthood had
to be instituted (§5.2) to perform holy rituals. They and the Levites
had a responsibility to guard the Tabernacle and prevent the approach
of any impurity which could threaten its holiness (§5.3). And since
impurity of some sort could not be avoided, it was necessary to
perform purification rituals periodically (§7.4). And if this was not
possible, it was expected that God himself would take active steps to
protect his holiness, as is illustrated by a number of narratives (e.g.
Lev. 10.1-3; Num. 16–17).[3]

35.15), מסך הפתח למשכן (Exod. 40.28), מסך פתח האהל (Exod. 39.38). Between
zones III and IV we find מסך פתח החצר (Num. 3.26), מסך שער החצר (Exod. 35.17;
40.8, 33), המסך לשער החצר (Exod. 39.40).

1. Some have considered that the earthly Tabernacle reflects an eternal heavenly
prototype, described as the pattern or blueprint (תבנית, Exod. 25.9, 40; 26.30; 27.8;
Num. 8.11) of the Tabernacle (Cassuto 1967: 322; 'das himmlische Urbild des
irdischen Heiligtums', Janowski 1983: 10). However, this is not necessary and
Hurowitz (1985: 22 n. 4) argues that ancient Near Eastern parallels do not require
that the model is of the heavenly temple.

2. Gorman (1990: 54) calls this a founding ritual. The significance of glory is
stressed by Struppe (1988: 72-73, 98-106).

3. The inviolability of the Tabernacle is affirmed by the story of Korah's rebellion. The offenders are consumed by fire (Num. 16.35), but the fire also sanctifies
the censers of the rebels. These cannot be returned to the secular sphere, and are
therefore incorporated into the altar of burnt offering (Num. 16.37-40 [H 17.2-5]).

4.3 *The Formal Description of the Tabernacle*

4.3.1 *The Lists and Summaries*
Lists of the various elements which make up the Tabernacle are found in a number of places, as summarized below:

List	Reference	Context of the Listed Items
List	*Reference*	*Context of the Listed Items*
Longer accounts		
A	Exod. 25–30 (prescriptive)	Yahweh instructs Moses to make the components (on Exod. 29–30, see below)
B	Exod. 36.8–38.20 (descriptive)	The workmen construct them
Briefer accounts and summaries		
C	Exod. 30.26-30	Yahweh commands Moses to anoint them (and priests) with the holy anointing oil
D	Exod. 31.7-10	God has appointed the craftsmen to make them
E	Exod. 35.10-19	Moses summons the people to come and construct them
F	Exod. 39.33-41	The people bring them for Moses' inspection
G	Exod. 40.2-8	Yahweh instructs Moses to assemble them
H	Exod. 40.9-15	Yahweh commands Moses to anoint them (and priests)
I	Exod. 40.18-33	Moses assembles them

There are two main sequences in which the items are described very fully (A, B), and a number of others where they are mentioned more briefly.[1] The lists occur mainly in pairs, one giving the instructions to carry out a certain action, and the other describing the action's fulfilment (A/E→B; D→F; G→I; C/H→Lev. 8.10-12).

There is little variation in the order in which the Tabernacle and its furniture is described, whatever the detail or the context in which the list occurs. The texts describing its commission, construction and dedication are largely set out in accordance with the principle of graded holiness. The most important items are at the centre of the Tabernacle and are described first.[2] This may be seen from the following table:

---

1. Scott (1965: 261-64). Hurowitz (1985) argues that several temple building accounts from the ancient Near East (in addition to 1 Kgs 6–9) exhibit a typical story pattern. The description in the command and fulfilment sections are two elements of this pattern, and could be almost identical.

2. E.g. Dillmann (1880: 279), Finn (1914: 479), Cassuto (1967: 328), Levine (1965: 307). There is no hint that the number of summary lists in Exod. 25–40 (seven) is a deliberate symbolic choice. Another sequence is found in Num. 3.31 (ark, table, lampstand, altar, veil [I–II]).

Zone	List →	A	B	C	D	E	F	G	H	I
I+II	Tent	6	1	1	1	1	1	1	1–8[1]	1
I	Ark	1	4	2	2	2	3	2		2
	Cover	2	5		3	3	4			3
	Cherubim		3	6						
I–II	Veil	7	2			4	2	3[2]		4
II	Table	4	7	3	4	5	5	4		5
	Menorah	5	8	4	5	6	6	5		6
	Altar	13	9	5	6	7	7	6		7
II–III	Screen	8	3			8	8	7		8
III	Altar	9	10	6	7	9	9	8	9	9
	Laver	14	11	7	8	10	10	9	10	10
III–IV	Court	10	12			11	11	10		11
	Screen					12	12	11		12
Clothes	Aaron's	11	13	8[3]	9	13	13	12	11[4]	
	Sons'	12	14	9	10	14	14	13	12	

In the above table, the numbers indicate the position of the given items in the respective list. Variations between the lists arise for several reasons.[5] Some are brief summaries, and the utensils and extras (e.g. the stand of the laver) may or may not be mentioned. When an article is named, it may include pieces closely associated with it.[6] The description may also proceed strictly in terms of the spatial dimension (as in the table above; CDGI), or the structure of the inner sanctuary may be described before the furniture (BEF). There are also a number of alternative names for the same piece of furniture.[7]

1. Indicated in Exod. 40.9 (את המשכן ואת כל אשר בו).

2. In Exod. 40.3, כפרת for MT פרכת is found in the Samaritan Pentateuch, but this is probably an error (Dillmann 1880: 368; Cassuto 1967: 479).

3. When Aaron and his sons are anointed (Exod. 30.30), this will include their clothing (see next note).

4. It is carefully noted that Aaron and his sons are clothed (Exod. 40.13-14) before they are anointed (v. 15).

5. The reasons for the different order of items in the LXX lie outside the scope of the present study (see Finn 1914 and Gooding 1959: 78-98).

6. Thus the cherubim are of one piece with the cover, and both can be counted as one. A reference to 'ark' may even include the cherubim as well as the ark cover with it (Cassuto 1967: 335-36).

7. E.g. the golden altar (Exod. 39.38) instead of the incense altar (both are combined in Exod. 40.5, מזבח הזהב לקטרת); the bronze altar (39.39) instead of the Altar of Burnt Offering; the Tent of Meeting (אהל מועד, Exod. 30.26; 31.7) instead of tent (אהל).

The main series A (Exod. 25–30) has an unusual order which has caused commentators some difficulties. It is reasonable that the furniture of the sanctuary (I and II) is described before the Tabernacle structure (I+II), followed by the altar of the court (III) and the outer enclosure (III–IV). But the incense altar (II, Exod. 30.1-10) and laver (III, Exod. 30.17-21) are described last, whereas in the descriptive account they occur in the expected order (Exod. 37.25-28; 38.8).[1] These two items are usually assumed to be later additions, but the question remains why they were not added in the appropriate place.[2] It is possible that the items here were considered less important than those which occurred in the main series,[3] and thus the association between them was merely verbal.[4]

4.3.2 *Numbers and Shapes*

The standard measurement used for the Tabernacle description is the cubit.[5] The lengths and numbers of the various parts are dominated by the numbers 5 and 10 (also the multiples 20, 50, 100), while the two- and three-dimensional character of the Tabernacle is modelled after the rectangle and the square (רבוע), both of which are associated with the number four.[6] In accordance with the usual reconstruction of the Tabernacle, some important measurements and figures are listed below:

1.   The order in Exodus 30 is: (1) vv. 1-10 incense altar (cf. 4.5.3), (2) vv. 11-16 ransom money (cf. v. 10), (3) vv. 17-21 bronze laver, (4) vv. 22-33 holy anointing oil, (5) vv. 34-38 altar incense (cf.v. 7). Only the fulfilment section (38.8) notes that the bronze laver was made from the mirrors of the ministering women. However, strict repetition is not be expected (a parallel is adduced by Hurowitz 1985: 27).
2.   Noth (1962: 192) suggests that the incense altar was excluded deliberately from the main series to exclude illegitimate attitudes to incense, but this is unlikely.
3.   Durham (1987: 351) describes Exod. 30.1-38 as an appendix dealing with four accessories to worship.
4.   Cassuto (1967: 393) points out the verbal link (the כפר root) between the incense altar (Exod. 31.10) and the half shekel ransom money (vv. 12, 15, 16), and the association between washing and anointing (p. 396). He also (p. 390) suggests that the incense altar alone did not belong to the heavenly dwelling (whose furniture is described in Exod. 25–27), but rather to human worship. However, houses could contain incense burners, and their use was not exclusively cultic. Cf. also Scott (1965: 264).
5.   The symbolism is not affected by the size of the cubit.
6.   It would be interesting to compare the measurements of other temples and secular buildings.

Zone and Item		L	B	H	Square[1]	Rectangular
I.	Holy of Holies	10	10	10	section, plan, end	
	ark	1.5	2.5	1.5	end	section, plan
II.	The Holy Place	20	10	10	end	section, plan
	table	2.5	1	5	section, plan, end	
	incense altar	1	1	2	plan	section, end
III.	The Court	100	50	5	half-court plan[2]	section, plan, end
	altar	5	5	3	plan	section, end

Critical scholarship has generally assumed that the numbers are merely technical details, largely derived from the measurements of the first Temple.[3] This was partly in reaction to the arbitrary and subjective character of past attempts to decipher the symbolism of the numbers, a practice which has had a long and varied history.[4] Even the more cautious suggestions lack support in the Priestly text.[5]

Traditional explanations have generally focused on the numbers in isolation. A structural approach draws our attention to the relations between numbers and figures, rather than the numbers themselves. The repetition in itself reflects a characteristic Priestly concern for order and unity (§4.3.3). The unique cubic shape of the Holy of Holies, each side measuring 10 cubits, suggests a special kind of distinctiveness appropriate to its great sanctity.[6] A similar contrast may be suggested by the fact that the walls of the holy place are double the height of those of the court walls.[7]

---

1. The incense altar (Exod. 30.2 = 37.25) and the altar of burnt offering (Exod. 27.1 = 38.1) are both specifically described as square (רבוע). In the personal dimension, the term is also used of the breastplate of the High Priest (Exod. 28.16 = 39.9; 1 span square: cf. § 5.2.3). See further the symmetrical arrangement of the tribes around the four sides of the Tabernacle (§5.4.1).

2. Although not mentioned specifically in P, the standard reconstructions plausibly locate the Tabernacle on the boundary of the half-court, so that the ark is in the centre of the half-court.

3. Friedman (1981c: 48-52; cf. 1980) has recently challenged this assumption. Whether he is correct or not (see the critical review in Davies 1983b), the question of symbolic significance remains.

4. For a selection of early unconvincing attempts, see Childs (1974: 547-49).

5. Such as those suggested by Driver (1911: 259-60).

6. Sarna (1986: 207). Ten often denotes completeness (Brongers 1966: 34).

7. Cf. Philo, *Vit. Mos.* 2.90.

There may also be a number contrast between the static and dynamic aspects of the cult (§3.2). The numbers 4, 5 and 10 are frequently found in the description of the tabernacle, which is a stable structure.[1] The number seven, on the other hand, is dominant in the dimension of time,[2] and a seven-day period is often mentioned in connection with rituals (Appendix 2, §§5.2.1, 6.3) and calendrical celebrations (Chapter 7).[3]

It is interesting to speculate further on the significance of 4 and 10 in the light of their significance as 'natural numbers', numbers closely associated with the human body. Mary Douglas has pointed out that the body is a natural symbol of the world and society.[4] The Tabernacle also reflects the geographical orientation of the body in terms of the four directions. Absolute directions were taken from the rising of the sun, which was 'to one's face' (לפני) or 'to the front' (קדם).[5] The location of the entrances to the Tabernacle and the positions of the tribes (§5.4.1) affirm that the east also has priority according to the divine pattern of things embodied in the Tabernacle.

It must be admitted that these suggestions are difficult to prove. Small numbers can serve many functions, and need not imply a symbolic force. Further, numbers were only occasionally associated with the social, economic and religious life of Israel. There was thus a limited material basis from which to develop a symbol system for numbers. Yet the patterns pointed out above remain intriguing, and point to aspects of the Priestly conception known to be important on other grounds.

1. A material factor encouraging the use of these numbers is that counting is simple in base 10, and a square or rectangular building is relatively easy to erect.

2. Tsarpati (1968) suggests that the prime number 7 is unique in the first 10 numbers in not being associated with one of the natural numbers as a multiple or part. There are other explanations for the symbolic significance of 7, such as the existence of 7 planets, and the fact that the lunar cycle can be divided into four 7 day periods. Both these suggestions maintain the association of 7 with time. Brongers (1966: 40-45) also stresses the close relationship between 7 and 10, both of which can express completeness. The Priestly creation account (Gen. 1.1–2.3) suggests the pre-eminence of the seven in the dimension of time (cf. §§7.3.1, 8.3).

3. Labuschagne (1982; 1984a) has postulated certain groupings of divine speech formulae, but even if valid (they are criticised by Davies and Gunn 1984; cf. Labuschagne 1984b), they show how purely formal observations provide a meagre basis for theological reflection. His calculations based on gematria (e.g. Labuschagne 1985) suffer from the same weakness.

4. Douglas (1966: 3, 72, etc.).

5. Childs (1962b), Har-El (1981). See also Gordon (1971).

4.3.3 *Repetition*

The previous two sections have illustrated how pervasive and varied repetition is in the Priestly texts, particularly those that describe the Tabernacle. Large sections are repeated almost verbatim (e.g. Exod. 25–31 and 35–40; Exod. 28–29 and Lev. 8–9), as are similar actions in a narrative (e.g. Num. 7). The furniture and framework of the Tabernacle occur time and again in different contexts and in varying detail (§4.3.1).

The significance of this repetition has been explained in various ways. The documentary hypothesis proposed that they were due to sources of different dates. However, this could explain at best only some of the cases,[1] and it has become clear that repetition is an important feature of the Priestly literary style.[2] Further, whatever the history of the text,[3] P is now a literary work, and it remains to be explained why so much repetition was preserved in the final text.

Some have sought to explain this feature by appealing to an oriental delight in it.[4] Repetition can also serve to unify and further a plot, and subtle variations in the paradigm are of utmost significance. However, such observations are more appropriate to narrative than to ritual texts,[5] and entertaining narrative is not prominent in the Priestly cultic texts.

A more fruitful approach is to look for a correspondence between

1. Mere repetition is not decisive in judging a text supplementary (Noth 1962: 274-75). The criteria of duplications and repetitions to distinguish different sources are questioned by Cassuto (1961: 69-83) and Whybray (1987: 72-91).

2. Haran (1978: 149).

3. Some repetitive texts have been traced to an origin in archival records (Levine 1965). Hurowitz (1985) considers that the repetitions in Exod. 35–40 reflect a common literary pattern (see Durham's 1987: 473-75 review of interpretations of this section). Cassuto (1967: 453) refers to the repeated sections in the Ugaritic story of Keret (e.g. *CTA* 14, 125-36 = 249-61 = 268-80).

4. E.g. Cassuto (1967: 453) on Exod. 35–40, McEvenue (1974: 7) on Exod. 25.31-36. Num. 7 is a good test case. Is the twelve-fold repetition of the gifts tedious and pedantic (Gray 1903: 74) or delightful repetition (Alter 1981: 88-89)? Is it intended to emphasize the significance of the contents of the sanctuary (Noth 1968: 63), the generosity of the leaders (Sturdy 1972: 62), the equal commitment of the tribes to Israel's worship (Wenham 1982: 93), or the honouring of tribes through their leader (Milgrom 1985: 222)?

5. Most studies of repetition are on narrative or poetic texts, rather than cultic texts (e.g. McEvenue 1971).

the form and the content of ritual texts. Deliberate repetition and variation is a common characteristic of many ritual texts, both in what is said and in what is done.[1] Several similar symbols and repeated actions and words are often used to reinforce the same point. This need not be excessive 'magical' persuasion (§3.3.2). Rather it reinforces the significance and importance of the action and the reality of the divine dimension being approached. A ritual will often embrace psychological, social and theological dimensions in exploring vital beliefs from various points of view. It is therefore reasonable to suggest that the formal repetitions of the Priestly texts reflect the central significance of the new cultic order set up at Sinai, focused on the Tabernacle.

The correlation between form and content may be categorized in two further ways.[2] The first is, '*more of form is more of content*'. The repetition of lists, materials and descriptions establishes the most fundamental aspects of Israel's ordered world. The Tabernacle chapters provide a basic orientation to the spatial and temporal universe in which Israel moves. Within the description of the Tabernacle there are further distinctions. The more important parts of the Tabernacle are often more fully described.[3] It may be inferred that what is mentioned only occasionally or briefly is less fundamental and, perhaps, more open to change and divergent interpretations.[4]

The normative world order also includes Israel's obedience to its God.[5] This is formally expressed by the almost exact correspondence between the prescriptions of Exodus 25–31 and the description of how these instructions were carried out in Exodus 35–40. Content and

1. P gives very little information about what was said, if anything, in the priestly cult. Kaufmann (1960: 303) even suggested that 'The priestly temple is the kingdom of silence'.

2. The two principles are taken from Lakoff and Johnson (1980: 127-33).

3. Thus there are unequal numbers of verses devoted to the various sections in the description of the Levitical tasks (Num. 4.4-33). The cover (כפרת) is described more fully than the ark, and could have been more important in the cult (de Vaux 1961: 300). In the sacrificial instructions (e.g. Lev. 1; 4), the later sections may assume parts of the initial description. Budd (1984: 46) suggests that the Kohathites require the most detailed description because they are most exposed to danger in handling the holy items.

4. The argument from silence can be a weak one, but in this context it probably has some force.

5. Elliger (1952: 130) asserts that this, rather than the importance of the object, is indicated by the repetition, but both themes could be present.

form coalesce in the recurrent execution formulae (e.g. 'just as Yahweh commanded Moses').[1] These occur at significant points in the Priestly narrative, and a significant seven times when the Tabernacle is set up (Exod. 40.19, 21, 23, 25, 27, 29, 32).[2]

A second principle evident in the literary form of the text is what Lakoff and Johnson call the '*me-first*' orientation.[3] The member of highest value generally comes first, and, in the Priestly description of the Tabernacle, this reinforces the priority of the holy items in the centre over those which are peripheral (§4.3.1). This priority is also expressed in the materials used in the construction of the Tabernacle, to which we now turn.

4.4 *The Material Gradation of the Tabernacle*

4.4.1 *The Furniture and Framework*
The principle of graded holiness controls the choice of materials (and fabrics §4.4.2) in the Tabernacle.[4] The distribution of materials indicates how the holiness of the various parts of the Tabernacle are graded in accordance with the spatial dimension. The costliness of an item is proportional to its closeness to God. The accounts of the people's offerings list the metals in the order gold, silver and copper (Exod. 25.3 = 35.5).[5] The clearest differences are found at the poles of the spectrum: copper is absent from the Holy of Holies, and there is no gold in the court.[6]

---

1.   Blenkinsopp (1976: 276-77). Levine (1965b: 310) calls this the 'compliance formula'. The pattern of word and fulfilment is an important theological theme unifying the Priestly writing (McEvenue 1970; 1971: 61 n. 54). Childs (1985: 158-60) refers to other repeated key phrases in Leviticus and comments, 'the highly formalized effect of such massive amounts of repetition serves to involve the reader in a manner equally effectively as the homily' (p. 159).

2.   Childs (1974: 638) includes v. 16 as an eighth occurrence, but this could be a fuller formula introducing the specific stages of the erection (Cassuto 1967: 480).

3.   Lakoff and Johnson (1980: 127-33). Similarly, in word pairs the priority normally belongs to the first element. Holy is usually placed before profane, and clean before unclean (on Lev. 10.10 see §2.2.1).

4.   See Haran (1978: 158-65). Others have noted this briefly (e.g. Dillmann 1880: 265-66, Driver 1911: 264, Henton Davies 1961: 501-502).

5.   Baentsch (1903: 221). Elsewhere the order of mention is silver-gold, probably because silver was the more common (Kessler 1986: 86).

6.   Dillmann (1880: 266). Contrast Josephus (*Ant.* 3.149), who mentions gold decoration on the altar of burnt offering. Beer (1939: 130) suggests that iron was not

Practical considerations have probably influenced some of the details.[1] The smaller items are of solid gold, but the larger items are wood overlaid with gold. The visible aspects of the furniture (cf. §4.5) convey the significant symbolism. Precious metals other than gold are used for the weightier items outside the Holy of Holies. But taken together, the materials form a code which indicates distinct grades of holiness:

Zone		Item	Material	Exodus
I.	Holy of Holies	ark	pure gold (over wood)	25.11 = 37.2
		cover	pure gold	25.17 = 37.6
		cherubim	beaten gold[2]	25.18 = 37.7
II.	The Holy Place	table	pure gold (over wood)	25.24 = 37.11
		menorah	pure gold	25.31 = 37.17
		incense altar	pure gold (over wood)	30.3 = 37.26
III.	The Court	altar	copper (over wood)	27.2 = 38.2
		laver	copper	30.18 = 38.8

The entrances to the court, the Holy Place and the Holy of Holies (§4.2.1) are described in some detail, and exhibit a similar material gradation (see also §4.5.2). The gradation applies to the rest of the framework (compare Exod. 27.9-19 and 38.18-20), but the texts do not fill in all the details. The materials of the posts, hooks and sockets of the entrances illustrate an overlapping gradation:

Entrances		Text in Exodus	Posts (עמודים)	Hooks (ווים)	Sockets (אדנים)
I–II	veil	26.32 = 36.36	gold (over wood)	gold	silver
II–III	screen	26.37 = 36.38	gold (over wood)	gold	copper
III–IV	screen	27.17 = 38.19	copper[3]	silver	copper

Gold thus predominates in the furniture, framework and entrances of the central regions I and II, which are most closely associated with

---

used, because of its association with weapons, and hence death and impurity. On the other hand, the materials may be traditional and derive from a time which preceded the Iron Age.

1.   A more consistent system is sometimes preferred by the LXX, when it refers to solid gold or silver items (Gooding 1959: 22-23, 28).

2.   זהב מקשה refers to gold worked with a hammer rather than poured (Durham 1987: 356-57), so pure gold was probably used, as for the rest of the interior furniture.

3.   These are banded (מחשכים, Exod. 38.17; cf. 27.17) with silver.

God's presence. There is a difference between the furniture, which is of a higher sanctity and of pure gold, and the framework, which is only 'gold'.[1]

The material grading in the spatial dimension is also reflected in the personal dimension. Pure gold characterizes a number of the garments of the high priest, who is the paradigm of holiness and dedication to God (see Chapter 5). These include the ephod, the chains (connecting ephod to breastplate, Exod. 28.14, 28.22 = 39.15), the bells (39.25; only 'gold' in 28.33), and the diadem (Exod. 28.36 = 39.30).

Gold has no inherent holiness, unlike the specially compounded holy oil and incense, which are forbidden to the people. Indeed, the people have to be restrained from offering too much (Exod. 36.3-7). Nevertheless, the quantity of gold in the Tabernacle represents a marked contrast to the rarity of its occurrence outside. Further, it attains a special holiness after the Tabernacle is consecrated. The initial dedication of the gold by the people (Exod. 25.1-9) marks the movement of gold from the secular to the divine sphere,[2] but it can still be worked by the craftsmen, and only attains a communicable holiness when it is anointed by oil (§4.2.2).

The predominance of gold in the Tabernacle can be related to its valued physical properties and great social significance. This is the basis for the analogies which are made between the human and the divine spheres, and a close connection between gold, divinity and holiness is evident throughout the ancient Near East.[3] Gold is rare, desirable, and very costly, and fittingly represents the dignity and power of those who are able to possess it, to a pre-eminent degree, God. The same message is conveyed by the use of other precious materials in the Tabernacle (e.g. silver, spices, oils, woven cloth). Further, gold is chemically stable (see also §4.6.1) and so free from mixture, tarnishing and ageing. Silver is second, both because it is less valuable and because it tarnishes.

1. Haran (1978: 163-64). Compare the differences between pure blue (תכלת טהור) and blue (תכלת, §4.4.3).
2. Similarly the gold ladles of the tribal leaders (Num. 7.84) are dedicated, and are on a par with the sacrificial animals (v. 87) fit for the anointed altar (v. 88).
3. E.g. Kedar-Kopfstein (1977b: 537-40). The golden form of the idolatrous calf in Exod. 32 is a striking contrast to the legitimate use of gold in the Tabernacle (Childs 1974: 570; Moberly 1983: 47). Whatever the relation of Exod. 32–34 to the surrounding Priestly material, the present redactional juxtaposition is very fitting.

4.4.2 *The Woven Materials*

The fabrics of the Tabernacle reinforce the graded holiness apparent in the metal gradation.[1] Several of the weaves and fabrics are mentioned in Exod. 35.35 (cf. 38.23):

English (NRSV)	*Hebrew*
He has filled them with skill to do	מלא אתם חכמת-לב
every kind of work done	לעשות כל-מלאכת
(a) by an artisan	חרש
(b) or by a designer	וחשב
(c) or by an embroiderer	ורקם
in blue, purple and crimson yarns	בתכלת ובארגמן בתולעת השני
and in fine linen	ובשש
(d) or by a weaver	וארג

The highest grade of weave (חשב) is mentioned first, followed by the two other main kinds of workmanship (רקם and ארג). The two highest grades consisted of coloured wool (the blue, purple and scarlet),[2] and fine twisted linen (שש משזר).[3] This mixed character is in itself indicative of holiness (§3.5.2), and may be aligned with the mixed character of the cherubim, which were probably figures of mixed human and animal or bird character.[4] The designs on the curtains and veil of the Tabernacle were described as כרבים מעשה חשב (Exod. 26.1 = 36.8; similarly 26.31 = 36.35). The presence of cherubim in the Tabernacle provides a striking contrast to the prohibition of images outside (Exod. 20.4).[5] The second grade (מעשה רקם) is likely a form of

---

1. Haran (1978: 160-74).

2. Ziderman (1987) has demonstrated that the scarlet was purple with a blue tinge. The order of colours is the same for the Tabernacle fabric (e.g. Exod. 25.4) as for the Priestly garments (e.g. Exod. 28.6; cf. §5.2.3). Haran (1978: 160) considers that the list order is one of importance and that this is correlated with their cost (blue is the most expensive).

3. The normal translations of the terms have been used. Scott (1965: 25-38) argues that בד is the general term for linen, שש is bleached linen, and שש משזר is linen canvas for hard wearing.

4. 'A class of mixed being [*Mischwesen*]', Freedman and O'Connor (1984: 333). Although the חשב kind of weaving is often thought to comprise figures (*Bildwirkerei*), it seems unlikely that the High Priest would wear such clothing. Perhaps abstract patterns of an artistic nature (*Kunstwirkerei*) were used, whereas the רקם weaving was a regular pattern (Dillmann 1880: 275).

5. Cassuto (1967: 407-408) suggests that this is because of their imaginary nature. There was no danger of confusing them with divinities.

patterned weave, while the plain weave (מעשה ארג) is of simple linen.

The grades of weave correspond to their occurrence in both the spatial and personal dimensions. The correlation is indicated in the following table:

	Designed	*Embroidered*	*Woven*
Materials	Wool + Linen	Wool + Linen	Linen
Grade	First	Second	Third

Spatial Dimension: Tabernacle

I–II	veil (פרכת)		
	(26.31 = 36.35)		
II–III	curtains (יריעת)	screen (מסך)	
	(26.1 = 36.8)	(26.36 = 36.37)	
III–IV		screen (מסך)	curtains (קלעים)
		(27.16 = 38.18)	(27.9, 18 = 38.9, 16?)

Personal Dimension: High Priest

	Ephod (אפוד)	sash (אבנט)	
	(28.6 = 39.3)[1]	(28.39 = 39.29)	
	breastplate (חשן)	robe of the Ephod[2]	tunic (כתנת)
	(28.15 = 39.8)	(מעיל האפוד)	(39.27)

The use of the same types of weave for the Tabernacle and the High Priest aligns the holy pole of the personal and spatial dimensions (see also §5.2.3). Although the High Priest can be defiled, this was strictly forbidden while he was ministering in the sanctuary. His holiness while performing the high priestly tasks was represented by the clothes he wore in the sanctuary. The most important items (the ephod and the breastplate) are of the highest grade of weaving, but the other types of weave are also found, possibly for practical reasons.

4.4.3 *The Tabernacle on the Move*

When the Israelites moved camp, the Tabernacle was dismantled and transported by the Levites. Although the task of the Kohathites was to carry the holy vessels (קדש הקדשים, Num. 4.4), only the priests were allowed to dismantle the inner sanctuary. They covered the holy vessels with special cloths (Num. 4.5-14), which vary in number and material:

---

1. Compare the decorated band of the ephod (חשב האפוד, 8× in P).
2. Although it is described as woven (ארג, Exod. 28.32 = 39.22), it was decorated with coloured pomegranates (Exod. 28.33 = 39.24), and so was probably embroidered.

	Item	Pure blue כליל תכלת	Blue תכלת	Scarlet תולעת שני	Purple ארגמן[1]	Dolphin תחש	Text Num.
I	Ark	3		1 = veil (פרכת)		2	4.4-6
II	Table		1		2	3	4.7-8
	Menorah		1			2	4.9-10
	Altar		1			2	4.11
	Vessels		1			2	4.12
III	Altar[2]				1	2	4.13

The ark was appropriately unique, and stood out by virtue of its special inner covering of the highest order of sanctity (the veil) and its pure blue outer covering.[3] It also had three coverings, whereas the others (except for the table of presence) only had two.[4] There is an intriguing structural contrast in that the ark was the item of furniture most hidden when the Tabernacle is stationary. But when the Tabernacle was on the move, the ark's importance was stressed by the opposite symbolism—it was the most visible.[5] It may also be noted that the items of highest sanctity (the ark) and of lowest (the altar in the court) were marked out by coverings of distinctive colour.[6]

1. The meaning of תחש is uncertain, but the structural contrast is unaffected whether it is translated badger (RV), dolphin (NJPSV), goat (RSV), seal (RV), dugong-hide (REB, BDB), porpoise (RV mg, NEB), fine leather (GNB, NJB, NRSV), or monodon monoceros (Aharoni). For references and discussion see Cross (1947: 62 n. 22) and Haran (1978: 162 n. 28).

2. LXX and Samaritan insert a note about the laver and its stand, which are to be covered with a purple cloth. But this is a later insertion based on its place in other lists (Dillmann 1886: 23). Although it too is holy (e.g. Exod. 40.11), it also marks the boundary between the pure and the holy (§4.2.2), and this may explain why it does not need to be covered.

3. Blue (תכלת) could have been chosen because it was most expensive, but it is also the colour of the sky, the location of the divine dwelling place (Wenham 1982: 73). P does not stress the representation of the divine-human polarity by the high-low contrast, but this is an early, widespread and natural interpretation of the colour (Josephus, *Ant.* 3.183).

4. Dillmann (1886: 22), Noordtzij (1983: 44).

5. Gray (1903: 34), followed by Budd (1984: 50), suggests that this abnormal order is for ease of identification, but the shape of the covered ark would surely be distinctive enough.

6. If the colours are graded in importance, there remains the question why the altar is covered by the more holy purple, whereas the table is covered by scarlet, which elsewhere appears in third position.

4.5 *Gradation and the Senses*

4.5.1 *The Sense of Touch*

The holiness of the Tabernacle could be transmitted in various ways. This has often been discussed in terms of contagion, which is normally associated with touch. However, the symbolic and cultural character of communicability (§3.3.3) explains why in certain cultures this power can also be attributed to other senses.[1] The Priestly perception of holiness is that it may be transmitted by sight as well as by touch. The importance of the sense of smell is demonstrated by the prominence of incense in the cult (§4.5.3).

The graded sanctity of the Tabernacle is therefore correlated with the various laws and restrictions which determine who may approach, touch and see the various holy items or regions.[2] According to P, it is forbidden even for a clean person to touch or approach the central holy sanctuary, and for an unclean person to even enter the court. The priests and Levites have a duty to prevent this happening, the priests on the inside (guarding I–II), and the Levites on the outside (guarding III). The integrity of the Tabernacle is maintained by God himself in cases where the human guard fails (e.g. Lev. 10.1-3). Any approach that could result in sight or touch is forbidden: 'any outsider who comes near shall be put to death' (NRSV הזר הקרב יומת, Num. 1.51; 3.10, 38; 18.7).[3]

4.5.2 *The Sense of Sight*

As would be expected, the greatest restrictions applied to the Holy of Holies.[4] The High Priest could enter only once a year (Lev. 16.34),

---

1. Meiggs (1978: 311) describes a culture where all five senses can pollute. Hall (1966: 107-22) discusses the visual, tactile and olfactory perception and grading of space in contemporary society, and the way they are controlled by 'cultural taboos' (see §3.3.4).

2. Haran (1978: 175-88); cf. Milgrom (1983b: 252). Compare the similar prohibitions for Sinai, which is covered with smoke (Exod. 19.18) and the cloud (24.15-16). The mountain must not be touched (נגע, Exod. 19.12) and the people are warned not to break through to Yahweh (הרס, Exod. 19.21, 24), in case they see him and die (Exod. 19.21).

3. Milgrom (1970a: 5-59). See also Haran (1978: 182-83).

4. For later evidence of the sight prohibition see Schwartz (1986).

and even then his sight was restricted from seeing the cover by a
cloud of incense (Lev. 16.12-13). The unique significance of the day
and its ceremonies was also communicated by the command that no-
one is allowed in the Tent of Meeting while the High Priest performs
the central atoning rites (Lev. 16.17). This would restrict seeing the
rituals as well as coming into contact with the holy area.

As for the Holy Place, the High Priest, and probably his sons (§5.2),
were allowed to enter twice a day for the regular cultic worship (the
תמיד, §7.1.2). All others, including Levites, were barred from observ-
ing the inner ritual (cf. Num. 18.3). The same prohibition of seeing
the most holy furniture was maintained when the sanctuary was dismantled and moved. Only the priests could do this, and the Levites
were explicitly warned not even to look on the holy things (Num. 4.20),
let alone touch them (v. 15). The penalty for unlawful seeing was the
same as for unlawful approach, death (v. 20). The coverings acted as
a barrier to sight, and a safe distance was maintained by the provision of poles for the ark, table and altars, and a carrying bar (מוט,
Num. 4.10, 12) for the other bundles. As for the holiest object, the
ark, the blue covering could have served to warn that special care was
needed in approaching it.[1]

The material gradations confirm that the invisible parts of the
Tabernacle had a higher sanctity than the visible.[2] The sockets of the
tent were silver (Exod. 26.21 = 36.26), but those visible at the entrance
were copper (26.37 = 36.38; see §4.4.1). Similarly, the clasps that
couple the tent strips were gold for the first layer (26.6), and only
copper for the second outer layer of goats' hair (26.11).[3]

---

1. Even the priests would not need to see the ark if it was first covered with the
veil (Num. 4.5).

2. Milgrom (1970a: 81 n. 300; 1980: 3-5). Invisibility perhaps associated an
item metaphorically with God, whom likewise human beings could not see and live.
This could be a factor in the greater sanctity and value of the interior materials. The
interior silver sockets are explicitly noted as being a reminder before Yahweh
(יהוה לזכרון לפני), Exod. 30.16).

3. The hooks and bands are also of gold, while the sockets are of less precious
metals. This could be a practical consideration arising from the weight of the sockets
(cf. Exod. 38.24-31), or it could be that the sockets are the parts most likely to be
seen.

4.5.3 *The Sense of Smell*

It is likely that incense[1] was an early and important part of Israel's worship, but it was also a multivalent symbol that could be interpreted in different ways. In this section, the main interest is the way in which the various kinds of incense offering are structured and aligned with the spatial and personal dimensions. This underlies the Priestly laws of incense, whatever the meaning attributed to a particular offering.[2]

Incense may be classified both by its composition and by the mode of offering. There is a fragrant incense (קטרת סמים), which is a pure and holy (טהור קדש, Exod. 30.35) mixture of a number of rare spices (Exod. 30.34-38), and an ordinary incense (קטרת), the composition of which is unknown.[3] Although it is not called incense (קטרת), frankincense (לבונה) was a major ingredient of the fragrant incense, and was used in its own right as an addition to sacrifices,[4] and thus can be included as a third kind. The first two types could be offered in a censer

---

1. קטרת in P refers to incense or to the incense offering. The wider meaning of קטר is 'to make a religious smoke' (Durham 1963: 308), and in P the verb (which occurs only in the *hiphil*) can refer to either an incense offering or a sacrificial offering. Haran (1978: 230-31) has suggested that the verb was used of sacrifices because incense was frequently added to mask the stench of burning flesh. However, this is speculative, and may take the analogy between divine and human smell too far (Durham 1963: 394).

2. Interpretations vary from the abstract symbolic to the grossly material. Gray (1925: 80) writes of 'a symbol of the pleasure of God in the due discharge of his service'). Neufeld (1971: 62) provides a hygienic and apotropaic interpretation (it kept flies from the meat!).

3. Haran (1978: 230-45). Durham (1963: 394-95, 416-17) argues that the use of incense was more flexible. The special incense could be taken outside the sanctuary, and other incense could be burnt on the altar. Nielsen (1986: 69-70) disagrees with Haran completely, arguing that קטרת סמים is the same as קטרת, and P has added סמים to stress its holiness. However, קטרת סמים need not be a fixed technical term, and the context can indicate the type. It is not surprising that the cumbersome מזבח קטרת הסמים (Lev. 4.7) is used only once. Further, it is unlikely that Korah and his sons could have had access to the special incense in the quantities required, and it is assumed that theirs is a legitimate offering, but by illegitimate personnel (see below).

4. Nielsen (1986: 89-107) deduces from this that incense is only added when there is mention of incense in the text. However, the accounts of sacrifices are often very abbreviated, and the explicit exclusion in two cases (Lev. 5.11, the reparation offering; Num. 5.15, the jealousy offering) implies that they were exceptions to the rule.

or upon an altar, but frankincense was apparently only a constituent of some sacrificial offerings.

The different types of incense offering can be analysed according to the dimensions of the Holiness Spectrum.[1]

Dimension	Fragrant[2] (Censer)	Fragrant (Incense altar)	Ordinary (Censer)	Frankincense (Bronze altar)
Spatial	I	II	III	III
Personal	high priest	high priest	priest	priest
Temporal	once a year	twice daily	occasional[3]	with the *minḥâ*
References	Lev. 16.12-13	Exod. 30.8[4]	Lev. 10.1; Num. 16	Lev. 21.1-2, 15-16 Lev. 6.15 [H 8]

There are three cases in which the illegitimate use of incense is noted, and these illustrate the need to maintain clear boundaries in accord with the Holiness Spectrum. Alien incense (קטרת זרה, Exod. 30.9) is not to be offered upon the incense altar, and this probably refers to incense that does not conform to the proper formula (Exod. 30.34-37).[5] The holy incense may not be offered outside the Tabernacle (Exod. 30.37),[6] and other incense may not be offered inside. These

1. It is likely that only certain kinds of incense are prohibited outside the cult (Nielsen 1986: 89-107), since incense had great practical usefulness (Neufeld 1971). The Priestly acceptance of domestic incense is implied by the availability of censers in Num. 16, and by its presence in the offering of the tribal leaders (Num. 7.14, etc.). Archaeological evidence for non-cultic incense burners is reviewed by Shea (1983) and Fowler (1984).

2. קטרת סמים דקה ('finely ground aromatic incense', Lev. 16.12, NJPSV, NJB). This corresponds to the fragment incense, which was also beaten fine (הָדֵק, Exod. 30.36, from the same root דקק).

3. No fixed or compulsory times for the censor incense offering are noted in P. The occasion of blood sacrifices would be particularly appropriate, since these are to be a soothing odour before the Lord. Numbers 16–17 is since these are to be a soothing odour before the Lord. Numbers 16–17 is a special case, but it may indicate the link between offering incense and the priestly enjoyment of the sacrificial flesh, probably one of the causes for the Korahite rebellion.

4. קטרת התמיד (see §7.1.2).

5. Dillmann (1880: 317), Driver (1911: 331). Durham (1987: 398) translates the phrase 'profane incense', but the adjective stresses the illegitimate character of offering any other type of incense than that ordained.

6. Similarly, the Israelites are prohibited from compounding the holy anointing oil, which is also made of choice spices (Exod. 30.32-33).

laws thus reinforce the grading found in other spheres.

The other two cases are narratives rather than general laws. In the illegitimate offering of Nadab and Abihu (Lev. 10.1-3), it is probably not the incense but the fire that is alien (אש זרה, v. 1). Fire not taken from the altar of burnt offering lacks the necessary holiness for the holy incense offering.[1] The coals, the type of incense, the person offering, and the place of offering must all be of an equivalent grade of holiness. Nadab and Abihu, though qualified priests, violated the first of these conditions and God acted directly in order to preserve the integrity of the sanctuary.[2]

The third occasion concerns the challenge to the Aaronic priesthood mounted by Korah and his followers (Num. 16–17). The issue is focused by the question of who may legitimately offer incense, and the divine punishment confirms the Priestly view that only an Aaronic priest may offer. The theme of incense integrates the two chapters (Num. 16–17), and the successful atonement by the legitimate High Priest through an incense offering (Num. 17.11) confirms his legitimacy in the same terms in which it was challenged.[3]

4.6 *The Symbolism of the Tabernacle*

4.6.1 *The Living God*
The discussion so far has demonstrated the highly structured character of the Priestly portrait of the Tabernacle. Structure, however, rarely exists for its own sake, and the structural polarities embodied in the Tabernacle witness to the central concerns of the Priestly authors, particularly the character of God, and the nature of his dwelling with Israel. The spatial gradation of the Tabernacle presents these themes in terms of the basic human experience of space. The visible and physical features of the Tabernacle are able to give substance and orientation to less tangible aspects of the Priestly theology.

The theme of life appears in numerous different contexts in discussions of Tabernacle symbolism. Although many of these 'life' motifs are implicit, the cumulative evidence that this was a central reference

---

1. Aaron must take fire from the altar (אש מעל המזבח) for his incense offering in Num. 16.46 [H 17.11].

2. Haran (1978: 232). Others, however, consider that another condition has been violated (Greenstein 1989: 56-64).

3. Budd (1984: 198). Others see here an apotropaic meaning (Noth 1968: 130; Haran 1978: 241), one also witnessed in Lev. 16.12-13 (Nielsen 1986: 86).

point for Priestly symbolism is impressive. Thus gold is not only precious, it is also extremely stable, and remains unchanged throughout the generations. It is therefore a fitting material for the heart of a structure that represents the living God who abides forever (§4.4.2).[1] The theme is also communicated by its opposite. All who have come into contact with death (i.e. the impure) are unclean and rigidly excluded from the sanctuary.

The description of the floral bowls and the tree-like shape of the lampstand suggests the 'tree of life' theme known from elsewhere in the Bible and the ancient Near East.[2] The associated ritual of lighting the lamps is part of the daily ritual (§7.1.2) that never ceases and is an 'everlasting statue throughout the generations (חקת עולם לדריחם)' (Lev. 24.3). A link with this theme in the personal dimension is also to be found. The priestly clothes are never to be torn in mourning (Lev. 21.10), and must be worn for the inner ritual by the High Priest in every generation (Num. 20.26).

The same theme is found in connection with sacrifice, the principal ritual performed in the Tabernacle. Although the blood of the animal is poured out in death, this is the means of renewed or enhanced life for the offerer (cf. Lev. 17.11). And although the way in which this happens is still disputed (see Chapter 6), it is difficult to discuss sacrifice without reference to the central issues of life and death.

4.6.2 *The Presence of God*

A second theme that promises to draw together a great number of Tabernacle texts is the presence of God.[3] This has occasioned an

---

1. Other analogies have been suggested. Toorn (1985: 27-28) draws a comparison between gold's luminosity and the 'glowing' skin after washing or anointing. Josephus (*Ant.* 3.184, 187) associates gold and its sheen with sunlight and God.

2. Meyers (1976: 180-81). Compare also the golden frontlet (ציץ, literally 'flower'; cf. KB 959) worn by the high priest (Exod. 28.36 = 39.30; Lev. 8.9), which is probably a symbol of life (de Vaux 1961: 399; de Buck 1951: 18-19).

3. A number of authors have found the key to Priestly theology in the presence of God (e.g. Roth 1954; Saebø 1980: 369, 373). Fishbane (1975: 18) comments, 'Like Sinai, it [the tabernacle] concretizes social space as sacred space and gives expression to the cohesion and blessing of Israel around God's presence'. Durham's recent commentary on Exodus is a *tour de force* of presence theology. However, there is a danger that all possible theological themes are reduced to this common factor, thus reducing the diversity of the Priestly theology.

extensive discussion, particularly because of the contrast which von Rad drew between a theology of presence (*Präsenztheologie*), and one of manifestation (*Erscheinungstheologie*).[1] Von Rad considered that the latter was dominant in the Priestly writings. However, it is difficult to exclude either perspective,[2] and they are perhaps complementary ways of viewing the central place of God in the cult from the static and dynamic points of view (§3.2.1).

Thus the name for the Tabernacle (*miškān*, משכן) suggests the permanent dwelling of God, as do the phrases 'before Yahweh' (לפני יהוה), and 'bread of the presence' (לחם הפנים). The contents of the Tabernacle (the tent and its furniture, which includes a chest, table and bread, and lamp), together with the regular attention paid to them (§7.1.2) also imply that a permanent dwelling place is meant.[3] Although this imagery is qualified by its evident symbolism, it does not undermine the positive significance of presence. Israel is assured of ready access to God in his sanctuary.

Elsewhere, God's presence is conceived more dynamically, and it has a temporary character. The purpose of the sanctuary is that God might meet (נועד, Exod. 29.42, 43) with his people, and the frequent use of 'Tent of Meeting' (אהל מועד, e.g. Exod. 29.44) is a transparent reminder of this theme. On appropriate occasions, God's glory (כבוד) is said to appear (נראה) to Israel or to Moses (Lev. 9.6, 23; cf. Exod. 29.43; 40.34-35; Lev. 9.4; 16.2).

The Holiness Spectrum provides an interesting way in which these two perspectives may be kept together.[4] The close association of presence and holiness (e.g. Exod. 29.42-44; Lev. 16.2) suggests that presence as well as holiness can be a graded quality, and both be exhibited

1. Von Rad (1931).

2. Janowski (1982: 295-354) surveys the discussion and writes of 'the condescending (reigning/meeting) presence of the transcendent God' (p. 347; my translation). This formula seeks to avoid a one-sided solution to the problem, but also illustrates the difficulty of applying sophisticated theological concepts to ancient texts.

3. Haran (1969: 254-55).

4. Many see a historical and polemical development lying behind these two aspects (e.g. Seow 1984: 191; Mettinger 1982: 80-97). Yet these attempts require extensive qualifications, and an alternative synthesis which resolves the tensions theologically is worth considering.

and manifested.[1] It can be considered to have an intensity which varies according to the graded dimensions of the Holiness Spectrum. In addition to a static character ('dwelling'), presence can also be a dynamic concept ('meeting'). Thus on the Day of Atonement, God promises to appear over the cover of the ark (Exod. 25.22; Lev. 16.2). This is the most appropriate place for God to reveal himself, since it is at the holy heart of the Tabernacle.[2] On normal occasions the presence is less evident, but it is invoked by Israel's use of incense in 'smell worship' (§4.6.3).[3] The confinement of the holy fragrant incense to the Tabernacle is one more way to stress that God is present there to an extent not found outside. But this does not prevent God from manifesting himself to all Israel, or from taking a great interest in Israel's affairs.

4.7 *Conclusion*

It is clear from this chapter's survey that the principle of grading pervades the spatial dimension of the Priestly cult. This happens at many levels, including the literary form of the Priestly texts (§4.3), the materials (metals and fabrics) of which the Tabernacle is made (§4.4), and the laws that determine who may go where and do what in the Tabernacle (§4.5). This grading is not just a theoretical structure, but is related to central aspects of the Priestly theology, particularly the character of God himself and his relation to his people (§4.6).

It is already apparent that the spatial dimension is closely aligned with the personal dimension. In particular, there is an important distinction between holy space (the sanctuary and the altar), which is on a par with the holiness of the priests, and other space, in which the laity may move (§4.2.1). The next chapter explores this correlation in more detail.

1.   Brueggemann (1976b: 682) comments, 'Israel's impressions and images ran the gamut from *full presence*, which denied his freedom, to *full freedom*, which made his presence quite uncertain' (author's italics).

2.   Durham (1987: 359) describes the ark and the cover as 'the two [objects] most intimately associated with Yahweh's immanent Presence'. However, P tends to emphasize the significance of the cover.

3.   Durham (1963: 366-67). The cost of the incense implies the same symbolism as that of gold (see above), but in a dynamic ritual context. The symbolism of the cloud or smoke (Lev. 16.12-13; Exod. 40.34-38) may also reflect the way in which God's revealing is also a concealing (Jenni 1976: 352).

Chapter 5

THE PERSONAL DIMENSION

5.1 *Introduction*

5.1.1 *The Personal and the Spatial Dimensions*

Chapter 4 focused on the graded holiness of the Tabernacle, particularly as portrayed in the book of Exodus (Exod. 25–31; 35–40), noting a close correlation between the holiness of the Tabernacle and the priests. In this chapter, the observations concerning the way in which the spatial and personal dimensions are correlated will be considered more closely. The material is drawn primarily from the portrait of the priestly hierarchy in Leviticus, and that of Israel in Numbers.[1]

The priestly class heads the social hierarchy of the personal dimension (§5.1.2). The priesthood is characterized by a unique grade of holiness (§§5.2.1, 5.2.3) that calls for special rules concerning the behaviour of priests (§5.2.4) and their families (§5.2.2) with regard to the holy and the unclean. They are assisted at the sanctuary by the Levites, who are graded according to clan and role (§5.3). At the broad base of the hierarchy are the remaining Israelite tribes. The arrangement of the camp orders the tribes in relation to one another, as well as to the priests and the Levites (§5.4.1).

Three other classifications merit further discussion. The distinctions between clean and unclean (§5.4.2), and between men and women (§5.4.3) apply to all Israelites, and cut across the hierarchical divisions. Israel is also to be distinguished from the nations around in various ways (§5.4.4), although this relationship is not a central concern of the cultic laws.

---

1. The independent perspective of Numbers has been stressed by Childs (1979: 190-201), Budd (1984: xvii-xxxii), Olson (1985) and Ackerman (1987). Nevertheless, it clearly belongs to the P tradition (see the remarks on the unity of P in §1.3.2).

5.1.2 *A Hierarchical Society*

According to P, Israel consisted of a harmonious hierarchy of clans and tribes, priests and laity, leaders and followers.[1] Role and responsibility in the cult depended primarily upon one's place in the hierarchy, although active participation in the cult required the appropriate status of purity. However, the implications of the Holiness Spectrum for Israel were not confined to the cultic sphere, but embraced various aspects of everyday life as well (§§2.2, 3.4, 3.5). Just as P's classification of significant space extended beyond the Tabernacle, so too holiness and purity affect the behaviour of the entire nation in and out of the sanctuary.

The texts illuminate the personal dimension of the Holiness Spectrum in various degrees of detail. As would be expected, P is particularly interested in the priestly classes, and any others who have significant cultic roles (particularly the Levites). The various social groups may be approximately ordered according to their distance from the cult:

Group	*Main Divisions*
The founder of the cult	Moses
The priests	Aaron/the high priest
	The sons of Aaron
	The priests
	The priestly family
The Levites	The Kohathites
	The Gershonites
	The Merarites
The other tribes	The tribes in order
	The leaders of the tribes and clans
	The clan or family
The unclean	Those with minor impurity
(cf. Appendix 2)	Those with temporary major impurity
	Those with a permanent major impurity
Non-Israelites	The sojourner and his or her family
	The nations

These groups are, for the most part, determined by family descent, and it is therefore impossible to transfer from one group to another.

---

1.   Compare Wellhausen (1885: 127): 'according to the representation given in the Priestly Code, the Israelites from the beginning were organised as a hierocracy, the clergy being the skeleton, the high priest the head, and the tabernacle the heart'.

Those not of Aaron's direct family cannot become high priests (Exod. 28.1; §5.2.3), the Levites cannot become priests (Num. 16–17), and members of the other tribes cannot fulfil Levitical functions (Num. 8.14).[1] The division of labour represented by the special tasks of the different groups is authorized by divine command through Moses,[2] or sometimes Moses and Aaron,[3] and has become part of the given order. To challenge and try to change this order is therefore a rebellion against God himself (Num. 16.11).

The hierarchical ordering in the table above is not to be understood rigidly.[4] As with the zones of the Tabernacle (§4.2.1), the extent of differentiation between the groups can depend upon the context. The high priest is sometimes distinguished from the priests, but he also shares much in common. Further, the criteria for making these distinctions vary. In terms of political leadership, Moses and Joshua lead the people (although they may call on divine guidance, mediated through the priesthood), but Aaron and Eleazar are at the head of the priestly hierarchy.

The population of the groups tends to be inversely proportional to its hierarchical order. The most cultic responsibilities fall on the one family of priests. Next come the three families of the Levites, with their limited cultic role, and finally come the other tribes, for whom the communication with God is mediated through the priesthood. On

---

1.   Haran (1971: 1073). Like many priestly laws, the actual practice was probably considerably more flexible. Genealogies tend to be adapted to reflect political and social realities (e.g. Wilson 1977).

2.   Moses does not fit easily into any one category, but transcends them all in his unique role as overall leader, sole law-giver, and high priest (Cazelles 1986: 43-44). In P he is a Levite of the Kohathite clan and the brother of Aaron (Exod. 6.18, 20; §5.3.1), but his genealogy does not limit his role as it does others.

3.   Like Moses, Aaron is portrayed as a unique individual as well as the first high priest (Rivkin 1976: 1-2). However, it is often difficult to tell whether laws addressed to Aaron are for him alone, or also for his high priestly successors. Fortunately, the complex historical problem of the rise of the priesthood does not greatly affect the treatment here.

4.   Wenham (1982: 46) is rather too systematic when he writes, 'Numbers distinguishes at least four grades of permanent holiness: lay, Levitical, priestly and high priestly; one grade of temporary holiness was acquired through taking a Nazirite vow'. Similarly, Ackerman (1987: 80) confuses the initial and continuing aspects of the cult when he writes, 'at the absolute centre of all the concentric circles stands Moses—the unique means of revealing the divine will'.

significant cultic occasions they are represented by their chiefs. The varying sizes of the groups correspond to the arrangement of the camp (§5.4.1).

A high status in the hierarchy brings with it great privileges, although there are not unlimited.[1] The priests had several sources of income and support, including a sizeable share in the booty and the tithes, although they could not own land (Num. 18.20).[2] The Levites were also given sources of income, in addition to cities with their pasture lands. The privileges were the reward for great responsibilities. The priests were not only required to sacrifice, they were also to guard the sanctuary from encroachment.[3] The Levites were also guards, but outside the sanctuary.

Although it could be said that Yahweh has a place at the head of the hierarchy, his uniqueness and distinctiveness are clearly acknowledged. He has supreme status and absolute power, and the authority of Moses stems from his special position as the mediator of Yahweh's commands. But Yahweh did not limit himself to Moses. His will could be communicated by means of the cloud (e.g. Num. 9.15-23; 10.11), and through the consultation of the Urim and Thummim by the high priest (Exod. 28.30; Lev. 8.8).[4] This was probably how Yahweh's will was ascertained in difficult religious (Lev. 24.10-14; Num. 15.32-36) and civil (Num. 27.1-11) cases.

---

1. It may be useful to make a distinction between status and power. In India, priestly castes have the higher status, but others have the greater economic and political power (Dumont 1980).

2. The war booty (Num. 31.25-47) is shared between people, Levites and priests in the ration of 489:10:1. The tithe (Num. 18.26) is also shared between people, Levites and priests in the ration of 90:9:1. When the relative numbers of the groups is taken into account, the priests and Levites would receive a substantial amount. In 11QT 58.13 the proportions are 1/10 (the king), 1/100 (the Levites), 1/1000 (the priests). Num. 18.8 implies that the offerings would amount to a generous stipend (Professor J.R. Porter, personal communication).

3. Some transgressions are punished by God. Milgrom (1970a: 5-8) distinguishes between a death penalty carried out by God (יומת *qal*) and by men (יומת *hophal*).

4. These are probably black and white stones contained in the חשׁן (Lipiński 1970), which could therefore be called the breastplate of judgment (חשׁן המשׁפט, Exod. 28.[15], 30). Joshua asks for guidance with their help (במשׁפט האורים, Num. 27.21).

5.2 *The Priests*

5.2.1 *The Ordination of the Priests*

The principle of graded levels of holiness is central to the outworking of the personal dimension. Israel could be called holy, but this was not intended to diminish the special holiness of the priests, for whom it was the necessary and defining attribute. There was to be a clear distinction between the people (including the Levites, §5.3.1) on the one side, and the priests on the other.[1] The holiness of the priests, when understood in this narrower sense, was of the same order as that of the holy areas of the Tabernacle.[2] The priests could thus perform cultic acts on behalf of the Israelites, who had to remain at a distance from the holy things.

However, only God was holy in the absolute sense, and the narrative records the way in which Israel became a stratified society. The initiation of the priesthood along with the institution of the Tabernacle (§4.2.2) took place at Sinai. The initial ordination of Aaron and his sons is described in great detail (Exod. 28–29 = Lev. 8–9), because it concerns the elevation of one family among many to a unique and permanent status of holy priesthood. Three elements essential to the priesthood are emphasized (Exod. 28.41): the donning of special vestments (§5.2.3), the anointing with holy oil, and the offering of a special ordination sacrifice.[3] Priesthood is implied by any of these elements, but all are needed in the full ritual and are closely associated with consecration and holiness (see also below).[4]

It is possible to label the various stages of the ordination (Lev. 8–9) in terms of a *rite de passage* (§3.2.4). Those undergoing the ritual

---

1. 'Since the priests are holy and permanently before Yahweh in their service, their separateness from the common Israelites is stressed' (Koch 1959: 101-102; cf. Cody 1969: 191-92).

2. Haran (1971: 1080). See also Haran 1983b.

3. Durham 1987: 389. The phrase מלא את־היד (lit. to fill the hand) is a difficult one (see Snijders 1984: 881-84 for a recent discussion). It could refer to the complete ordination ritual (e.g. Exod. 29.35), or to the special ordination sacrifice (the איל המלאים, Lev. 8.22).

4. E.g. 'you shall anoint them and ordain them and consecrate them' (Exod. 28.41; cf. 29.33); similarly for anointing (30.29-30—both Tabernacle and priests) and Exod. 40.9-15. The oil is holy (Exod. 30.25), as are the clothes (28.2) and the sacrificial portions (29.33).

were initially separated from the community and hence from their previous role in it (the rite of separation). Then there follows an intermediate period with appropriate rituals, during which they were in a marginal or 'liminal' state. Finally, a special rite of aggregation reintegrated them into society, though now with a new status.[1]

Initial state

Aaron and his sons are clean.

Aaron and his sons wear normal clothing.

Rite of separation (Lev. 8)

Moses washes Aaron and his sons with water (v. 6).[2]

Moses dresses Aaron and sons in their special clothing (vv. 7-9, 13).

Moses anoints and consecrates the Tabernacle (vv. 10-11).

Moses pours the anointing oil on Aaron (v. 12).

Moses offers 3 sacrifices (vv. 14-29) —*ḥaṭṭā't* (bull), *'ōlâ* (ram,), *millŭîm* (ram).

Moses sprinkles anointing oil and blood on Aaron and his clothing.

Moses sprinkles anointing oil and blood on Aaron's sons and clothing (v. 30).

Marginal state

Aaron and his sons remain in sanctuary for seven days (vv. 33, 35).

Rite of aggregation (Lev. 9)

Aaron offers a representative selection of sacrifices.[3]

    (a) for himself (vv. 8-14) —*ḥaṭṭā't* (calf), *'ōlâ* (ram)

    (b) for Israel (vv. 15-21) —*ḥaṭṭā't* (goat), *'ōlâ* (calf and lamb, 1 year old)

                                  —*minhâ* (grain), *šᵉlāmîm* (ox and ram)

Aaron blesses the people by himself (v. 22) and with Moses (v. 23).

The glory of Yahweh appears (v. 23).

Fire from Yahweh consumes the sacrifices (v. 24a).

The people respond by shouting and prostration (v. 24b).

Final state

Aaron and his sons are priests.

As a result, the priests were elevated to a holiness equivalent to that of the sanctuary in which they were to serve. However, the exercise of

---

1. Adapted from Leach (1976: 89-91). Leach considers the rite of separation to end before the ram of ordination is sacrificed, but it is best to maintain the unity of the initial ritual complex.

2. While strictly redundant, this could imply that something more than mere purification was involved.

3. They include most kinds of offering (the אשׁם is for specific offences) and most kinds of animals, except birds, which are generally reserved for the poor (Wenham 1979b: 149).

priesthood still required a clean status and a preliminary purification ritual by washing at the laver (Exod. 30.17-21), as well as donning the appropriate clothes. While the priests were fully consecrated, they lost their full holiness when they left the sanctuary. The preliminary rituals recalled the initial consecration and confirmed that the priestly holiness was once again effective, and that it was safe for them to take on the priestly role.

The ordination, in form and content, is closely associated with the sanctification of the Tabernacle. Thus the instructions to ordain Aaron and his sons, and their fulfilment, follow immediately upon the instructions to consecrate the Tabernacle and their fulfilment (Exod. 40.8-11/12-15; Lev. 8.10-11/12-13). Moses acts as the agent of divine sanctification for both, and the principal act of consecration was anointing with oil. During the ordination, both the altar (Lev. 8.15) and the priests with their garments (Lev. 8.30) were purified by the blood of a חמאת (§6.2.2).

5.2.2 *The Priestly Hierarchy*

Aaron stands at the summit of the priestly hierarchy and was the first of the high priestly line. He was the priest *par excellence*, and could be referred to simply as 'the priest' (Exod. 29.30; 'Aaron the priest' in 31.10; Num. 3.6).[1] Yahweh sometimes spoke to him directly (Lev. 10.8; Num. 18.1, 8, 20), and he was even able to correct Moses on a cultic matter (Lev. 10.16-20).[2] His special ministry in the inner sanctuary led to his being subject to certain laws which imply a special degree of holiness (§5.2.4). He had to take great care to ensure the highest standards of purity, even while outside the sanctuary.

Aaron was ordained together with his sons, and the priesthood from then on was a hereditary job taken over by the Aaronides in general.[3] The sons of the high priest shared some of his special pre-eminence,

---

1. Sometimes Aaron (and his sons) is identified specifically, while at other times he is referred to as the high priest or the anointed priest (Bailey 1951). The varied terminology may reflect several eras, a certain fluidity in the language, or an emphasis upon Aaron's role as the first high priest or the priest *par excellence*.

2. Gunneweg (1965: 140) considers that the tradition has magnified Aaron by recording that he was Moses' older brother (Exod. 7.7).

3. The priestly accounts concentrate on Aaron's immediate family, but the laws imply that the priesthood was more extensive.

and were given various responsibilities.[1] The death of Nadab and Abihu (Lev. 10.1-3) stressed that these responsibilities entailed strict obedience, and disobedience would evoke divine sanctions. Following this, Eleazar and Ithamar were warned about certain types of behaviour which would compromise their fitness as priests (Lev. 10.6).[2]

The eldest son of the high priest held the second highest position in the hierarchy. Eleazar had overall leadership of the Levites (Num. 3.32), and he supervised the sanctuary vessels carried by the Kohathites (4.16). The younger son, Ithamar, oversaw the other two Levitical clans (Gershonites 4.28; Merarites 4.33; 7.8), who carried the less holy materials of the sanctuary, and who thus had a less dangerous task. Ithamar was also in charge of the inventories of the Tabernacle (Exod. 38.21).

Eleazar, instead of Aaron, also performed priestly roles for the whole community when there was some danger of defilement from corpses (Num. 17.2; 19.3). This was no doubt because Aaron's primary ministry was in the sanctuary, and for this he would have had to maintain the highest degree of purity. In the same way, Eleazar's own son, Phinehas, performed the same function for him (Num. 31.6) once he was high priest (Num. 20.22-29).[3] This close relationship between the high priest and his sons suggests that the sons could take Aaron's place if he became unclean and was not able to minister in the holy sanctuary. In Lev. 10.6, Aaron's sons are commanded not to mourn, a law applicable to the high priest (Lev. 21.10), suggesting that in certain contexts they had high priestly status.[4]

1. Koch (1959: 102): 'The different grade of holiness determines a distinction of class between the high priest and his "sons" '. The historical questions about the origin of the high priesthood in Israel, and how much royal ideology underlies the Priestly portrayal, will not be pursued (see the summary in de Vaux 1961: 400-401).

2. The nature of Nadab and Abihu's disobedience, and its relation to the instructions to Eleazar and Ithamar are unclear (but see §4.5.2). See Gradwohl (1963), Laughlin (1976), Kiuchi (1987: 68-71).

3. Gray (1903: 420). Budd (1984: 330) suggests that Phinehas is sent out because Eleazar would have to perform the purification rites on return from war. But the only qualification is that the sprinkler should be clean (Num. 19.18), and this need not be a priest, especially since the sprinkler is inevitably defiled (v. 21). Phinehas' important priestly role is reflected in the tradition, in which he exhibits great moral and religious zeal. In Num. 25.1-13 he deals with a grave sexual sin which poses a threat to the religious integrity of the nation (Pedersen 1940: 187).

4. Kiuchi (1987: 70). Some texts imply that only the high priest is anointed and

Although the priesthood was exclusively male, the entire extended family of priests was affected by priestly status. The special role of the priests meant that they had no inheritance in Canaan (Num. 18.20), and were supported by the Israelites. Aside from the sacrificial portions (§6.4.5), they obtained a portion of the Levitical tithe (Num. 18.26-29), the firstborn and the firstfruits (Num. 18.12-19), and 1/1000 of the booty (Num. 31.25-29). The priestly family included the slaves, but not hired workers or daughters married to a non-priest (Lev. 22.10-16). The latter were able to return and eat again of these offerings if their husband had died or divorced them and they had no offspring (v. 13).[1] The laws of the cult are again aligned with Israelite social and legal structures.

The priestly privileges entailed a greater responsibility for obedient behaviour and a correspondingly severe punishment for serious sins. A priest's daughter who had become a prostitute was to be burnt (Lev. 21.9), though the standard form of execution was stoning (Deut. 22.21).[2] Sexual sins may have constituted an offence against the special holiness of the priestly line,[3] since she is said to profane her father (את־אביה היא מחללת, Lev. 21.9).

is subject to strict mourning customs (Lev. 21.10), and this is generally interpreted as an earlier stage than the texts which describe the anointing of the sons (Exod. 29.21) and their subjection to mourning restrictions (Lev. 10.6-7; Noth 1962: 230; 1965: 86). However, it is likely that the sons acted as high priest on certain occasions (e.g. when Aaron was unclean), and so a contextual approach to the final text is plausible.

1.   Contrast the way in which the children born of a levirate marriage ensured the continuation of the 'name' of the husband (Deut. 25.5-10).

2.   Vos (1968: 95-97). A similar severe punishment is indicated for a man taking both a wife and her mother in Lev. 20.14. The burning may only refer to the treatment of the corpse after stoning (Josh. 7.15, 25; Amos 2.1; Keil 1882: 427; Dillmann 1880: 561).

3.   Some find overtones of cultic prostitution, for which the daughter of a high priest would be an especially eligible candidate (Elliger 1959: 289; Porter 1965: 370-71; Vos 1968: 96-97). Or H may be subsuming ethical action under the holiness category. In Lev. 19.29, *ḥll* (חלל) is used in connection with anyone allowing a daughter to commit harlotry. But more may be implied in context. The female members cannot be holy in the stricter sense, since they are not consecrated and are forbidden to enter the holy places.

124 · Graded Holiness

5.2.3 *The Priestly Garments*

Groups with special roles are often distinguished by their clothing, and for P the priestly garments had an important ritual and symbolic function.[1] The special garments worn during their ministry in the sanctuary distinguished the priests from the lay. They also suitably expressed the holiness of a priest at these times, in contrast to the everyday clothes worn in the camp, where it did not matter greatly whether the priest was unclean or not.

As was found for the description of the Tabernacle furniture (§4.3.1), there is a correlation between the order in which the clothes are described and their importance:

Clothing	A Exod. 28.6-43	B Exod. 39.1-43	C Exod. 28.4	D Exod. 29.5-9	E Lev. 8.7-9	F Lev. 16.4	G m. Yom. 7.5
1. Ephod	1	1	2	3	4		6
2. Breastplate	2	2	1	4	5		5
3. Robe	3	3	3	2	3		7
4. Rosette	4	9*			7		8
Diadem[2]		9*		6	7		
5. Tunic	5 (1s)	4* (+s)	4	1 (1s)	1	1	1 (+s)
6. Turban	6	5	5	5	6	4	3 (+s)
Headdress	(3s)	6		(3s)			
7. Sash	7 (2s)	8	6	(2s)	2	3	4 (+s)
8. Under- garments	8* (+s)	7				2	2 (+s)

Key: s   indicates the garments of the sons of Aaron

+s the garments for Aaron and his sons are described together

*   indicates that the item is marked off from the previous items in some way

Some of the lists probably give the order in which the garments were put on (D, E). The undergarments covered the genital regions (Exod. 28.42-43),[3] and so were the first to be put on for ministry

---

1.   Surveyed by Gabriel (1933), Haulotte (1966: 44-54), Haran (1978: 165-74). The NRSV translations have usually been followed.

2.   נזר in Exod. 39.30 (ציץ נזר הקדש זהב טהור; cf. Lev. 8.9 ציץ הזהב נזר הקדש) could have a concrete or a symbolic reference; i.e. 'the frontlet for the holy diadem of pure gold' (NJPSV; cf. Exod. 29.6, where the phrase is replaced by נזר הקדש), or 'a rosette of pure gold as a symbol of their holy dedication' (NEB; cf. Lev. 21.12; Num. 6.1-21).

3.   Their purpose was to cover בשר ערוה, and בשר ('flesh') is probably a

(Lev. 6.3). This law can be associated with the careful regulation of sexual matters in relation to the cult (§3.5.2).[1] The other garments were 'for glory and beauty' (לכבוד ולתפארת, Exod. 28.2, 40; cf. Sir. 45.12-13; 50.5-14).

The order indicates clearly the superior grading of the high priest in the personal hierarchy, and his special role in the Tabernacle. The high priest wore an elaborate set of eight garments, while the ordinary priests wore only four.[2] And whereas the high priest wore a turban, the priests wore headdresses (מגבעות or פארי מגבעות), which were probably less elaborate items.[3] Only the four high priestly garments, which were highly symbolic, are described in detail. Although all the priestly garments were holy,[4] those of the high priest were distinct from the others, in accord with the way that Aaron is often treated separately from his sons (e.g. Exod. 31.10; 35.19; 39.41). The transfer of the high priestly office is bound up with the transfer of these garments (Exod. 29.29-30; Num. 20.28).

The holiness of the high priestly garments is expressed by the way their materials (gold thread, §4.4.1) and weave (§4.4.2) are aligned with the materials of the Tabernacle.[5] When Aaron and his sons are

euphemism for the genital organs (cf. Lev. 15.2, 3, 7; KB 157; Bratsiotis 1973: 852). They are therefore mentioned as a separate item at the end of list A (Dillmann 1880: 313; Keil 1882: 205), and the lists can assume this preliminary stage (C, D, E).

1. Cf. Exod. 20.24-26, which forbids steps to an altar. This law has been thought to deny Canaanite fertility practices, or the custom that priests minister naked (Childs 1974: 466-67).

2. The distinction between the two sets of garments is made clearly in Exod. 28.5-43 (contrast the summary in 28.4, 41, in which Aaron and his sons are mentioned together). In Exod. 39 the first three high priestly garments are described, then those in common, and then after a break the final high priestly item (v. 31 עליו = Aaron).

3. Haran (1978: 170).

4. בגדי קדש characterises the garments of Aaron (Exod. 28.2; 29.29; 39.1; Lev. 16.4) and his sons (Exod. 28.4; 35.19). In Exod. 39.30 the phrase נזר הקדש (holy diadem) is used, and in Exod. 28.36 = 39.30 the frontlet (ציץ) is engraved 'Holy to the Lord' (קדוש ליהוה).

5. In P, the stress is on the fact that the high priest's clothing and sanctity are of the same order as the sanctuary (§4.4.2). The Tabernacle is also anointed (Exod. 30.26-30; 40.9-15). A number of these garments and materials correspond to royal vestments (e.g. the turban, Ezek. 21.31; the crown נזר, 2 Kgs 11.12 = 2 Chron. 23.11), and the high priest is anointed like the king (e.g. 1 Sam. 10.1). This is

consecrated, the donning of the priestly clothes is an essential part of the ritual (Exod. 28.41; 29.5-9 = Lev. 8.7-13; Lev. 8.30). The blood of the ram of ordination is sprinkled on Aaron and his clothes, and on his sons and their clothes (Exod. 29.21 = Lev. 8.7-15). Other garments are worn outside the sanctuary for ordinary life in the camp (implied by Exod. 28.43; cf. Ezek. 44.19).

The order in the accounts that describe the making of the garments offers a better guide to their relative importance (A, B; cf. G). The breastplate was probably the most important,[1] not only because of its primary place in two of the summary lists (Exod. 28.4; *m. Yom.* 7.5), but also because of its material and function. It was made of the most costly material (precious stones and pure gold), and contained the sacred oracle, the Urim and Thummim (Exod. 28.30). The stones represented the 12 tribes of Israel (28.21, 29; see §5.4.1), and these, together with the Urim and Thummim, were given a special function in the ministry of the high priest in the holy place (28.29-30).

The garments of the high priest were elaborate and striking:

Clothing	Coloured	Material	Checkered	Weave	Lev. 16
1. Ephod	gold	fine twisted		designed	–
(אפד)	28.6 = 39.2-3	28.6 = 39.2		28.6 = 39.2	
2. Breastplate	gold	fine twisted	checkered	designed	–
(חשׁן האפד)	28.15 = 39.8	28.15 = 39.8	28.20 = 39.13	28.15 = 39.8	
3. Robe	pure blue[2]				–
(מעיל)	28.33 = 39.24				
4. Rosette		pure gold			–
(ציץ)		28.36 = 39.30			
6. Turban		fine linen			linen
(מצנפת)		28.39 = 39.28			

frequently regarded as a sign that the high priest has taken over the position and attributes of the king (e.g. Wellhausen 1885: 150; de Vaux 1961: 400-401). In terms of the Priestly redaction, this would emphasize the status of the high priest as head of the hierarchy.

1. The ephod is first in some of the lists, probably because it provided the support for the breastplate (Exod. 28.25-27 = 39.18-20; Cassuto 1967: 373). The squareness of the breastplate (רבוע, 28.16 = 39.9) could be a further mark of its holy character (cf. §§4.3.2, 5.4.1).

2. The robe is simply described as woven (Exod. 28.32 = 39.22). However, it is blue and is decorated with coloured pomegranates (28.31 = 39.22) and golden bells (28.34 = 39.25). This suggests that it is one of the higher grades of weave (cf. §4.4.2).

Clothing	Coloured	Material	Checkered	Weave	Lev. 16
7. Sash) (אבנט)	coloured 39.29	fine twisted 39.29		embroidered 28.39 = 39.29	linen
8. Under-garments (מכנסי בד)			fine twisted 39.28		linen

Explanation of terms:

a. Coloured — blue, purple and crimson (תכלת וארגמן (ו)תולעת שני)

b. Gold (coloured) — gold threads worked in as well (זהב תכלת וארגמן (ו)תולעת שני), 39.3)

c. Material — linen (בד), fine linen (שש), fine twisted linen (שש משזר)

d. Checkered — חשבץ (39.13); מוסבת משבצות זהב (Exod. 28.20) or משבצים זהב (28.4) or שבצת (28.39)

e. Weave (§4.4.2) — designed (חשב), embroidered (רקם), woven (ארג)

f. Lev. 16 — refers to the garments worn by the high priest on the Day of Atonement (Lev. 16.4; see §7.4)

The quality and materials of the garments are similar to those of the Tabernacle (§4.4.2). The high priestly garments exhibit a mixed character appropriate to a high degree of holiness (§3.5.2). Several garments contained coloured wool in addition to the basic linen garment, and gold threads were worked into the weave of the two most important items, the Ephod (28.6 = 39.2) and the breastplate (28.15 = 39.8), and these are also chequered. It is a reasonable assumption that the high priestly garments communicated holiness,[1] whereas those of other priests did not. Ordinary priests had regular close contact with the people on numerous occasions, such as the offering of sacrifices or the performance of rituals outside the camp, and the danger of accidental contact and transmission of holiness would have been unavoidable.

The 12 stones on the square breastplate of the high priest contain the names of the Israelite tribes, and the four-fold arrangement may be compared to the similar symmetry of the Israelite camp (§5.4.1).[2]

---

1.   It is occasionally noted that Aaron plays a high priestly role outside the sanctuary (Num. 20.26; cf. 16.46 [H17.11-12]). The communicable holiness of the garments implies that precautions would have been taken to prevent any contact with non-priests. However, as is often the case in P, it is uncertain whether this external role is to be regarded as unique or paradigmatic.

2.   However, no information is provided by P about the order of names on the stones.

This complements the names of the tribes of Israel engraved on two stones on the shoulder straps of the ephod. The high priest represents Israel and brings them to remembrance before God when he enters the holy place, thus evoking his effective intervention (אבני זכרן for the ephod, 28.12 = 39.7; לזכרן for the breastplate, 28.29 = 39.29).

5.2.4 *Marriage and Mourning*

The degree of holiness affected not only cultic behaviour, but also the restraints on family and community life. This is particularly noticeable in the *rites de passage* (§3.2.4) of marriage and mourning. The laws set out a way in which high priest, priest and Israelite took on distinct behaviour patterns (Lev. 21.1-15), and the literary form of this passage conveys the graded structure of the priesthood. It begins with the rules about the priests in mourning (vv. 1-6) and marriage (vv. 7-9), and this is analogous to those for the high priest (mourning vv. 10-12,[1] marriage vv. 13-15), except that the demands on him are stricter.[2]

The spectrum of allowed partners, mourning customs and is set out below.[3]

	High Priest	Priest	Israelite	References
Choice of Wife				
virgin (בתולה)	Yes	Yes	Yes	Lev. 21.13-14; Ezek. 44.22
widow (אלמנה)	No	No	Yes	Lev. 21.7, 14; Ezek. 44.22
priestly widow	No	Yes?	Yes	Ezek. 44.22
divorced (גרשה)	No	No	Yes	Lev. 21.7, 14; Ezek. 44.22
prostitute (זנה)	No	No	No?	Lev. 21.7, 14

1. Verses 10-12 are unified by a double reference to anointing oil at the beginning and end of the section, and this highlights the contrasting impurity of the corpse (v. 11).

2. The wife of the high priest is not mentioned, perhaps because defilement was unavoidable if she died suddenly (Döller 1917: 135). One verse could suggest that P sought to present such an ideal picture of the undefiled high priest that he always remained in sanctuary (Lev. 21.12). However, this text is better taken to refer to the period of ordination (Haran 1978: 177 n. 4), since garments and anointing oil are mentioned. Alternatively, it could refer to the specific occasions when the high priest was required to minister in the sanctuary and was informed about the death of a relative (cf. Lev. 10.3-7).

3. Not all the cases are explicitly treated in P (or elsewhere). However, some are also found as general prohibitions, and for others an *a fortiori* principle can be reasonably applied.

Mourning Custom

dishevelled hair (פרע ראש)	No?	Yes	No?	Lev. 21.10
torn clothes (פרם בגד)	No	Yes	No?	Lev. 21.10
baldness (קרח קרחה בראש)	No?	No	No	Lev. 21.5; Deut. 14.1
beard shaved (גלח פאת זקנים)	No?	No	No	Lev. 21.5; 19.27
flesh lacerated (שרט שרטת בבשר)	No?	No	No	Lev. 21.5; 19.28; Deut. 14.1

Mourning of Partner

Intentional defilement by corpse of   Lev. 21.1-4, 11; Num. 19

wife	Yes?	Yes	Yes
close relative[1]	No	Yes	Yes
any Israelite	No	No	Yes

Anyone who partakes in mourning practices and who incurs corpse defilement is touched by death, and for a priest this gives rise to a tension with his call to be holy and serve the living God. The tension is expressed in a set of laws for mourning, graded according to the level of holiness. Some of the customs which were allowed for ordinary Israelites were forbidden for the priests, and some of these were forbidden for the high priest, who had to be at the furthest remove from any taint of death. Other priests had a lesser grade of holiness and were not concerned with ministry in the inner sanctuary, so the restrictions were less severe. The laws thus affirm the incompatibility between death and the cultic personnel, while also recognizing the inevitable occurrence of death. The graded distancing from death points to the character of the living God who dwelt at the centre of the sanctuary, who could not be touched by death at all (§4.6.1).

Some customs were completely forbidden to all, and in these cases their repetition in the texts setting out priestly duties emphasizes the necessity for the priests to observe them with great care. It is likely that their participation in the reality of death crossed the boundary of legitimate symbolism, since they concerned the mutilation of the body, not just disordering hair and tearing clothes. Their practice was a

---

1. I.e. father, mother, son, daughter, brother, virgin sister.

deliberate attempt to seek death and thus a denial of Israel's confession (§3.5.1).

The laws regarding marriage normally involved matters of purity and fitness, which were of central concern only to the priests. The high priest had to marry a virgin of his (priestly) kin (בתולה מעמיו, Lev. 21.14),[1] but this is not stated explicitly for the priests, who were probably allowed to marry a priestly widow as well as an Israelite virgin.[2] The priests were forbidden to marry prostitutes,[3] especially because, like a divorcee or non-priestly widow, she would have had sexual relations with a non-priest.[4] The penalty for a high priest partaking in these forbidden customs is not mentioned, possibly because it was unthinkable that such an offence could occur without divine judgement (cf. Lev. 10.1-3).

5.3 *The Levites*

5.3.1 *The Initiation of the Levites*
Levites as well as priests had a close relationship to the sanctuary, but it was of a very different kind, according to P.[5] As was the case for the priesthood (§5.2.1), the initiation of a group with important cultic

---

1. Wenham (1972: 336-38) suggests that virgin (בתולה) implies an adolescent. Less certain is his suggestion that older women or widows could come under the suspicion that they had illicitly misused the freedom following bereavement or divorce (1979b: 292).

2. This is the law of Ezek. 44.22 ('They shall not marry a widow, or a divorced woman, but only a virgin of the stock of the house of Israel, or a widow who is the widow of a priest', NRSV).

3. Lev. 21.7 refers to זנה וחללה (וחללה זנה, v. 14; *BHS* wishes to read וזנה). This may refer to a woman who has lost her virginity in some way (from חלל = to pierce; e.g. NEB, KB 307 ['entjungfert']; Amorim 1986: 181 n. 1), but Zipor (1987) has recently argued that the variation is characteristic of hendiadys. It is taken from חלל = to profane) and refers to the woman who profanes the holy priestly stock by being a prostitute (cf. v. 9). The rabbinic interpretation refers it to the offspring of a mixed marriage (e.g. high priest/widow, ordinary priest/divorced woman; Snaith 1967: 99; Rashi on Lev. 21.7).

4. G.I. Davies (personal communication). Israelites would no doubt have been discouraged from marrying a prostitute, but no OT law explicitly prohibits this (cf. Exod. 20.14; Num. 25.1; Deut. 22.21; Hos. 1.2).

5. There is as little scholarly consensus about the history of the Levites as for the priests, but the Priestly portrait is relatively clear.

responsibilities is described in detail (Num. 8.13-22), but a comparison shows significant differences:

Priests: Initiation (Lev. 8)	*Levites: Initiation (Num. 8)*
Moses	Moses
washes them with water	sprinkles them with the water of
clothes Aaron and anoints him	purification (מי חטאת, v. 7)
(vv. 7-9, 12)	Levites
clothes Aaron's sons (v. 13)	shave (v. 7)
offers the standard sacrifices	wash their clothes (v. 7)
offers the ordination sacrifice	Aaron
puts blood on extremities (vv. 23-24)	separates them (הבדיל, v. 14)
offers them as a *tᵉnûphâ* (v. 27)	offers them as a *tᵉnûphâ* (v. 11)
	Levites offer sacrifices (vv. 12, 21)
Purpose: to consecrate them (vv. 10, 30)	Purpose: to purify them (v. 21)

Priests: Role	*Levites: Role*
offer sacrifices (Lev. 1–7)	hard labour (עבודה) for the sanctuary (Num. 8.19, 21)
disqualified by impurity and blemishes (Lev. 21–22)	disqualified by impurity (but not by blemishes?)[1]
serve in the holy place (לשרת בקדש) (Exod. 28.43; 35.19; cf. Num. 4.12)	serve (שרת) Aaron (Num. 3.6; 18.2), and the people (Num. 16.9)
guard the holy place and the altar (לשמר משמרת, Num. 18.5)	guard Aaron and the tent (לשמר משמרת, Num. 18.3)
superintend packing of the Tabernacle (Num. 4.16, 28, 33)	carry and transport Tabernacle items (Num. 3.21-37; cf. §§4.4.3, 5.4.1)

The initiation of the Levites was a purification, and they are never described as holy. Nevertheless there are elements in the ritual which hint at an ordination and consecration. The Levites took the place of the first-born, whom God consecrated to himself at the Exodus (הקדשתי אתם לי, Num. 8.17),[2] and were presented as a *tᵉnûphâ* (תנופה, Num. 8.11, 13, 15, 21),[3] normally a sacrifice and thus holy. While the

---

1.   The rabbinic opinion is that age but not blemishes disqualifies a Levite, while the reverse is true for priests (*b. Ḥul.* 24a; Rashi on Num. 8.24).

2.   In Num. 8.17 God's consecration of the first-born of men and beasts to himself can be associated with the wider sense of holiness, rather than the special priestly holiness (cf. Haran 1978: 59).

3.   Traditionally translated 'wave offering'. Milgrom (1983a: 133-58) argues that 'elevated offering' is more correct, but Anderson (1987: 133-35) prefers 'additional offering'.

initiation ritual results only in their purification, this should probably be considered to be of a higher quality than normal.

Whereas the community played a minor and passive role in the ordination of the priests (Lev. 8.3-4), the Israelites laid hands (סמך) on the Levites (Num. 8.10). This probably indicates that the Levites were identified as taking the place of their first-born (Num. 8.16-18). The way in which the Levites substituted for the firstborn of the other tribes is worked out in precise numerical detail. An imbalance in the numbers, found after a census of the Levites (Num. 3.14-39), required that the firstborn without a Levitical equivalent had to be redeemed (פדויי) for five shekels each (Num. 3.40-51). The principle was extended to the livestock as well, which were also included in the Exodus narrative (Exod. 11.5,7; 12.29). However, exact equivalence does not seem to have been necessary for animals (Num. 3.41, 45).

The Levites' subordination to the priests is clearly expressed in the Priestly presentation of their role.[1] In texts which mention both Levites and priests, the Levites are mentioned second, as in the records of their genealogies (Num. 3.1-4 before 3.5-13), tasks (18.1, 6 bracketing 18.2-5), and maintenance (18.8-20 before 18.21-24).[2] The appointment of the Levites (Num. 8) also comes after that of the priests (Lev. 8), whom they are commanded to serve.

There was a clear division of labour: the Levites were to guard the sanctuary, while the priests protected the holy items inside.[3] The Levites were not allowed access to the holy things on pain of death (Num. 4.15).[4] They were directed to serve Aaron, and were under the authority of him and his sons (§5.2.2). They did not serve Yahweh directly in the sanctuary, as did the priests; rather they guarded the sanctuary from defilement on the outside and performed the hard labour (עבודה) of its dismantling and erection. Only the priests could safely pack and cover the holy items (Num. 4.5-20; §4.4.3), and subsequently the coverings provided the necessary barrier between the

---

1. This is also expressed formally.
2. Horbury (1983: 53).
3. Spencer (1984) points out that the normal military meaning of שמר (guard) and צבא (a military unit) should be retained.
4. 'According to the priestly school. . .all the functions of the Levites are performed outside the cultic sanctity. The Levites have no place inside the priestly circle' (Haran 1978: 61).

holiness of the Tabernacle and the Levites.[1]

The priority of the Aaronides is confirmed in the narrative of Korah's rebellion (Num. 16–17).[2] Korah was of Levitical stock (16.1) and challenged the authority of Moses and the assignment of a special degree of holiness to the Aaronic priests. He asserted that 'all the community are holy, all of them' (v. 3). Since God was in Israel's midst, there was no need for a special priestly class. An appropriate priestly function was chosen for the test, and Yahweh's judgment on Korah, together with the successful priestly action of Aaron (atonement by the incense offering, Num. 17.11; see §4.5.3), reaffirmed the given order. The postscript (17.17-26) confirms this in narrating how the rod of the tribe of Levi with Aaron's name on was the only one that budded. This was stored in the Tent of Meeting and acted as a permanent expression of Aaron's supremacy and holiness before Yahweh.

Although the Priestly portrait of the Levites is normally interpreted as reflecting disputes over the identity of the priesthood, there is no overt downgrading of the Levites. The choice of the Levites to assist the priests was a practical, valuable and necessary contribution to the ordered exercise of the cult.[3] The Levites were relieved of agricultural work and military duties,[4] and were supported by the tithes of the Israelites (Num. 18.24) and a share of booty (Num. 31.25-43). In the land they were to be given cities with their associated pasturelands (Num. 35.1-8).[5]

The intermediate place of the Levites in the Israelite hierarchy is also expressed in the genealogy (Exod. 6.16-25):

---

1. Other tasks were doubtless performed, such as assisting offerers in the slaughtering of animals. The priests had special responsibilities for communal sacrifices but the Levites could assist (cf. 2 Chron. 29.34).

2. The literary analysis of Num. 16–17 is complex (see recently Milgrom 1981d; Magonet 1982; Ahuis 1983), but the relevant Korah passages are usually assigned to P (Budd 1984: 181-91). Whatever the historical circumstances, the Holiness Spectrum is able to illuminate the issues.

3. Milgrom (1970b) points to a Hittite text that refers to two classes of guard, both of which have their responsibilities and privileges.

4. They were not numbered in the military censuses (Num. 1; 26), but were counted separately for the first-born calculations (Num. 1.47, 49; 2.33; 3).

5. Milgrom (1982).

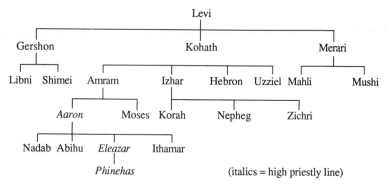

The genealogy reflects the peculiar status of the Levites. They are aligned with the rest of the Israelites in that the tribe is not to be identified with the priestly clan. On the other hand, they are far closer to the priests than anyone else, and their genealogical relation to them (a common tribal ancestor, Levi) is reflected in their special Levitical role.[1]

5.3.2 *The Families of the Levites*
The three Levitical clans are graded by location and by task, a point emphasized when the text records their details in an order other than birth (see the table on the next page). The first census (Num. 3) follows the birth order, as would be expected, but not the second, in which the tasks are given in detail (Num. 4). The formal structure of the texts thus once again stresses the grading. The location in the camp and the level of difficulty and danger involved in their tasks are all aligned with the relative importance of the clans.

Kohath is probably first because Aaron belonged to this clan (Exod. 6.18, 20), and they were given charge of the most holy (and dangerous) part of the sanctuary, the furniture (שׁמרי משׁמרת הקדשׁ, Num. 3.28).[2] As always, privilege is commensurate with responsibility,

---

1. Wellhausen (1885: 121-22). Gunneweg (1965: 155) also describes the Levites as 'a kind of minor cleric. . . a kind of priest of a lower rank without priestly rights in the narrower sense' (p. 139; my translation). Pedersen calls them 'lower priests, who have some holiness' (1940: 283).

2. Kohath also has the most males. However, Merari has more eligible for service aged between 30 and 50 (first Merari 3200, second Kohath 2750, third Gershon 2630; Num. 4.44, 36, 40).

and the Kohathites are singled out for warning (Num. 4.18-20). The other two clans dealt with the hangings and the framework, which were not communicably holy and needed less supervision and participation by the priests (§5.2.2).

	Kohath	*Gershon*	*Merari*
Order (importance)	first (Num. 4.1-20)	second (Num. 4.21-28)	third (Num. 4.29-33)
Numbers (males) (from 1 month)	first (8600) (Num. 3.28)	second (7500) (Num. 3.22)	third (6200) (Num. 3.34)
Orientation in Camp (§5.4.1)	south (second) (Num. 3.29)	west (third) (Num. 3.23)	north (fourth) (Num. 3.35)
Charge (משמרת)	furniture[1] (Num. 3.31)	woven materials (Num. 3.25-26)	framework (Num. 3.36-37)
Means of Transport	poles on shoulder (Num. 7.9; §4.4.3)	2 wagons 4 oxen (Num. 7.7)	4 wagons 8 oxen (Num. 7.8)
Order of birth[2]	second	first	third

5.4 *The People*

5.4.1 *The Camp*

When we turn to the people as a whole, one of the clearest ways in which the graded relation between the various groups is expressed is by the architecture of the camp (Num. 2–3).[3] In the square or rectangular encampment, the tribes and Levitical clans are graded both by distance from the centre, and by orientation. The east is the most privileged direction (and then clockwise, south, west, north), corresponding to the eastward orientation of the entrances to the Tabernacle (Exod. 27.13 = 38.13).

---

1. This included the innermost screen (מסך, normally called the פרכת, see §4.2.1), while the Gershonites carried the other two entrance hangings, the screens for the Tent of Meeting and the court (Num. 4.25-26).

2   Cf. Gen. 46.11; Exod. 6.16; 1 Chr. 6; Num. 3.17, 21-37.

3.   Compare also the order in which the tribal leaders present their offerings (Num. 7.12-83): Judah, Issachar, Zebulun; Reuben, Simeon, Gad; Ephraim, Manasseh, Benjamin; Dan, Asher, Naphtali. This corresponds to that of the camp if priority is accorded to (1) the east, (2) the central position, (3) the last side (numbering the tribes clockwise from the east, 2 1 3; 5 4 6; 8 7 9; 11 10 12).

Zone	East	South	West	North
Inmost (I–III)	The Tabernacle, Yahweh's dwelling			
Inner ring (IVA)	Aaron (Num 3.38)	Kohath (Num 3.29)	Gershon (Num 3.23)	Merari (Num 3.35)
Outer ring (IVB) centre tribe status	Judah fourth of Leah (royal house) (Num 3.2)	Reuben firstborn of Leah (Num 3.10)	Ephraim firstborn of Rachel's son (Num 3.18)	Dan firstborn of Bilhah (Num 3.25)
Outside camp (V)	The place for the dead and those with major impurity (Num. 5.2; see §5.4.2)			

In terms of a schematic map of the camp:

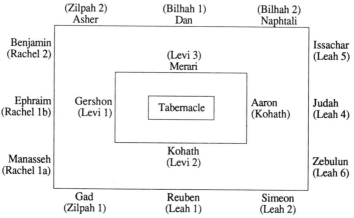

Key: 1, 2, 3 = order of birth;
a, b = grandchildren

Some of the grading criteria conflict (e.g. genealogy, size, importance of role), but it is possible to suggest reasons for the way P has resolved these.[1] The arrangement of the tribes has close connections with the genealogical order known from the patriarchal narratives, particularly the account of the birth of Jacob's sons.[2] With the understandable exception of Levi (who inhabits the inner circle), the sons of

1. The historical background to the tribal system is not discussed here (cf. Olson 1985: 55-81).
2. The genealogies assigned to P (Gen. 35.22-26; 46.8-27; Exod. 1.1-5) list the sons by mother and then order of birth.

Leah, Jacob's first wife, are to the east and south, and the three Rachel tribes occupy the west. Three of the four sons of the maidservants are to the north, the least privileged orientation (Dan and Naphtali to Bilhah, Rachel's maidservant, and Asher to Zilpah, Leah's maid-servant). Gad fills the sixth place on the more privileged south side, leaving the middle position in the north to Dan. This suggests that orientation was preferred to a central position (otherwise Gad and Dan would change places). The tribe nearest the previous side also has priority and is the elder son (Issachar, Simeon, Joseph–Manasseh) or belongs to the favoured mother (Zilpah).

Although Joseph was Rachel's firstborn, his two sons have independent status, to preserve the twelvefold character of the outer camp, since the inner ring consists of the tribe of Levi. Of the brothers, the firstborn usually takes on the privileged middle position of the groups, and they set out first on the march (see below). The inferior position of Joseph's firstborn (Manasseh) is reflected in the genealogies as well as in the order of the lists of leaders (Num. 1.10; 7.48-59), and census results (1.32-35).[1] The pre-eminent position of Judah is anomalous, since he was not one of the firstborn, and Reuben, Leah's firstborn, might be expected to take prime position (as in the genealogies and the censuses Num. 1.20-21; 26.5-11). The arrangement may reflect Judah's priority in monarchic times, or the setting of the priestly school in Judah.[2]

It is likely that the ordering of the camp had a military defensive purpose, and in Num. 1.1–10.10 a number of military measures are taken (e.g. the census of the tribal military hosts, Num. 2). The tribal and Levitical gradings also take on a military significance in the order of the tribes on the march (Num. 10.11-28):

1.   The reversed priority is assumed in Gen. 48.3-6 (P; cf. v. 13-14). The birth order recurs in Num. 26.28-37, perhaps because Manasseh now surpassed Ephraim in size and more genealogical information was to be recorded (Budd 1984: 289).

2.   As the largest tribe it is well fitted for the vanguard position, but the numbers may also reflect later historical realities (cf. Gray 1902; Budd 1984: 24-25). Judah and Reuben are also prominent in the ingenious numerological interpretations of Barnouin (1969: 358; cf. 1977; Wenham 1982: 64-66), who stresses the importance of six and its multiples (60, 3600, 6,000, 600,000) in the various figures. six might then significantly characterize the personal dimension (cf. §4.3.2). However, the complexity and indirect nature of his calculations suggest caution.

Unit	Function	Tribe or Family		
1. First group	vanguard	Judah	Issachar	Zebulun
2. Levites	carry Tabernacle frame	Gershonites	Merarites	
3. Second group		Reuben	Simeon	Gad
4. Levites	carry holy vessels	Kohathites		
5. Third group		Ephraim	Manasseh	Benjamin
6. Fourth group	rearguard	Dan	Asher	Naphtali

The most important personnel and equipment, those associated with the cult and its paraphernalia, are flanked by tribal groups. The Gershonites and Merarites set out after the first group (10.17), since the Tabernacle had to be set up before its furniture was unpacked (10.21). The furniture is transported by the Kohathites (accompanied presumably by the priests), and is in the centre, the most protected position.

5.4.2 *The Unclean*

A person's status of holiness, purity or impurity determined the range of areas in which he or she was able to move:

Category	Status		Forbidden Area	Restriction Lifted
High Priest	holy	קדוש	Holy of Holies	once a year
Priests	holy	קדוש	The Holy Place	times of ministry
Laity	clean	טהור	holy areas	never
Priests and Laity	minor impurity	טמא	The Tabernacle	until clean (1 day)
Priests and Laity	major impurity			
	corpse	טמא לנפש	camp	until clean (7 days)
	skin disorder	מצרע	camp	healed (+ 7 days)
	discharge (m)	זב	camp	for 7 days
	(f)	זבה	camp	(for 7 days)
	menstruation	נדה	(camp)	for 7 days
	childbirth	יולדת	(camp)	for 7 days

The Holiness Spectrum thus correlates the personal with the spatial dimension. In normal circumstances a person's social status and location in the camp depended on the family and tribe (§5.4.1), but different rules applied if a major impurity was contracted. The purity–impurity classification cut across genealogical lines, and affected priests as well as non-priests. Purity was a necessary presupposition both for a priest, if he was to minister in the sanctuary, and for a non-priest who wished to enter and offer sacrifice. Even minor impurity had to be kept far from the cult, since the sanctuary embodied the presence of the living God (§4.6.1).

A separation from what was holy was the only restriction on those with minor impurity. This included not touching any sacrificial food (cf. קדש in Lev. 12.4) as well as staying away from the sanctuary. Minor impurities affected only the individual concerned, and there was no need for him or her to be isolated or marked out as unclean in the camp. In contrast, the communicable character of major impurity (§§3.4, 3.3.3) had serious repercussions on everyday life, since it could affect other people and things (Lev. 15). Polluted persons were isolated or banned from the camp altogether. Although space was clean or neutral unless otherwise indicated, the appropriate location for major impurity was outside the camp.

No blame was attached to the condition and the restrictions were precautionary rather than punitive. There was no danger, provided that the spread of the impurity was limited and the correct procedures for purification were followed (§6.3). It would be dangerous if those with a communicable impurity were allowed freely through the camp, since they could defile a person going to visit the sanctuary. Purity was the normal state of things, and was required for special occasions (particularly the domestic celebration of the Passover, Num. 9.1-14).

Three cases of major impurity, skin disorder, discharge[1] and corpse impurity, entailed particularly severe consequences. Anyone with them had to remain outside the camp (Num. 5.1-3).[2] In accord with the close relation between impurity and death (§§2.2, 3.4), it is not surprising that someone with corpse impurity was excluded. Further, a person in this state is akin to a dead one in that he or she had to withdraw from the normal activities of life, both social and cultic. Graves were also placed outside the camp or city, since they transmitted corpse impurity (Num. 19.16).

---

1. For practical reasons, it would be difficult to apply the law to women who had just given birth or who were menstruating, and so these women are isolated rather than expelled.

2. *m. Kel.* 1.1-4 has a graded list of sources of impurities, including (in decreasing order) דם הנדה, זב, זבה, מצרע, מת. Elsewhere skin disorder is last (e.g. *m. Nid.* 10.4; *m. Ker.* 2.1). The usual order is discharges (men, women), childbirth, skin disorder (e.g. Elijah of Vilnah in Danby 1933: 803; *m. Nid.* 10.4; *m. Hal.* 4.8). In P, the impurities are not listed in a graded order (Num. 5.1-3; Lev. 15.1-31).

The major impurity *ṣara'at* is not a precise medical term and described a wide spectrum of skin disorders. It is almost certain that it did not include what is now called 'leprosy' (Hansen's Disease). The details of the Priestly laws indicate clearly that *ṣara'at* is treated as a ritual disorder rather than a disease or a punishment for sin.[1] It is unlikely that it was contagious, so 'quarantine' is a misleading description of what is primarily a ritual category and dealt with by ritual not civil procedures.[2] Purification, not cure or forgiveness, is the goal of the rituals which the cured leper must undergo.[3]

ṣara'at has an unusually extensive discussion and was probably a paradigmatic case of impurity, being given a special symbolic weight because of the way it embodied fundamental Priestly values.[4] In particular there is a close analogy between *ṣara'at* and death (see the next table; cf. also §6.3.3).[5]

Houses and garments could also contract a condition called *ṣara'at*, probably a type of fungus or mould, and similar measures were taken for its confirmation and treatment.[6] The common element is probably the similar appearance of the various kinds of *ṣara'at* and death. The

---

1. Although it is a punishment for sin in Num. 12.10-11; 2 Kgs 5.27; 2 Chron. 26.16-21. 'Skin disorder' (cf. the vague NJPSV 'scaly affection'!) is thus a preferable translation to 'malignant skin-disease' (NEB). Harrison (1980: 137) still considers that true leprosy could be included, but this is very unlikely (Hulse 1975; Wilkinson 1977; Wilkinson 1978).

2. In Israel confinement was usually a temporary condition pending a proper judicial decision (de Vaux 1961: 160). Lev. 13 assumes a sedentary society. Thus stones must be removed from a diseased house and deposited in an unclean place outside the city (14.41, 45). Normally P reflects a wilderness location with all the people dwelling in the camp in tents (so Num. 5.1-3).

3. Döller (1917: 82).

4. Skin disease was also a paradigmatic illness in Mesopotamia (Toorn 1985: 30-31, 72-75).

5. *ṣara'at* was imposed on Miriam as a punishment for her rebellion (Num. 12.9-15; cf Deut. 24.8-9), and it was compared to the appearance of a dead foetus. There may thus be a connection between the disease and death at the level of appearance (Frymer-Kensky 1983: 400; Lewis 1987). However, the narrative is non-Priestly, and the vivid metaphor may not be significant.

6. These chapters are complex (e.g. Seidl 1982). The diseased house assumes a settled context, in contrast to the tents and the camp of the other two cases (e.g. Lev. 14.8). Nevertheless, similar procedures have been adapted to the different subject (Wenham 1979b: 212).

objects classified together are appropriate ones, since in the Bible there is an intimate connection between clothing, the home of a person, and the person himself (cf. §5.2.3).[1] In setting out a comprehensive understanding of the world, P employs concrete legal and cultic classifications of bodily phenomena.

Aspect	Skin Disorder (Lev. 13–14)	Death (Num. 19)
Character	major impurity	major impurity
Spatial Dimension	outside the camp	outside the camp
	defiles what is under the same roof (Lev. 14.46)[2]	defiles what is under the same roof (Num. 19.14)
Ritual Response[3] (cf. §3.5.1)	rent clothes	rent clothes
	hair dishevelled	hair dishevelled
	upper lip covered[4]	
Purification (cf. §6.3)	ritual involving	ritual involving
	hyssop, scarlet, cedarwood	hyssop, scarlet, cedarwood
	three-stage ritual:	two-stage ritual:
	initial blood rite (1st day)	sprinkling (3rd day)
	shave, wash, bathe (1st, 7th)	sprinkling (7th day)
	final sacrifices	

5.4.3 *Men and Women*
The cult was of great significance to all Israel, including the women.[5] For many cultic actions women had an equal status with men, although they could not become priests.[6] Both men and women could offer

1. Cf. 1 Sam. 24; Haulotte (1966: 11-13, 71-113), Hönig (1957: 150-51). Clothing can be a powerful social and theological symbol (anthropological perspectives may be found in Polhemus 1978).

2. Döller (1917: 106).

3. There is a structural contrast in the injunctions to the priests not to rend their clothes or dishevel their hair during ministry (§§3.5.1, 5.2.4).

4. Cf. Ezek. 24.17, 22. The various mourning customs mentioned in this section may have been examples from a wider range forbidden to priests.

5. See the detailed reviews in Vos (1968: 60-132) and Gruber (1987).

6. Hayter (1987: 64-73) considers that this was due largely to a polemic against fertility religion, with its cultic prostitutes, but that it also had a sociological factor (priesthood was a profession). She adds a 'theological aspect' (pp. 67-70), which refers to a woman's inferior grade on the scale of sanctification because of her greater uncleanness. The language of grading is inappropriate, since men as well as women could incur major impurity. But it would certainly be true that there would be difficulties because of the regular character of female impurity.

sacrifice,[1] and at the start of life the same sacrifice was offered for a newborn female child as for a male. It is explicitly stated that women as well as men could undertake a Nazirite vow and become holy (Num. 6.2, 8; cf. §2.2.3).

Elsewhere the differences between men and women were of great importance in the cultic law, and (like the clean–unclean classification) they cut across genealogy and hierarchy. Men and women took on complementary roles. The offerings for the Tabernacle came from all (Exod. 35.22-24; 36.3-6), but the women supplied the jewelry and wove the necessary fabrics, while the craftsmen were men (31.1-11). There is also an allusion to a band of women who had a serving role at the sanctuary (38.8), in a similar way to that of the bands of Levites.[2]

Both men and women were subject to major and minor impurities, but their character could differ. A discharge from the sexual organs (זוב, Lev. 15.2) rendered both men and women contagiously unclean (Lev. 15), but their nature was probably not identical.[3] Skin disorder (ṣaraʿat), however, is not specific to sex, and the occasional reference to women (e.g., איש או אשה, Lev. 13.29, 38) indicates that the law applied to women and men equally.[4]

The most distinctive of the exclusively female purity laws concerned the two-stage impurity of a mother following childbirth (Lev. 12). There was an initial major impurity, indicated by its comparison to menstrual impurity (v. 2 כימי נדת דותה), her status as being 'in a state of blood purification' (NJPS v. 3: בדמי טהרה, similarly vv. 5, 7), and the seven day duration of the impurity. The second stage lasted longer, but the impurity was minor and so did not entail serious economic or social repercussions (§5.4.2). The duration of the impurity, but not the sacrifice at the end, depended upon whether the woman had given birth to a son or daughter:[5]

---

1. Gruber (1987: 39) points out that נפש and אדם in the sacrificial laws reflect non-sexist language (cf. Num. 5.5-7). Several sacrifices are compulsory for women (Lev. 12.6; 15.29).

2. Compare 'the women who served (הצבאות אשר צבאו) at the entrance to the tent of meeting' (Exod. 38.8; cf. 1 Sam. 2.22) with the Levites who came to serve there (הבא לצבא צבא, Num. 4.23; 8.24; Gruber 1987: 36).

3. Blood for women, and white emissions for men, according to *m. Zab.* 2.1.

4. Vos (1968: 77-78).

5. However, the sacrifices are the same for male and female, and the differentiation is in terms of the wealth of the offerer. The עלה and חטאת are

Purification	Male	Female
major impurity	7 days	14 days
minor impurity	33 days	66 days
Total	40 days	80 days

The seven day purification for a male infant led to the circumcision ceremony on the eighth day (v. 3). This would allow the mother to be present and not defile those participating in the ceremony.

Numerous explanations have been given for the different times of purification for male and female infants.[1] A structural interpretation might relate the inequality of time to the general inequality of impurity with regard to men and women.[2] Although men and women could suffer the same degree of impurity, the regularity and universality of menstruation and childbirth suggests a quantitative difference.[3] The different times of purification establish from the beginning of life the social, sexual and purity distinctions which will characterize the rest of life in both the domestic and the cultic spheres.

This structural contrast is not necessarily related to the authority of the father or husband in other contexts (e.g. in vows, Num. 30). The role differentiation of men and women in a society is a complex and many-sided phenomenon. Economic factors may be significant, as when sacrificial animals males are preferred (§6.4.4). The higher values placed on males for vows (Lev. 27.1-8; cf. Num. 18.16) may reflect the standard prices for slaves.[4]

normally a yearling lamb and a bird (pigeon or turtledove), but for the poor two birds.

1. See Döller (1917: 10-44), Vos (1968: 68-70). Explanations include (1) physical: some of the rabbis thought that the female foetus took longer to develop than the male (*m. Nid.* 3.7, *b. Ber.* 60a), (2) hygienic: the lochia for a female baby were slightly more toxic than for a male (Macht 1933), (3) demonic: evil spirits were doubly active for a girl (Snaith 1967: 69), (4) social: a male birth in a patrilineal society was a mitigating factor (Eilberg-Schwartz 1990: 191).

2. Gruber (1987: 43 n. 13) stresses that this inequality is not necessarily a value judgment on the inferiority of the female.

3. The more extended times of impurity of women may be the reason that only men were priests. Vos (1968: 193) also points to the full-time character of the priesthood, the physical demands of slaughter, and the demanding role of motherhood.

4. Wenham (1978). The figures are (in shekels) (a) 1 month up: 5 shekels for male, 3 shekels for females (60%) (b) 5 years up: 20 shekels for male, 10 shekels for

Two important passages in the Holiness Code define the boundaries
of legitimate marriage and sexual intercourse (Lev. 18.6-23; 20.10-
21). They list a number of sexual offences, including incest, adultery,
bestiality and homosexuality. From a structural point of view, many
of these can be understood as an illegitimate confusion of classes
which should be kept distinct (§3.5.2).[1] But sexual integrity had a
fundamental social and religious dimension. At the heart of the Priestly
view of man and woman was a belief that the order of the world and
society was based on marriage and the extended family. Any deviation
from the norm threatened the stability and structure of Israel's existence as a holy people and was subject to severe legal sanctions (in
most cases death).

P contains little about marriage and marriage customs,[2] but the
two major texts list those with whom marriage is not permitted, so
defining the inner circle of partners with whom marriage would be
incest (i.e. the exogamous boundary).[3] The outer circle (the end-
ogamous boundary) is ideally the nation (cf. Num. 25; but see
Lev. 24.10), but in special cases the tribe (for inheritance purposes,
Num. 36.6-9; or for priestly purity, Lev. 21.4 and see §5.2.4).

The incest laws have a minimum content (the prohibition of
marrying the mother is so obvious that it is omitted), but it is likely
that the more distant kinships were often regarded with disapproval
rather than legally forbidden, and the Levitical laws represent one
stage in the development of a coherent legal system. The punishments
for incest were graded in accord with the distance from the immediate
family circle. Thus Lev. 20 distinguishes between marriages where
the partners are to be cut off (vv. 17-18), and those in which the
couple will be childless (vv. 20-21).

---

females (50%), (c) 20 years up: 50 shekels for male, 30 shekels for females (60%),
(d) 60 years up: 15 shekels for male, 10 shekels for females (67%).

1.   The restrictions on priestly marriage (§5.2.4) can also be understood in structural terms. Widowhood, divorce and harlotry brought the possibility of confusion of
genealogical lines and names.

2.   The following discussion is based on Mace (1953: 150-59), where a detailed
discussion is found. See also Neufeld (1944: 191-212). Wenham (1979: 40) argues
that the law of Deut. 24.1-4 extends the theological logic of the Levitical incest laws.

3.   Rattray (1987: 542) points out the the mention of close kin (שאר בשרו,
Lev. 18.6) assumes that the immediate family (שאר הקרוב אליו, Lev. 21.2) is also
forbidden (i.e. mother, sister, daughter).

The rules defining incest depend both on consanguinity (a direct blood relation) and affinity (relations through the married partner). In P the former are worked out more thoroughly than the latter. Some of the special laws (e.g. a woman and her sister are not to be married together) reflect the weakness of the affinity relation, and may be practical measures to preserve the harmony of a household (cf. Gen. 29–30). The rule therefore holds only so long as the wife lives (Lev. 18.18).[1]

5.4.4 *Israel and the Nations*

P is interested primarily in the cult and Israel's behaviour as a nation called to holiness and obedience. Nevertheless, Israel existed in the midst of the nations, and some of the laws imply that Israel had a distinctive identity in relation to them.[2] Various laws reflect this awareness of a distinction between Israel and the nations.[3]

In connection with the food laws (Lev. 11; 20.22-26), it is stated that Yahweh had made a separation (הבדלתי, 20.24, 25; cf. 11.47) between Israel and the nations. This is aligned with the separation (הבדלתם, 20.25) which Israel was to make between clean and unclean animals. The recognition that there was a close relation between animals and human beings is found frequently in P,[4] and was employed to mirror social and religious realities.[5] The same passage relates obedience to the food laws with Israel's call to holiness, on the basis of

---

1. The ultimate rationale for incest prohibitions is not clear. A structural rationale would be that it guards against confusing roles: a mother could not be at the same time a wife (Lev. 18.8 = 20.11). But the universality and force of the prohibitions implies that they reflect a basic aspect of human identity.

2. Many laws have been considered to refer implicitly to customs in neighbouring cultures, either as a borrowing or polemical rejection (cf. §3.4.1). This section discusses the explicit references, many of which are found in H (§1.3.4). These are assumed to contribute to the overall Priestly perspective on the matter.

3. Other texts discussing the nations lie outside the cultic texts. For marriage, see the last section.

4. Wenham (1981b: 10-11). Examples include the law of the firstborn (cf. §5.3.1) and participation in the blessings and curses (Lev. 26.22).

5. This may be a late meditation on the meaning of the food laws, for which other classificatory laws are given in Lev. 11 (§3.4; Porter 1976: 165). Nevertheless, it is more than an arbitrary juxtaposition based on הבדיל as a catch-phrase (Noth 1965: 151).

Yahweh's holiness (v. 26).[1] Holiness takes on a broad meaning
(§2.2.3) because the context is that of God dwelling in the midst of the
whole people.

It is possible to extend the parallel to include a correspondence
between the three classes of the animal world (sacrificial, clean and
unclean animals), and the three divisions of the human world (priests,
Israelites and Gentiles).[2] The strongest evidence for this is an alignment between sacrificial animals and the priestly class in the two lists
of blemishes. Those which disqualify a priest from entering the sanctuary to offer sacrifice (Lev. 21.17-21) are very similar to the defects
(מום) which bar a sacrificial animal from being slaughtered (Lev. 22.17-
25).[3] The threefold division is not attested explicitly, and may reflect a
late systematization. Nonetheless, it indicates a development which was
consistent with the Priestly interest in systematic classification.

In the same context appear warnings against sorcery and necro-
mancy (Lev. 20.27), implying a negative contrast to Israel's obedience
to the food laws. These practices exemplify why the nations were to
be expelled from the land (v. 23). The Holiness word group is used in
other places to describe prohibited religious offences prevalent among
the nations, such as giving sons to Molech.[4]

While Israel as a nation is distinct from other nations, it is recognized that there may be foreigners resident in Israel's midst. A
number of laws stress that the *gēr* or sojourner (גר) has rights and
privileges equal to the native Israelite (אזרח; particularly Lev. 19.33-
34). Along with these principles, there was an obligation to keep
various civil laws (e.g. the laws of redemption, Lev. 25.45, 47). The

---

1. Zimmerli (1980: 511-12) stresses that the separation, and thus the nature
of holiness, is different for Yahweh and Israel. Israel's obedience depends on
Yahweh's prior redemption, which resulted in Israel's separation from the nations.
This is indicated by the various 'I am Yahweh' formulae (e.g. Lev. 19.2, 36), which
recur in H.

2. Milgrom (1963: 295), Douglas (1975: 267-68), Wenham (1979b: 170-71,
177 n. 34); cf. Arist. Exeg. 139-71, where the distinction is developed in ethical
terms.

3. Wenham 1979b: 295.

4. Lev. 20.3 (cf. 18.21) describes the consequences of this particular action as
compromising Yahweh's holiness ('defiling my sanctuary and profaning my holy
name').

gēr must also respect the cultic laws, following the legitimate purification rituals (Lev. 19.10) and sacrificial procedures (Lev. 17.8-9,
10-13), and refrain from abominations such as sacrificing to Molech
(Lev. 20.2; cf. 18.26; 24.16).

Although the *gēr* is clearly identified as such in the laws, there is a
tendency in P to assimilate him or her to the Israelite community.[1]
Grades of identification with the Israelite community are indicated by
the option of being circumcised and eating the Passover (Exod. 12.48-
49; Num. 9.14). Participating in the ritual was probably a significant
step in becoming part of the Israelite community.[2] It is possible that a
geographical and spatial definition of 'Israel' could take priority over
genealogical status (i.e. the personal dimension). There are no clear
instructions about marriage rules (contrast Ezra 9), and it is possible
that the children of a *gēr* could eventually become full citizens and
receive an Israelite genealogy (cf. Deut. 23.1-8).

5.5 *Conclusion*

According to the Priestly world-view, Israel's social order demonstrated a harmonious and closely related hierarchy of groups, each of
which took on particular roles in relation to the cult. Priests, Levites
and members of the tribes played roles corresponding to their distance
from the sanctuary and their status. The priests were consecrated
(§5.2.1) and had responsibilities in the sanctuary, while the Levites
were appointed to guard it (§5.3.1). Within these groups there is further grading and differentiation, so that the high priest was superior
to his sons (§5.2.2), the Kohathites to the other two Levitical clans
(§5.3.2), and Judah to the other tribes (§5.4.1).

Other significant gradings occur in the texts. From time to time
individuals belonged to the class of those with major impurity. These
had to be isolated or live outside the camp (§5.4.2), although there
was always a way back to the sanctuary once the conditions for
purification had been fulfilled (§6.3). From a wider perspective, Israel

---

1. Martin-Achard (1974: 410). Scholars are rightly way of identifying the גר
with the later institution of proselytism, although Kellermann (1973: 988) considers
that in the later strata of P 'the גר is regarded largely as a Proselyte'. It is likely that
the process of social and religious identification was not a clear-cut conscious matter.

2. Thus in Exod. 12.45 the dweller (תושב) and hired servant (שכיר) are not
allowed to eat the Passover.

as a whole had a distinctiveness based on Yahweh's redemption and his call to holiness. Israel was to respond by obedience to Yahweh's laws, which could concern ethics, the cult, or matters of purity (particularly the food laws, §5.4.4).

Chapter 6

THE RITUAL DIMENSION

6.1 *Sacrifice and Ritual*

6.1.1 *Introduction*

In the last two chapters the more stable aspects of the Priestly conception of the cult have been explored. Life, however, entails change and movement on the physical, social and religious levels. Ritual provides a framework for such changes to take place in an ordered and safe way, and the ritual dimension of the cult takes up and develops the gradings already met in the spatial and personal dimensions. Grading unifies and controls the rituals so as to bring them into accord with the larger Priestly world-view.[1]

The paradigmatic ritual in the ancient world was sacrifice,[2] and the meaning of sacrifice continues to challenge the interpretative skill of both anthropologists[3] and biblical scholars (§6.1.2).[4] I have found it

---

1. This chapter will concentrate on the sacrifices described in Leviticus, especially Lev. 1–7. Numbers records a number of new laws and institutions that supplement or modify those of Leviticus (e.g. Lev. 4.13-21→Num. 15.22-31). Diachronic aspects of sacrifice are important, but for the purposes of clarity have not been treated in detail.

2. De Vaux (1961: 415), Hecht (1976: 49), Fortes (1980: v, ix).

3. Anthropological studies of sacrifice are reviewed by Bourdillon (1980), Fortes (1980) and Ashby (1988: 5-25). They include Evans-Pritchard (1956), Lévi-Strauss (1966: 223-28), Turner (1977), Rigby (1980), Hecht (1982) and de Heusch (1985). For structural perspectives on Old Testament sacrifice see Collins (1977) and Davies (1977).

4. Aside from the commentaries, the entries in *EM*, *IDBSup*, *JewEnc*, *THAT* and *ThWAT* are important (especially those by Haran, Levine and Milgrom). For surveys of sacrifice, see de Vaux (1961: 415-67), Levine (1971b) and Sabourin (1985). Other important studies are by Rendtorff (1967), Janowski (1982), Kiuchi (1987) and by Milgrom in numerous articles (a number of which are collected in 1983a).

most helpful to approach sacrifice by means of several models or basic metaphors. These can be related to the Priestly sacrificial texts with varying degrees of success, but they can all be structured to manifest various degrees of grading (§6.2). A particularly important and far-ranging model is that of purification, which also applies to rituals other than sacrifice (§§6.2.2, 6.3). The survey of grading in the various types of sacrifice (§6.2) is complemented by the study of grading with reference to the various dimensions (§6.4).

6.1.2 *The Interpretation of Sacrifice*

An interpretation of sacrifice in P depends upon a number of factors, including the general approach adopted with regard to the scope and unity of P (§1.3.2). A synchronic approach which treats the final text as a seamless whole may overestimate the coherence of the Priestly view. On the other hand, a diachronic approach may miss levels of meaning and coherence in the final text.[1] In addition, there are a number of issues involved in the interpretation of ritual and symbolism. These have been of great interest to the anthropologists (§3.2.4), and some of the distinctions they make can be helpful in assessing the approaches of Old Testament specialists.

One approach has been to search for a general pattern in the sequence of the ritual (§3.2.4). Hubert and Mauss set out a three-phase scheme of sacrifice, characterized as entry, ascent and descent.[2] In P, the sacrificial rituals comprise several main stages,[3] but these too can be analysed as having a beginning (the approach), a middle (the slaughter and blood manipulation), and an end (the distribution of the parts). Each of these may be the starting point for constructing significant variations.

Since there are features common to most sacrifices, it is also possible to compare and contrast the differences between alternative rituals, both for the same sacrifice, and for different types of sacrifice. This comparison will be the main concern in this chapter, since it

---

1. Childs (1985: 170) writes of these two approaches in terms of the 'Scylla and Charybdis of Gese and Milgrom'.

2. Hubert and Mauss (1964: 19-49). The similarity of this scheme with that of a *rite de passage* was noted by van Gennep (1960: 184). Hubert and Mauss's theoretical presuppositions have been criticized by de Heusch (1985: 1-6), among others.

3. Rendtorff (1963: 5-11; 1967).

leads to further insight into the significance of grading and the Holiness Spectrum in P.

The Priestly sacrificial system makes use of a limited repertoire of basic symbols, movements and actions. Past studies have often concentrated on the individual aspects in explaining how sacrifice 'works'. The 'dynamistic' approach attributes the effectiveness of a ritual to the power of the particular symbols and actions of which it is comprised. The symbols themselves are understood to convey power and bring about the result.[1] However, the dynamistic approach tends to isolate the symbols from the larger context of the ritual, particularly its personal dimension (cf. §3.3.2). Furthermore, it does not take sufficient account of the variety, richness and ambivalence of many common symbols.[2] Not all of these potential meanings will be active in a particular ritual.

Similar problems beset the attempt to find a verse which can provide a key to the meaning of sacrifice. The verse normally discussed in this connection is Lev. 17.11,[3] but it is not as helpful as is sometimes supposed. There are not only considerable exegetical difficulties

1. See Bertholet (1926). Many examples of this approach might be given. For Füglister (1977: 162), water, oil and blood are 'kraftvermittelnden Substanzen'. Elliger (1966: 34) employs a material metaphor in his interpretation of כפר as 'das Übertragen von seelischen Fluidem'. Heller (1970) connects the fat with the 'strength' of a person, which can be magically absorbed in sacrifice. Although grading can be subsumed to this view, there is a significant shift of perspective. Thus Kedar-Kopfstein (1977a: 263) refers to 'the carefully graded manipulations of blood. The nearer it is brought, the holier it is and the more significant the sacrifice' (my translation). Milgrom's view of graded impurity is similarly dynamistic (see below). This approach is often associated with the concepts discussed in §3.3.

2. Turner (1967: 28-30) suggests that important symbols (which he calls 'dominant ritual symbols') can have three properties: (1) they condense various ideas and context, (2) they unify disparate concepts, (3) they polarize meaning into a 'sensory pole' (which represents universal experience) and an 'ideological pole' (which refers to more abstract realities). They generally have strong associations with basic human experience (e.g. blood), and have been called 'natural symbols' (see Bourdillon 1980: 21-23, Douglas 1970).

3. Janowski (1982: 242) refers to it as the 'Summe der kultischen Sühnetheologie'.

in its interpretation,[1] but it is not certain how far it can sum up all aspects of Priestly theology.

Instead of an atomistic approach, it is preferable to begin with the movement and structure of the sacrificial ritual as a whole, since this larger context should determine the primary significance of the individual symbols. The value of a structural approach is that it looks for patterns at the level of the complete ritual. The symbols and actions will be combined in such a way as to communicate the nature and purpose of the sacrifice. Certain meanings of a multivalent symbol will not be stressed in a ritual in which they are unnecessary.

Admittedly, this approach need not be a total explanation. There may be anomalies, for which a historical approach is more appropriate. There is a conservative tendency in the cult to preserve actions and symbols when their original function has ceased, although it is also the case that the symbols can be reinterpreted in a way consistent to the new context. Further, the meaning of individual symbols may transcend the specific purposes of a ritual.

The structure of ritual has been compared to that of language, with the complete ritual equivalent to a sentence or discourse, and the words being the basic actions and symbols.[2] The problem of interpreting ritual is akin to interpreting sentences, particularly when they are highly metaphorical. A word derives its particular force from the context, as does a symbol, and the multivalence of a symbol can be compared to the fruitful ambiguity of poetry. Blood, for example, may have signify life or death, and water may purify or revive.

One of the most helpful approaches to sacrifice has been to explore the basic experiences of the world which appear to have been used to

1. The meaning attributed to Lev. 17.11 depends on (1) the structure of the verse, (2) its role in the context of the chapter (e.g. does it refer to the שלמים or to all blood sacrifices), (3) the symbolic significance of blood (purification, life, or death; cf. Kedar-Kopfstein 1977a), (4) the meaning of כפר (see §6.2.2), (5) the interpretation of the ב in בנפש (*beth pretii* or *beth* of exchange, *beth instrumenti*, or *beth essentiae*). See the various interpretations of Milgrom (1983: 96-103), Levine (1974: 67-70), Brichto (1976: 22-36), Füglister (1977), Janowski (1982: 242-47), Schenker (1983), Kiuchi (1987: 101-109).

2. E.g. Lawson (1976), Fernandez (1977), Wheelock (1982). The comparison of ritual to language codes is an important aspect of the theories of Douglas (e.g. 1970: 40-58).

shape a sacrificial ritual.[1] These are the so-called theories or models of sacrifice, of which a great number have been proposed. Because sacrifice is the primary religious act of the ancient world, it is not surprising that several different models have been found to apply.[2] It is helpful to recognize that sacrifice cannot be reduced to any one theory, and many of them are complementary. The value of any one will largely depend upon context and perspective. This does not obviate the problem of judging which models are more suitable, but it does safeguard against interpretations which are too literal, all-encompassing or abstract. A good model should have substantial support from the text's vocabulary, symbolism and content, and be linked with matters of social and theological importance.

It is also necessary to ascertain how far a particular model can be developed. Interpreters have often put too much weight on the full outworking of a single model, both in advocating and rejecting it. It is not always simple to know how far to draw legitimate analogies. For example, sacrifice as food for the deity is a complex idea, since food is a rich social and theological symbol, as well as good to eat. An offering of food may not be for consumption; the primary emphasis may be that the one receiving it is owed honour and tribute. In exploring the limits of a model, it is important to realise that the larger Priestly world view should set limits to speculation.

Models may be too crude, but they can also be too general or abstract. Even in human terms 'gift' can have many different nuances, depending upon the context. In discussions of sacrifice as a gift, it is rarely clear how it is to be understood, either from the 'native' or the interpreter's point of view.[3] The ambiguity of the notion of gift has

---

1. The literature on model (e.g. Black 1962) and metaphor (e.g. Ricoeur 1978) is extensive and has served as an inspiration rather than a guide to the discussion here. The dynamic juxtaposition of a basic experience with a more abstract theme is common. Thus 'the essence of metaphor is understanding and experiencing one kind of thing in terms of another' (Lakoff and Johnson 1981: 5), and note Turner's description above of a dominant ritual symbol. 'Metaphor', 'symbol' or 'symbol system', 'theory' and 'model' all indicate that an analogy is being made between two realms of experience.

2. E.g. Rowley (1967: 112), Wenham (1979b: 111), Fortes (1980: xiii), Kidner (1982).

3. The gift theory of sacrifice is often associated with Gray (1925: 1-54). Hecht (1976; cf. 1982) has suggested that Western scholars were attracted to the economic

influenced what action is regarded as sacrifice. It is helpful to distinguish sacrifices from offerings[1] and purifications (§6.3), since they do not involve the cultic destruction of a material and the rituals are often very different.

While holding to a single model can lead to simplistic interpretation, mixing models can lead to confusion and incoherence.[2] Elements of several models are typically found in a sacrifice, but it is plausible to suppose that the context and content of a sacrifice will highlight one model and background the others. A specific sacrifice will tend to take on a distinctive character. On the other hand, the common symbolism and procedure of a sacrifice will recall all the others.[3] Any animal sacrifice will require certain common features (such as the need to deal with the blood, and the disposal of the remains), but different sacrifices tend to focus upon different aspects of the ritual.

Several significant models of sacrifice deserve brief discussion, keeping in mind the qualifications that have been made. An attempt will be made to describe the 'pure' models, with the basic human experience as prominent as possible. In practice, aspects of the model need not be developed, or may be mixed inconsistently.[4] In the following, the way in which the model lends itself to development along the lines of the principle of grading will be emphasized.

The principal source for knowledge about the Priestly sacrificial system is Lev. 1–7, which describes five main types of sacrifice:[5]

---

metaphor for historical reasons which often had little to do with the way those sacrificing understood their actions. The complexity of the idea of gift is stressed by Evans-Pritchard (1956: 287-82) and Kirk (1981: 74-75).

1. Firth (1963) and van Baal (1976). In P, offerings would include tithes (מעשׂר), votive offerings (נדרים) and other contributions (חרומות; see on these Milgrom 1976: 44-63; 1983a: 159-70).

2. Levine (1974), for example, relates sacrifice to impurity, demons, transmission of sins, ransom and substitution, but the coherence behind his analysis is not clear. Various aspects of his position are criticised by Milgrom (1976: 142-43).

3. Compare the phenomenon of dissimilation in language.

4. This does not necessarily mean that they are incoherent. For the distinction, see Lakoff and Johnson (1980: 94-95).

5. Lev. 1–5 describe the sacrifices from an officiant's and Lev. 6–7 from an offerer's point of view (Baker 1987: 193). There is still no consensus about the best translation, and those offered here are for convenience.

Sacrifice			*Lev. 1–5*	*Lev. 6–7*
burnt offering	*'ōlâ*	עלה	1.1-17	6.8-13 [H 1-6]
grain offering	*minhâ*	מנחה	2.1-16	6.14-23 [H 7-16]
peace offering	*šᵉlāmîm*	שלמים	3.1-17	7.11-21 [H 21-31]
purification offering	*hatṭā't*	חטאת	4.1–5.13	6.24-30 [H 17-23]
reparation offering	*'āšām*	אשם	5.14–6.7 [H14–26]	7.1-10

A ritual normally involved several sacrifices, and the procedural
order was the purification offering, the burnt offering, and finally the
peace offering (e.g. Num. 6.16-17).[1] Ideally, each sacrifice would be
assigned to one major model, but the reality is more complicated, and
there may be echoes of several models in a ritual. The following discussion stresses the distinguishing features of a sacrifice, rather than
what is held in common (for which see §6.4).

6.2 *Models of Sacrifice in P*

6.2.1 *Honouring of God*
Several factors suggest that the *'ōlâ* is the 'sacrifice par excellence'.[2] Its
characteristic feature is the complete burning of the animal offered
(cf. 'burnt offering'), so that not even the offering priest benefits
from it.[3] It is not generally associated with a benefit for the offerer,
such as atonement.[4] It is the only sacrifice offered as a regular daily
offering (Exod. 29.38-46; Lev. 6.9 [H 2]; Num. 28.4-8), and is the
most important festival sacrifice (Appendix 4). The purpose of the
sacrifice is described in general terms as 'pleasing' to God (לרצנו, Lev.
1.3).[5] It had to be a full blood sacrifice (contrast Lev. 5.11-13) and

1.   Rainey (1970); cf. Milgrom (1976: 70 n. 251, 82 n. 295).

2.   Clamer (1956: 30).

3.   The skin is given to the officiating priest (Lev. 7.8), but this does not significantly affect the symbolism of complete destruction.

4.   'Atonement' or 'expiation' refers to the important but disputed word כפר. It is
unlikely that the appearance of כפר in Lev. 1.4 is to be taken as the key to the purpose of the offering, although some have argued that it is the primary sacrifice which
deals with human sin (e.g. Wenham 1979b: 55-63; Milgrom 1971c: 69). It may be a
later systematization which associates atonement generally with blood (Elliger 1966:
36; Porter 1976: 14, 20; Rendtorff 1990a: 36-38). A similar anomaly is that ריח ניחח
is used only once of the חטאת (Lev. 4.31).

5.   The term ריח ניחח ('a pleasing smell', Lev. 1.9, 13, 17) also describes God's

only the more valued male animals may be offered (§6.4.4). All this
suggests that the *'ōlâ* is particularly associated with God, rather than
with Israel and its needs.[1] As such, it has a pre-eminent position in the
prescriptive lists (Lev. 1–7; Num. 28–29), even though it was not
offered first.

The divine orientation of the sacrifice has been variously expressed,
particularly in terms of 'gift' or 'homage'.[2] However, it is difficult to
be so specific when there are is no corresponding terminology in the
Hebrew. An appropriate interpretation may well depend on the larger
ritual context in which it plays a role. The kind of animal offered was
graded according to the occasion for which it was prescribed (cf.
§7.2.2) or the resources of the offerer (§6.4.4).

6.2.2 *Purification of Impurity*

In many cases, the *ḥaṭṭā't* is required for purification from an impurity to which no blame can be attached.[3] 'Purification offering' is
therefore a better translation than 'sin offering'. The nominal form of
the *ḥaṭṭā't* (חטאת) is related to the *piel* of *ḥāṭā'*, which (like the *hithpael*, Num. 8.21; 19.12, 13, 20; 31.19, 20) usually means 'purify'
(Exod. 29.36; Lev. 8.15; 9.15; 14.49, 52; Num. 19.19). *kpr* (כפר),
traditionally translated 'atone', is frequently the purpose of a *ḥaṭṭā't*
needed for purification.[4] The manipulation of blood of the *ḥaṭṭā't* is
required for cleansing from impurity (מן, 'from' in Lev. 14.19; 15.30;
16.16; cf. 12.6, 8; §6.3). The purification offering is also offered in
cases where there is no specific sin or impurity in view (e.g.

pleasure in the sacrifice, and the stench of burning flesh emphasizes the metaphorical
character of the use of the sense of smell in the cult (see §4.5.3).

1.   Köhler (1957: 184-85).
2.   'Gift' can take on overtones of bribe, contract ('I give you so that you give
me'), honour, homage, tribute, or all of these and more. Rendtorff (1990a: 79) has
recently suggested thankfulness as the theme ('It is a gift to God. . . to express his
thankfulness').
3.   E.g. childbirth (Lev. 12.6, 8), skin disease (Lev. 14.19, 22, 31), discharges
(Lev. 15.15, 30), and corpse impurity (cf. Num. 6.11; cf. 19.1-22; see §6.3.2). The
physical basis of the purification metaphor is implied by ideas of purging or absorp-
tion (e.g. by blood), and wiping (a possible etymology of כפר).
4.   Recent discussions of כפר include Janowski (1982), Schenker (1981), Lang
(1982), Kiuchi (1987: 87-109). It is often related to a 'ransom' model, which is
found clearly outside Priestly cultic texts (e.g. Janowski 1982: 103-81), and to the
interpretation of Lev. 17.11.

Lev. 8.14-17; 9.8; Num. 8.8; even possibly Lev. 16.3, but see §7.4). In these cases it is likely to be part of a comprehensive ritual to insure that purification is complete or fully assured.

Milgrom has helpfully drawn attention to the importance of the *ḥaṭṭā't* in purification, and also to the great significance of grading. However, his interpretation faces certain difficulties. He argues that only places, and not people, are purified.[1] However, it is closely related to personal impurity in most of its occurrences, and the person is cleansed as a result of the priest performing atonement (Lev. 12.8; 14.19-20; 16.19, 30; Num. 8.6-7, 15, 21). While blood is not applied to the person requiring purification, there may have been practical reasons for this. It seems reasonable to affirm that the *ḥaṭṭā't* dealt with impurity on both the divine (i.e. the sanctuary) and the human side.[2]

Milgrom also considers that impurity has a 'dynamic, aerial quality', and the graded purification of the purification offering (§6.4) is attributed to the graded power of impurity, whose spatial penetration increases in proportion to the seriousness of the offence.[3] Accordingly, the blood ritual for purification has to take place correspondingly closer to the heart of the sanctuary. In the light of references to impurity from the ancient Near East, Milgrom traces the origin of this power to the demonic. But since the Priestly texts pay little attention to the demonic in any form,[4] Milgrom suggests that humanity has become the demonic source of impurity in the 'Priestly theodicy'.[5]

1. Milgrom (1983a: 75-76).

2. Milgrom also assumes that the sanctuary is defiled immediately a person becomes defiled. Kiuchi (1987: 61) prefers to limit the spatial scope of defilement, so that the sanctuary is defiled only when the person presents himself to be purified. It may be that Milgrom is right for general corporate contexts (e.g. Lev. 15.31), whereas Kiuchi is right for the ritual response to individual impurity.

3. Milgrom (1983e: 78-80) and similarly Levine (1974: 67-91). The electromagnetic model encourages reference to mysterious powers characteristic of the dynamistic approach (§§3.3.3; 6.1.2), rather than the social and religious factors.

4. Wenham (1979b: 94-95). The 'goat-demons' (NRSV for שעירם) are found only once in a sacrificial context (Lev. 17.7), and this is an isolated polemical statement. Azazel (Lev. 16.8, 10, 26; see §7.4) appears in the unique context of the Day of Atonement, but any demonic associations are strongly qualified. Anthropological discussions (e.g. Douglas 1966; Meiggs 1978; Ikenga-Metuh 1985) show that it is possible to interpret purity laws without reference to the demonic.

5. Milgrom (1983a: 82-83). In a striking analogy to 'The Picture of Dorian

Milgrom, however, is here arguing on the basis of the unproven assumption that the demonic explains impurity in the Priestly texts. Parallels with other cultures have to be used with great caution, and other explanations for the negative and communicable character of impurity are available (Chapter 3).

6.2.3 *Forgiveness of Sins*

Leviticus 4–5 describes two sacrifices which are concerned with various sins, the *ḥaṭṭā't* (4.1-35 and 5.1-13) and the *'āšām*, (5.14–6.7 [H 5.14-26]).[1] In Leviticus 4 the sins are inadvertent or unwitting ones (חטאת בשגגה).[2] In all cases (except 4.3-12)[3] it is stated that the priest must atone for the offender (e.g. וכפר עליו), who is thereby forgiven (ונסלח לו 4.20, 26, 31, 35). In Leviticus 5 the action may be deliberate (5.1; 6.1-7 [H 5.20-26]),[4] and the sacrifices are characterized by a different animal grading from that in Leviticus 4 (§6.4.4). Other considerations also suggest it should be distinguished from the *ḥaṭṭā't* of Leviticus 4.[5]

The way in which the purification offering is related to sin in Leviticus 4–5 raises acutely the problem of the relation between the sin and the purification models. With Milgrom, it seems better to

---

Gray' (the title of the article), Milgrom asserts that 'sin may not leave its mark on the face of the sinner, but it is certain to mark the face of the sanctuary'.

1. Milgrom (1983b: 249-50). אשם (like חטאת) need not refer to a type of sacrifice (see §6.2.4).

2. In Num. 15.22-31 these are contrasted with deliberate sins, committed with a high hand (ביד רמה v. 30). They are described as 'hidden' from the offender (נעלם, Lev. 4.13; 5.2, 3, 4; cf. v. 7). Wenham (1979b: 92-93) distinguishes between inadvertent and hidden sins (the latter are sins of omission which 'slip the memory'), but 4.13 (נעלם) tells against this.

3. It is often assumed that this is an accidental omission (e.g. Noth 1965: 41). However, Kiuchi relates it to Lev. 16 (see §7.4.5).

4. In the Priestly system, sin and guilt are objective realities, and can exist even if the guilt is unrecognized or the sin inadvertent. This does not exclude the recognition of human responsibility in other contexts. Milgrom's (1976: 7-12) translation of the verb אשם as 'feel guilt' is too subjective (Childs 1985: 158; Toorn 1985: 92).

5. Milgrom (1983b: 249-50) hypothesizes that the sacrifice in Lev. 5.1-13 'is enjoined for failure or inability to cleanse impurity upon its occurrence'.

recognise the priority of the purification model for P. However, when 'sin' vocabulary (חטא and חטאת) is used of the offerer of this sacrifice, as in Leviticus 4–5, it is possible that the notion of an offering for sin is prominent.[1] The models can be understood to overlap if sin is understood to cause pollution of the sanctuary. Purification of the sanctuary and the offerer is then the way in which the forgiveness of sins is expressed.[2] Purification thus remains the common factor of the various occasions in which the *ḥaṭṭā't* is offered, but the significance of the purification is determined by the context.[3]

This may clarify the diversity of the *ḥaṭṭā't* rituals. If the problem is simple impurity (§6.2.2), then no forgiveness is required or attained by the *ḥaṭṭā't*. But when someone has sinned, then that person does not need cleansing (the טמא root does not occur in Lev. 4–5) so much as forgiveness. When specific sin is the reason for the *ḥaṭṭā't* (Lev. 5.1-13), forgiveness requires a correspondingly specific confession (התודה, 5.5).[4] The personal character of sin is reflected in the grading of the sacrifices in Leviticus 4 in accordance with the personal dimension (§6.4.2). In contrast, the simple purifying *ḥaṭṭā't* is fixed (though often with a poverty clause).

Although ritual impurity is not of itself sinful, it can become the occasion for sin. Minor impurity could become the occasion of sin through contact with the holy (Lev. 7.20-21; 12.4; 22.3-9; see §5.4.2), resulting in death (Lev. 22.9). A delay in purification for a major impurity was a serious offence, as was deliberately spreading impurity (cf. Lev. 13.45-46; 20.18). For this reason, a person who touched a

---

1.   The sin model is frequently taken to be the primary one, in accord with the common translation 'sin offering'. For example, Koch (1977: 868) perceives sacrifice as removing the sphere of sin, and impurity is a sign of how sin affects its surroundings. But this subordinates impurity to sin too strongly.

2.   Milgrom (1983b: 251) supposes that the growing power of impurity contaminates the sanctuary, but in so doing he does not sufficiently acknowledge the human side to these actions.

3.   Marx (1989) wishes to relate the חטאת closely to rites of passage, but Milgrom (1991) rightly stresses the predominance of the purification element.

4.   The absence of confession in Lev. 4 may suggest that the inadvertent sin was discovered by oracular means, and its specific content was not known. Rendtorff (1990a: 153) points out the increasing specificity of chapter 5 compared with 4.

corpse and did not purify himself (יתחטא) defiled (טמא) Yahweh's dwelling (Num. 19.13; cf. Lev. 15.31; 16.16).[1]

6.2.4 *Repayment of a Debt*

The distinctive feature of the *'āšām* (אשם) in Lev. 5.14–6.7 [H 5.14–26] is that it denotes guilt with regard to holy things that had financial consequences.[2] Little is said about the sacrifice, which indeed may be commuted (5.15), but reparation (the amount plus a fifth) is essential and must be rendered to the party defrauded (cf. Num. 5.5-10).[3] Economic offences had cultic as well as legal consequences, and conversely, some cultic offences could be regarded from an economic point of view (Lev. 14.10-32; 19.21-22; Num. 6.12).[4]

The economics of sacrifice have broader implications. Factors of expense and means have probably influenced the laws in a number of ways. The material cost of purifications and sacrifices was graded according to the seriousness of the offence. This affected the type of animal (or otherwise) and how many were to be sacrificed. The greater resources of the community allowed a greater number of sacrifices to be offered during festivals than was possible for individuals (§7.2.2). At the other extreme, poor offerers were provided with cheaper alternatives (especially birds; e.g. after childbirth or skin disease, Lev. 12.8; 14.21). The more common major impurities were also subject to an economic accommodation to reality (§§5.4.2, 6.3.3).

In one case, even grain could be offered instead of an animal for a *ḥaṭṭā't* (Lev. 5.11-13). This is sometimes regarded as qualifying the

---

1.   If the delay in purification defiled the sanctuary, it suggests that the sanctuary had become the register of Israel's sin and thus needed to be cleansed periodically.

2.   Porter (1976: 44). A great deal of confusion arises because of the different meanings of אשם. According to context, it could refer to a sacrifice of reparation, the penalty for guilt, or the state of guilt (Milgrom 1976: 1-12; Kiuchi 1987: 31-34). אשם in Lev. 4.1–5.13 describes the guilt which follows sin (Lev. 4.13, 22, 27; 5.2-5), while in 5.6 it probably refers to the sacrifice (the חטאת) that must be brought as the penalty for guilt. The אשם sacrifice is thus quite distinct from the חטאת and is dealt with in a different passage.

3.   The exception in Lev. 5.17-19 could be that because the defrauding is suspected, and no specific sums are concerned. The more severe penalties of the civil law (Exod. 22.6-8) were perhaps to encourage voluntary reparation (Milgrom 1976a: 114-15).

4.   Milgrom (1976a). The precise rationale for offering the אשם is often uncertain.

demand for a blood sacrifice for atonement and purification, but it may also be due to a competing principle which wins out. The necessity for even the poorest person to offer something took precedence over the symbolism (cf. Exod. 23.15; 34.20; Deut. 16.16-17). Milgrom has argued that the sacrifices graded according to means dealt with impurities or other offences which could not be avoided, including those which may have slipped the memory (Lev. 5.1-4).[1] The 'āšām, on the other hand, concerned frauds and sins which would normally concern only the comparatively well off.[2]

6.2.5 *Sharing a Meal*

The distinctive character of the peace offering[3] was the final stage of this sacrificial ritual, in which the flesh of the sacrifice was distributed to various parties, including the non-priestly offerer (§6.4.5). This was possible because it did not deal with with the faults of the offerer, and is never described as atoning, unlike the *ḥaṭṭā't* and the '*āšām*,[4] It was accordingly a voluntary sacrifice, whereas the others could be required on various occasions. Whereas the '*ōlâ* law focuses on the burning of the animal, the *ḥaṭṭā't* law on the blood manipulation, and the '*āšām* law on the additional reparation, the *šᵉlāmîm* law is concerned with the distribution of the parts of the sacrifice as food.

This sacrifice is commonly related to a communion or fellowship model, in which the parties involved in the sacrifice (i.e. God and the offerer) share in a meal and strengthen the bonds between them.[5] While the etymological link between *šᵉlāmîm* and *šālôm* ('peace') is

---

1. Milgrom (1983b: 252). In contrast, the violation of a specific prohibition, even inadvertently, meant a fixed sacrifice (Lev. 4).

2. Others consider the fixed sacrifice to point to the seriousness of the offence (e.g. Wenham 1979b: 108).

3. The normal term in P is זבח שלמים (e.g. Lev. 3), but שלמים and זבח are sometimes found on their own. Rendtorff (1990a: 118-29) favours the suggestion that the double term refers to the public and cultic aspect of the more general term זבח. 'Peace offering' is a disputed and possibly incorrect translation. Alternatives include sacrifice of well-being (NRSV), shared-offering (NEB), completion sacrifice ('Schlußopfer', Rendtorff 1967: 133) or community sacrifice ('Gemeinschafts-Schlachtopfer', Rendtorff 1990a: 125-26).

4. Milgrom (1983a: 153). At most, the blood manipulation considered in itself could be associated with atonement (Kiuchi 1987: 103).

5. A model often associated with Robertson Smith (e.g. 1927: 345).

uncertain, and ideas of 'communion' may be anachronistic,[1] the use of
the sacrifice for food is distinctive and significant. The nuanced distribution of the various parts of the sacrifice allow a 'culinary sacrificial
topology' to be developed,[2] which illuminates the grading in the personal dimension (§6.4.5).

The meal metaphor can illuminate aspects of other sacrifices as
well. Just as a meal is consumed by human participants, so are the
burnt parts of the sacrifice consumed by God. The 'pleasing aroma'
(Lev. 3.5, 16, etc.) and incense (§4.5.3) may suggest good cooking,
and some of the offerings are explicitly called 'food' (*leḥem*) for
God.[3] The different ways in which the *minḥâ* is cooked (Lev. 2.4-7)
no doubt reflected the ordinary cooking techniques of the Israelite
home.

However, the present text makes it clear that the model must be
carefully qualified.[4] Indeed, a number of scholars have argued that
šᵉlāmîm need have no association with a meal.[5] Its etymology does not
necessarily refer to the well-being or peace that follows a good meal.
Despite these qualifications, this model should not be rejected completely.[6] The positive symbolism (corporate harmony, physical
blessing) can be retained, while the qualifications point to significant
aspects of Yahweh's character and the way that the model is limited.
God does not enjoy food in the same sense as human beings do. He

1. 'Communion' can have unhelpful overtones of eucharistic theology or early
anthropological theories of totemism.

2. The phrase is from de Heusch (1985). Cf. Thornton (1982).

3. E.g. 'the bread of their God' (לחם אלהיהם, Lev. 21.6), 'food offered by fire
to Yahweh' (לחם אשה ליהוה, Lev. 3.11).

4. Kaufmann (1960: 111-12). The symbolic character of the cult makes it
unlikely that earlier forms of the rite were understood as crudely as has been
suggested. In Mesopotamian religion elaborate meals were prepared for the gods, but
they were not physically consumed (Oppenheim 1977: 191-93). A Babylonian priest
would probably be as amused as an Israelite one at the literalism of *Bel and the
Dragon*.

5. This facet is not stressed in P, though it is elsewhere (e.g. Exod. 12.8-10;
24.5). Porter (1976: 29-30) considers that it has lost this aspect in the Levitical
system and instead represents more a gift that brings about 'agreement' or 'recon-
ciliation'. The ritual is similar to the other sacrifices, and so atonement rather than
communion could be implied (the lack of a כפר reference could be accidental).

6. As it is by de Vaux (1961: 449-50). It is more than a 'linguistic vestige'
(Milgrom 1971c: 70; cf. Eichrodt 1961: 143-44).

does not eat but smells the burnt portions, and the portions devoted to him (the fatty parts) are different from those which the Israelites are allowed (Lev. 3.17; 7.23-25).[1] The turning of some or all of the sacrifice into smoke is an appropriate symbol of an immaterial God who dwells in heaven.[2] The same contrast is found in *minḥâ* ritual, in which only a handful is burnt (Lev. 2.2), and this is called 'the memorial offering' (זכרון), a term which stresses the non-physical significance of the sacrifice.

The *šᵉlāmîm* texts in P set out an animal grading (§6.4.4), but the choice was in all likelihood determined by different motives from the others. For a votive offering (נדר, Lev. 7.16), it is plausible to suppose that the animal chosen depended upon the nature of the vow and its response; for a thanksgiving (תודה, Lev. 7.12), the magnitude of the blessing; and for a freewill offering (נדבה, Lev. 7.16), the desire and capacity of the offerer to honour and praise God. The animal chosen would depend upon the wealth of the offerer and the character of the occasion on which it was offered.

6.2.6 *Summary*

Constructing models of sacrifice can be helpful, but any individual approach has its limitations. The various sacrifices exhibit similarities and differences. It is difficult to keep the models 'pure', and the failure of comprehensive theories of sacrifice highlight the differences between the types. None of the five models discussed is able to explain the system as a whole. However, one further model should be considered, since it is an extremely broad one, and fits in with the anthropological and structural perspectives introduced in Chapter 3.

This is the 'order' model, which has recently received a certain amount of attention (see further §8.3). Its application to the cult may be illustrated by the following two quotations.[3]

---

1. The structural contrast remains even if the Hebrews regarded the fat as the best and most desirable portion of an animal (Münderlein 1977: 954). The point is emphasized by the complete consumption of the עלה, the principal sacrifice (§6.2.1). The reason why the blood must be poured out on the ground and not eaten (Lev. 3.17; 7.26-27) is probably different (Lev. 17.11).

2. One possible explanation of the term עלה is that it is the participle of עלה (to go up) and describes the ascending character of the smoke. However, it could also describe the smell, the fire, or the offerer's ascent up to the altar (Kellermann 1987: 106; Rendtorff 1990a: 27 leaves the question open).

3. Blenkinsopp (1983: 108), Gorman (1990: 60).

> It follows from this world view [of P] that the purpose of the many cultic acts carried out in the temple was to maintain and, where necessary, re-establish this divine order. Sin was understood as a disturbance of that order, even when committed by inadvertence.

> The primary question addressed in examining specific parts of the larger Priestly ritual system concerns the way in which the rituals relate to the foundation, maintenance, and restoration of the divinely created order.

The 'negative' sacrifices (the *ḥaṭṭā't* and the *'āšām*), are the means by which the divine order, disturbed by impurity or sin,[1] is restored to an original harmony.[2] A 'fault' in the order of things can be personal (sin) or impersonal (impurity), unavoidable or deliberate, individual or corporate. It need not be directly associated with the cult (cf. §6.2.4), since Yahweh guarantees the world-order and there are religious repercussions to unethical behaviour in society. The *šᵉlāmîm* can also be assimilated to the model if they are regarded as reinforcing the value of the restored relation between God and man. They are the appropriate way to acknowledge positively God's goodness and any particular benefits which an individual may have received from Yahweh's hand.[3]

The model has considerable heuristic and theoretical interest, and provides a way to assimilate certain symbols, actions or words which cannot be assigned definitely to a more specific model.[4] It points to the limited scope of the previous models, and stresses that the models are

1.   'Sin is whatever disrupts the proper order of things in a society where every facet of life is governed by the precepts of the divine law' (Porter 1976: 11).

2.   Brichto (1976: 27-28) considers that *kpr* refers to the restoration of an equilibrium when an imbalance between two parties occurs. From an anthropological perspective, de Heusch (1985: 215) discusses sacrifice in terms of 'the metaphysical calculation of profit and loss', an economic metaphor. Schenker (1981) also develops the 'exchange' model.

3.   The עלה could even be understood as a sacrifice which acknowledges that God is the source of the cosmic order.

4.   The order model may be of use in understanding Lev. 17.11. The general character of the verse makes it difficult to link it closely with any of the specific models set out in §6.2. Interpreters are forced to use very general concepts such as ransom, exchange, representation and substitution. Lev. 17.11 fits a general exchange model quite well, since it stresses the relation between sin–impurity and death, and suggests that the life in the sacrificial blood deals with this conjunction and gives life back to the offerer.

not to be understood in a narrow way. Yet in turn, the order model has weaknesses. Its very generality makes it difficult to relate the model directly to specific words and texts in the Priestly writing. If the models are a second order interpretation of the reality of sacrifice, then 'order' is one stage yet further removed.

It is in the light of these considerations that the value of an approach in terms of grading can be perceived. Grading is common to all the models, and so provides a key to understanding the system of Lev. 1–7 in its diversity as well as its unity. It also provides the link between the specific models and the general order model. It has particular relevance for the model of purification, which is not restricted to a narrow cultic focus. So before considering the grading of the sacrificial system in detail, the Priestly system of purification will be discussed.

6.3 *Purification*

6.3.1 *Graded Purification*

Purification results in a movement from a state of major or minor impurity to one of purity. In terms of the Holiness Spectrum, it is a move from the right (the impurity pole) to the left, and is a response to the opposite process, defilement (§2.2). Purification is achieved principally by an appropriate ritual and a lapse of time.[1] Just as there are grades of impurity (§5.4.2), so there are corresponding grades of purification (see the summary in Appendix 2).

Most of an individual's life would be spent in a state of purity or of minor impurity, corresponding to the central part of the Holiness Spectrum. A minor impurity could be cleansed simply and easily by washing one's clothing, bathing, and waiting until evening. Major impurities were more serious, since they usually required not only water purification, but also sacrifice and a wait of seven days. In P, matters are ordered so as to minimize the danger of major defilement of the camp and minor defilement of the sanctuary. A person with major impurity is either isolated or kept outside the camp (§5.4.2).

Since purification is the reverse of defilement, it is not surprising that the materials of purification are often associated with life,

---

1. The discussion in this section tries to avoid any appeal to ideas of sympathetic magic or dynamism (§6.1.2).

corresponding to the death aspect of impurity (§3.4.3). Water unites the themes of cleansing and giving of life. Both life and death are probably associated with the most powerful means of purification, the sprinkling or application of the blood of a sacrificed animal. Although blood does not cleanse physically, it is essential to life (like water) and its loss leads to death.

The relative grading of purification of minor (water) and major (blood) purification may also be viewed from an economic perspective (§6.2.4). Sacrifice was expensive and used only for the more serious and rarer impurities, while minor impurities were cleansed with water, which was both cheap and accessible. The necessity for a long delay before a major impurity was dealt with reinforced the symbolism. A lapse of seven days was costly in terms of the restrictions it imposed upon the actions which could be performed, whereas minor impurity did not even entail isolation or expulsion from the camp. Economic factors may also have been a consideration in some anomalous purifications. It would have been prohibitively expensive to require a blood sacrifice for the purification of common major impurities (e.g. menstruation, corpses).

6.3.2 *Purification from Corpse Impurity*
The ritual for cleansing a person from corpse impurity is recorded in Numbers 19, and displays a number of peculiarities.[1] For example, the ritual is called a *ḥaṭṭā't* (v. 9), but it is a very unusual sacrifice. It takes place outside the camp, and the blood is not directed to the sanctuary or altar directly, but is merely sprinkled towards the Tent of Meeting.[2] Further, Eleazar, the son of the high priest, performs part of the ceremony (vv. 3-4), but another priest is involved in actions which incur minor impurity (vv. 6-7).

---

1.   Studies of this intriguing chapter illustrate well different approaches to ritual. Scheftelowitz (1921) illustrates well the confusion which results when the older ideas of primitive thought, magic, taboo and impurity are assumed (cf. §3.3). Wefing (1981) is primarily concerned with historical questions, and so does not discuss the meaning of the ritual at the level of the final text. Milgrom's (1983a: 85-95) valuable discussion is affected by his view of impurity (§6.2.2) and his psychological explanation that 'corpse contamination evoked an obsessive, irrational fear'. Closest to the treatment here is Gorman (1990: 191-214).

2.   Wefing (1981: 349, 354) denies it is a sacrifice, but Milgrom (1983a: 86-90) argues persuasively that it is.

An economic perspective can make sense of some of the unusual and unique features of this chapter. For example, a person touching an animal carcass suffers minor defilement, while corpse impurity generates major impurity. The different degrees of purification from animal and human death reflect the priority of humans in the personal dimension. But it is also a practical necessity in a rural or nomadic economy in which the farmers would frequently come across the death of domestic animals. The purification from such an impurity had to be relatively light.

Human death would also occur periodically,[1] but this sets up a dilemma. On the one hand, a human corpse generates the most extreme impurity in the Priestly system (§5.5.2),[2] and death is central to the idea of impurity (§3.4.3). On the other hand, it would be economically prohibitive to demand a sacrifice each time someone died, since a large number of people could contract corpse impurity.[3] The solution to this dilemma in Num. 19 is that the material of purification is complex, richly symbolic and expensive, but that its application is simple and cheap.

An expensive animal was to be used, one that was a rare colour (red, v. 2) and had not been used for ploughing (never yoked, v. 2). According to the *ḥaṭṭā't* ritual of Lev. 4.13-21, a bull was used to purify the congregation, whereas an individual offered a female of the flock (Lev. 4.28, 32). The choice of a cow rather than a bull perhaps combined the corporate (herd) and individual (female) aspects of the normal *ḥaṭṭā't* ritual. On the other hand, application was cheap because the large animal provided ashes sufficient for innumerable purifications. Not even the hide (which was normally given to the priests) was omitted, and a practical function of the cedar wood, hyssop and scarlet would be to increase the volume of the ashes.[4]

---

1. Death by accident or old age are not the only possibilities. Budd (1984: 211-12) suggests that it was redactionally appropriate for the ritual to be placed here after the deaths of Num. 16–17.

2. נדה is used elsewhere to describe the impurity of menstruation (Lev. 15.19, 20, 33). Noordtzij (1983: 170) states that this term is a technical one for an extreme degree of impurity, which is removed by the 'waters of impurity' (מי נדה, Num. 19.13, 20), but Milgrom and Wright (1986: 251-52) argue that it means 'cleansing' in this context.

3. Noordtzij (1983: 171).

4. Milgrom (1983a: 88-90) stresses the way in which the quantity of ashes was

The materials and actions of the ritual are unified in the way that they symbolise life, an appropriate theme for a ritual which corrects a state of impurity and death. The ashes were not used on their own, but were combined with 'living water' (מים חיים, v. 17) for sprinkling, thus reinforcing the double symbolism of water as purifying and reviving. Blood also speaks of the duality of life and death, and several of the materials echo the red colour of blood (the red cow, the scarlet thread, the blood manipulation).[1]

The application of the ashes and water must take place on the third and seventh days. The dual purification stresses the seriousness of the impurity, but it also raises the problem that the cleansed man was not able to approach the sanctuary on the third day, since he was still impure. This may explain why the blood manipulation and the burning of the red cow must take place outside the camp. The unusual place of slaughter and burning could indicate that the purification is effective there, rather than inside the sanctuary. Unlike the purification of the leper, where the initial blood ritual is not a sacrifice (Lev. 14.4-7), the ashes of the red cow lead to the benefits of sacrificial purification being attained without the need for further entry into the sanctuary.

6.3.3 *Purification from Skin Disease*

Next to corpse impurity, and in some ways more serious because it is a lasting impurity, is the person with skin disorder (see §5.5.3). The *mᵉṣōraʿ* (Lev. 14.2) must stay outside the camp, since a permanently unclean place was allowed in the wilderness, but not in the camp. His status in the personal dimension therefore corresponds with his location on the spatial dimension. Similarly, garments are destroyed (13.55), and houses pulled down, and their stones deposited in an unclean place (14.43-44), to remove 'diseased' items from the inhabited zone. Destruction by fire eliminates impurity completely, but it is impossible for stone houses, and immoral for people, for whom there

---

maximized. According to the Mishnah (*m. Par.* 3.5), only 7 or 9 red cows had ever been prepared.

1.   Blood, cedar, hyssop, scarlet thread and running water are also aspects of the purification of a person with skin disease (see §6.3.3). Wefing (1981: 351) suggests that the cedarwood and hyssop represent the totality of life (by merismus—the smallest and greatest), and the scarlet thread the fundamental principle of life (its colour recalls blood). Together the three materials point to all that makes up life.

is also the possibility of cleansing.[1] The instruction concerning an
'unclean place' (14.44-45) implies that even outside the camp, there is
a concern to limit the scope of impurity (cf. 13.46).

The unique character of the purification ritual for the $m^e s\bar{o}ra'$ who
had been healed emphasizes the special place which this disorder had
in the Israelite graded conception of impurity (§5.4.2). It took place
in three phases, with the spatial, social and cultic implications of the
change of status expressed by appropriate symbols and rituals:[2]

Location	Sacrifice	Purification	Result
1. outside camp (V)	bird set free	wash clothes	
1st day	bird slaughtered	shave all hair	clean
(Lev. 14.1-8)		bathe in water	(v. 8)
2. outside tent (IV)		shave all hair	
7th day		wash clothes	clean
(Lev. 14.9)		bathe in water	(v. 9)
3. before Yahweh (III)	*'āšām* lamb (m)	3× application of blood	
8th day		7× sprinkling with oil	
(Lev. 14.10-32)		3× application of oil	
	hattā't lamb (m)		clean
	'ōlâ sheep (f)		(v. 20)

The transition from the status of $m^e s\bar{o}ra'$ to full participant of society
is represented by entry into the tent, and the resumption of cultic
responsibilities is represented by offering three sacrifices. However,
these acts take place only after various rituals and a delay of a week.
From the point of view of the Holiness Spectrum, it requires an extended procedure to move from the extreme impure pole to the state
of purity necessary for the offering of sacrifice. But once this is done,
there is no further question about the rights and status of the purified
person. The declaration that the $m^e s\bar{o}ra'$ is clean is repeated three times,
each one at the conclusion of a different stage. It is probably anachronistic to say that different grades of purity are indicated,[3] but the

---

1.   Compare the graded treatment of vessels which have been in contact with a
major impurity. The earthenware vessels are destroyed but the wooden vessels are
scoured (Lev. 15.12; cf. 11.33, 35).

2.   Pilch (1981) stresses that 'cultural healing' has a social as well as a physical
dimension.

3.   Kiuchi (1987: 60). According to the Mishnah (*m. Neg.* 14.2-3), after the first
stage, the purified person has uncleanness like that of a creeping thing (ץרש); after the

context appears to imply some kind of intensification or completeness of purification. Only after the third stage is the person fully purified.

The first stage includes an unusual elimination ritual, one whose symbolism expresses the passage from impurity and death to life and purity (cf. §6.3.2).[1] There is also a symbolic counter-movement in the spatial dimension. Extreme movements away from the centre and toward it are balanced. As in the purification from corpse impurity, the life motif recurs several times. At the beginning, a living bird (הצפור החיה, Lev. 14.6) is set loose in an open field, and the other bird is slaughtered over running water (על המים החים, v. 6; lit. 'living water').[2] This is counter-balanced by the movement of the cured person from outside the camp (v. 3, the place of death and impurity) into the camp, and eventually to the central sanctuary.

The intermediate stage emphasizes a phased social reintegration. An identical triple set of lesser purity rituals occurs before and after this period, thus marking it out as a distinct period. The *mᵉṣōraʿ* has entered the camp, but remains outside his tent and is a liminal figure (§3.2.4). He is on the threshold of normal social life but not yet fully involved. The week's delay no doubt allowed time for readjustment to the implications of full adult life in the community. Although washing and bathing are the standard means of purification from minor impurity, the shaving of hair has been added to stress the new stage of life which is about to begin (§3.5.1).

On the eighth day there is a special blood application after an *ʾāšām* sacrifice (Lev. 14.12-18), which is similar to that of the ordination of the priests after the special ordination sacrifice (Lev. 8.23-24; §5.2.1). It ratifies a previous declaration by God, or by a priest speaking on

second, as one who has bathed on the same day; and after the third, he is clean enough to partake of the holy things.

1. Davies (1977: 396). The ritual is not called a חטאת (contrast Num. 19.9; §6.3.2) and is not a sacrifice in the strict sense (Milgrom 1983a: 90). But the creature (bird), the slaughtering (v. 5), the manipulation of blood, and the purifying action are all aspects of a sacrifice, suggesting that this ritual attracts some of the potency and meaning of a sacrificial ritual.

2. This is often compared with the scapegoat ritual of the Day of Atonement and assigned an early date and a primitive rationale. But in both cases, it is possible to find a symbolic fitness in the way an elimination of impurity in one direction balances a movement towards purity in the opposite (§7.4).

behalf of God. The result of the ritual is that the status of the person is raised, whether from a potential to a true priest, or from one like dead (§5.4.2) to that of a normal member of the worshipping community.[1] In terms of the Holiness Spectrum, they comprise a move towards the left: for the priests, from purity to holiness, and for the *mᵉṣōraʿ*, from impurity to purity.

The three main types of involuntary sacrifice mark the concluding ritual of the eighth day. All of them are part of the atonement ritual, but impurity is mentioned specifically only in connection with the *ḥaṭṭāʾt* (וכפר על־המטהר מטמאתיו, v. 19; see §6.2.2).[2] This emphasizes the comprehensiveness of the purification, as does the application of blood to the extreme limbs. The purified person is also confirmed as a fully capable member of the community, able to offer the entire range of sacrifices.

Houses may also contract this disorder (נגע צרעת, Lev. 14.34). When they are 'healed' (נרפא, v. 48), the priest carries out a purification ritual similar to that for a person to purify (לחטא, v. 49) the house. He pronounces it clean (וטהר, v. 48) once he has performed the atonement ritual for the house (כפר על, v. 53; see §6.2.2).

6.4 *Sacrifice and Grading*

6.4.1 *Leviticus 4 and Grading*
We now return to the main corpus of sacrificial laws at the beginning of Leviticus. Sacrifice is a complex ritual which allows numerous variations between types of sacrifice, and within the same type. These variations are, in the Priestly system, largely associated with the correlated gradings which characterize the Holiness Spectrum.[3] This may be illustrated by the description of the *ḥaṭṭāʾt* ritual in Leviticus 4. This chapter

---

1. This show the close relation between a *rite de passage* and a purification ritual. See now the debate between Marx (1989) and the response by Milgrom (1991).

2. וכפר עליו הכהן occurs in Lev. 14.18a and 20b, thus bracketing the atonement ritual which is focused on the חטאת (I owe this observation to Dr G.I. Davies). Contrast Lund's (1929: 115-16) analysis.

3. In the Mishnah (*m. Zeb.* 10.1-6), there is an attempt to arrange the sacrifices in an order of precedence according to the grade of holiness, the order of offering and the order of eating. However, the criteria for grading cut across the different types of sacrifice, and are somewhat arbitrary.

consists of five sections, each of which describes a particular case.

The variations between the five sections introduce the most important gradings found in the sacrificial texts of P, and there is a complex but clear correlation between the ritual and the other dimensions.[1] This is summarized in the following table, which also demonstrates how the order in which the text describes the sacrifices gives formal expression to the grading (cf. §4.3.3). The most serious faults are dealt with first and require the strongest purification rituals:

A. Major blood rite takes place in zone II (the Holy Place)

Lev. 4	Offender	Animal	Blood sprinkled (הזה)	Applied (נתן)	Food for[2]
3-12	anointed priest congregation	bull	7× in front of the	horns[4] of incense	no one
13-21		bull[3]	veil	altar	no one

B. Minor blood rite takes place in zone III (the Tabernacle Court)

Lev. 4	Offender	Animal	Blood sprinkled	Applied	Food for
22-26	leader (נשיא)	f goat		horns of	priests
27-31	anyone	f goat		altar of	priests
32-35	anyone	m lamb		'ōlâ	priests

This will be used as a starting point for a more general discussion of grading in the Priestly sacrificial system.

6.4.2 *The Personal Dimension*

The five *ḥaṭṭā't* rituals are distinguished primarily by the status of the persons for whom the sacrifice is offered.[5] The grading is thus by social status, which is not a significant grading in the other sacrifices (though see §6.4.5). This suggests that the *ḥaṭṭā't* is the sacrifice most directed to correcting a personal fault, even if the object of the ritual

---

1. The rituals associated with the seasonal or human rhythm of time (as opposed to lapse of time) are discussed in the next chapter.

2   See Lev. 6.24-30 [H 17-23].

3. The he-goat offering for the congregation in Num. 15.24 probably reflects a different tradition which relates this sacrifice to that typical of the festival offerings (Milgrom 1983d).

4. The horns of the altar were probably the holiest part (Pedersen 1940: 218; de Vaux 1961: 414; Durham 1963: 366-67).

5. 'Socio-religious status' (Milgrom 1983b: 249); 'theokratische Stellung' (Dillmann 1880: 413). Cf. Koch (1959: 103), Janowski (1982: 195).

is the purification of the sanctuary (as suggested in §6.2.3).

The rituals for the anointed priest and for the community are identical, and demonstrate the principle of hierarchy and representation which is significant in numerous other Priestly texts. The defilement of the anointed priest is so serious because he is the religious head of the community and represents the people, who are bound up in his guilt (לאשמת העם, Lev. 4.3). The sin of the congregation requires the same high degree of purification. This may be because the community requires more effective purification than an individual, or because the priests who are included require a high degree of purification.[1] The third alternative, unique for the leader (נשיא), is appropriate because the leaders occasionally have a special cultic role (e.g. Num. 7). Factors other than personal status determine the animal offered by the ordinary Israelite.

6.4.3 *The Spatial Dimension*

The grading of the *ḥaṭṭā't* on the human side (the personal dimension) is matched by the grading on the divine side, represented by the manipulation of the blood in the spatial dimension. The nearer the blood comes to the centre of the sanctuary, the more effective is the purification, and the two most important cases in Leviticus 4 have an identical blood ritual. The blood is brought into the Tent of Meeting (zone II, vv. 5, 16), sprinkled (הזה) seven times before the veil (vv. 6, 17, and applied (נתן על) to the horns of the incense altar (vv. 7,18). In the other three cases, the blood is applied (נתן) to the horns of the main altar (zone III), and there is no sprinkling of blood.

The distinction between these two alternatives, which may be called the major and the minor blood rites, is crucial to the Priestly system.[2] The two types are further distinguished by the kind of animal which is offered (§6.4.4), and the rules about the consumption of the flesh (§6.4.5). The pattern of correlation should be extended to include the Day of Atonement (§7.4).

---

1. Noth (1965: 40) traces the cause of sin to an individual who is unwilling or unable to offer the sacrifice himself. However, this is not the primary meaning of inadvertence (שגגה).

2. They have been called 'kleine/grosse Blutritus' (Gese 1977: 94; Janowski 1982: 222); 'kleine/grosse Sünderitus' (Koch 1959: 53); 'Sündopfer höheren Grades/niederen Grades' (Baentsch 1903: 322, 325).

A distinction in the spatial dimension may also distinguish the *šᵉlāmîm* from other sacrifices. Several times it is mentioned that the *ḥaṭṭā't* (Lev. 4.24, 29, 33; 6.18) and the reparation offering (Lev. 7.2; 14.13) were to be slaughtered in the same place as the burnt offering.[1] For the *šᵉlāmîm*, however, this took place at the entrance of the tent of meeting (פתח אהל מועד, Lev. 3.2).[2] This may reflect a feeling that the *šᵉlāmîm* were of a lesser holiness than the other sacrifices (cf. §6.4.5). The flesh of the *ḥaṭṭā't* (Lev. 6.29 [H 22]), the *minḥâ* (Lev. 2.3, 10; 6.17 [H 10]) and the *'āšām* (Lev. 7.1, 6) had the special status of being most holy (קדש קדשים, Num. 18.9-10), whereas the *šᵉlāmîm* were only holy (קדשים, see §6.4.5).[3]

6.4.4 *The Materials of Sacrifice*
Although some offerings do not involve animals (the separate *minḥâ*, Lev. 2; the libation *nᵉsēkâ*, נסכה), the majority entail the slaughter of a clean animal. The nature of the animal was an important part of the sacrificial code, and the animal grading was correlated with the spatial and personal dimensions. In Leviticus 4, bulls are offered in the two most important cases,[4] and the fourth and fifth sections of the chapter are distinguished only by the alternative sacrifices that a common person may offer, a female goat or a female sheep. The animal grading also differentiates the various types of sacrifice.

There were a number of criteria which defined whether an animal could be sacrificed or not, and for what kind of sacrifice it would be

1. This is identified as the north side of the altar (Lev. 1.11). This was probably for practical reasons (Dillmann 1880: 396-97), rather than theological ones (Porter 1976: 23). The laver was on the west side (Exod. 40.30), the altar steps on the south (following Josephus's description of the temple [*War* 5.225]; cf. Lev. 9.22, where Aaron descends from offering; Hoffmann 1905: 135-36), and the ash heap to the east.

2. A grading according to sacrifice follows the rabbinic interpretation (*m. Zeb.* 5.3-7; Hoffmann 1905: 164). Alternatively, it may have been that the smaller animals were slaughtered in a separate place, since the texts only refer to these classes of animals (Rendtorff 1990a: 72).

3. The rabbinic sources distinguish the most holy offerings (קדשי קדשים) from the lesser holy offerings (קדשים קלים; *m. Zeb.* 1.2; 5.1-8; Haran 1962b: 40-41). Rainey (1970: 487-88) calls קדש קדשים in this context, 'an administrative rather than an esoteric quality'.

4. Their similarity is emphasized by Lev. 4.20, 'He shall do with this bull just as is done with the [priest's] bull of sin offering; he shall do the same with it'.

appropriate. Some of these are summarized in the following table:

a. General	Sacrificial			Non-sacrificial
Status of Purity	clean (טהור)			unclean (ממא)
Social Character	domestic (בקר, צאן)			wild (חית שדה)
Perfection[1]	perfect (תם)			blemished (מום)

b. Specific	High Value			Low Value
Sex	male (זכר)			female (נקבה)
Size	large cattle (בקר)			flock (צאן)
Species	bull	sheep	goat	bird
Age	full-grown	2 years	yearling	recently born
Number	fourteen			one

A sacrificial animal had to be clean and domestic, such as an ox, a sheep or a goat, and it is probable that the birds which were sacrificed were also domesticated.[2] The animal also had to be free from blemish (תם), since it was to be offered at the sanctuary, and holiness was incompatible with blemishes (§3.4.2).[3] For some sacrifices, there were restrictions on the species and sex of the animal. The '*ōlâ* was always a male, and the '*ašām* was usually a ram (Lev. 5.14–6.7 [H 5.14-26]; 19.20-22; a male lamb [כבש] Lev. 14.10-32; Num. 6.12). The same animal was required for the ordination offering of a priest (Exod. 29.20-28 = Lev. 8.22-29).

Another set of criteria defined the type of sacrifice for which animals were fitted. The species of the animal was of great importance for the grading employed in the sacrificial code (§6.3.3). There is a close correlation between the effectiveness of the purification and the economic value of the animal, which in turn depended upon size, age, condition and sex. The grading is indicated by the order in which the alternative animals are listed in Leviticus 1–7 (see the next table).[4]

---

1. Arist. Exeg. 93 adds that the animals were chosen for their fatness as well as for their freedom from blemishes.

2. There was a long history of rearing pigeons and doves in Israel, so that they could easily be considered domesticated (Keil 1882: 289).

3. An animal of abnormal size (large or small) may be offered as a voluntary sacrifice (נדבה, Lev. 22.23). The criteria for the voluntary offerings were less severe than for the obligatory ones.

4. Cf. other occasions of sacrificing a bull (Exod. 29.36; Lev. 9.4, 18; 16.3; Num. 7.87-88; 8.12; 28–29), cow (Num. 19.2, 9), ram (Num. 7.88; Lev. 16.3, 5) and goat (Num. 7.87; 15.24, 27; 28–29).

The sacrificial animal of most worth was the bull or ox, the largest, most useful and most expensive domestic animal. It comes first in the lists of alternatives, both in P and elsewhere.[1] The male is also generally listed before the female (e.g. in Lev. 3).[2] In the lists of festival offerings (Num. 28–29), the community provides a number of animals which are offered as an *'ōlâ* , the first of which is the bull. The same animal is used on other communal occasions for both the *'ōlâ* and the *ḥaṭṭā't* (Lev. 9.4, 18; Num. 7).

		'ōlâ Lev. 1		*šelāmîm* Lev. 3		*ḥaṭṭā't* Lev. 4		*ḥaṭṭā't* Lev. 5.1-13		*'āšām* Lev. 5.14–6.7 [H 5.14-26]
bull[3]	m	1	3-9	la	1-5	1	3-12			
						2	13-21			
cow	f			1b	1-5	see §6.3.2				
sheep	m	2a	10-13	2a	7-11					5.14–6.7
	f			2b	7-11	5[4]	32-35	la	6	
goat	m	2b	10-13	3a	12-16	3	22-26			
	f			3b	12-16	4	27-31	1b	6	
turtledove		3a	14-17					2a	7-10	
or dove		3b	14-17					2b	7-10	
grain								3	11-13	

1. Blome (1934: 61-79), Rendtorff (1967: 28). The order שׁור–כשׂב–עז is found in Lev. 7.23; 22.27; Num. 18.17. The double listing in Num. 15.1-11 (see also below on the portions accompanying the sacrifice) emphasizes the grading by its structure (v. 3 bull, flock; then chiastically, sheep, ram, herd [4-10]; bull, ram, sheep, goat [11]). In the Marseilles sacrificial tariff (*KAI*, 69; cf. the Carthaginian tariff, *KAI*, 74), the animals are graded by a monetary equivalent in the order (1) ox (אלף), (2) calf (עגל) or ram (איל), (3) sheep (יבל) or goat (עז), (4) lamb (אמר) or kid (דגם) or young ram (צרב איל), (5) birds, (6) other non-animal offerings.

2. This probably reflects the human social hierarchy of a patriarchal society (Noth 1965: 22; Porter 1976: 21). There may also have been an economic factor, since females would be more useful for breeding (Levine 1971a: 1156).

3. *Key:* m = male; f = female; 1, 2, 3, 4, 5 = order of mention in the text; a, b = alternatives

4. The unusual order is perhaps because a goat was sacrificed as a חטאת on public occasions such as the festival offerings (Num. 28–29; see §7.2.2). In Num. 15.24 the חטאת for the congregation is a male goat (discussed in Budd 1984: 173-74). The customary association of the goat with the ritual was probably the reason why the normal priority of sheep over goat was reversed, though cattle remained the most effective offerings when the חטאת was the main purpose of the ritual.

At the other extreme, the poor were often allowed to offer birds (e.g. Lev. 5.7, 11; 12.8; 14.22) instead of the more expensive animals. The usual command was to offer two turtledoves (תר) or two doves (יונה), one for a *ḥaṭṭā't* and the other for an *'ōlâ*. They were required for purification after a discharge (Lev. 15.14, 29), possibly because this was a relatively common problem (§6.2.4). An economic motive may also be seen when they were offered for defilement incurred during a Nazirite vow (Num. 6.10), since this fault required a lamb as an *'āšām*. Birds were not offered as *šᵉlāmîm*, probably because of their minimum food value.[1]

The same grading is shown by the quantities of meal and oil (in the meal offerings), and the wine (in the drink offering) which accompanies the *'ōlâ* (Num. 15.1-11; 28–29):

Species		Flour (ephah)	Oil (hin)	Wine (hin)	Text
cattle	בקר	3/10	1/2	1/2	Num. 15.8-10; cf. 28.12, 14, etc.
ram	איל	2/10	1/3	1/3	Num. 15.6-7; cf. 28.12, 14, etc.
sheep or goat	שה בכבשים או בעזים	1/10	1/4	1/4	Num 15.4-5; cf. 28.4-7, 13-14, etc.

The *šᵉlāmîm* allows the widest range of species, sex and number (e.g. Num. 7.17). This is fitting for a sacrifice which is primarily for the benefit of the offerer or the community. The choice of animal was more restricted for the others, and individuals normally sacrificed just one animal.

6.4.5 *The Distribution of the Sacrificial Portions*
The parts of the sacrifice are dealt with in different, ways depending upon the type of sacrifice, the nature of the victim and its purpose. They may be burnt on the altar, given to the priests to eat or retain, returned to the offerer to eat, or disposed of outside the camp (see the next table).[2]

The fatty parts[3] of the sacrifice are always burnt, and there is most

---

1. Wenham (1979b: 89).
2. References in the table are to Leviticus unless otherwise indicated.
3. The fullest listing of the parts to be burnt is found for the שלמים for which the tail of the sheep is additionally specified (Lev. 3.9).

variation in the destination of the flesh.[1] The entrails (קרב) and the legs (כרעים) were usually carried outside the camp, possibly since they were associated with the excreta (cf. Lev. 4.11).[2] Dung is incompatible with holiness (Deut. 23.13-15; 11QT 46.13-16), though it is not specifically classified as ritually unclean. For the *'ōlâ* the entrails and legs were burnt, but only after washing (Lev 1.9). Curiously, the crop of a bird had to be placed on the ash heap (Lev. 1.16), possibly because it had eaten from unclean or dead animals.[3] The destination of the cuts of meat (נחתים, Lev. 1.12, etc.) depended upon the type of sacrifice. The way in which the various parts are distributed provides a three-dimensional spatial model of social relationships.[4] This is most true of the *šǝlāmîm*, which provide the fullest image of Israelite society in an alimentary code (§6.2.5).[5]

	Burnt	Priests	People	Outside
'ōlâ	fat, etc., pieces, head, suet, entrails, legs 1.7-9, 12-13	skin 7.8	–	–
minḥâ	handful 2.2; 6.8	rest; 2.3; 6.9-11; 7.9-10	–	–
ḥaṭṭā't (major)	fat, etc. 4.8-10, 19	–	–	skin, flesh, head, legs, entrails, dung 4.11-12
ḥaṭṭā't (minor)	fat, etc. 4.26, 31, 35	flesh, skin?[6] 6.19, 22; Num. 18.9-10	–	(entrails, legs)

---

1. The flesh (בשר) could include the priestly portions (מנה, Lev. 7.33).
2. The translation 'hind legs' is consistent with this concern (cf. Snaith 1967: 31). However, KB (p. 475) suggests shin (Unterschenkel).
3. See the discussion in Rendtorff (1990a: 76-78).
4. Thornton (1982: 543-44) applies this perspective to the covenant rituals in Gen. 15.8-11, 17-18 and Jer. 34: 18-19.
5. In Mesopotamian religion, there were lists that apportioned the sacrificial remains in great detail. The order of the lists and the quality of the cuts mirrored the priestly hierarchy (Oppenheim 1977: 190; McEwan 1983).
6. The Mishnah (*m. Zeb.* 12.3) states that the skin of an animal that is offered by individuals belongs to the priest, though this may be a later systematization.

	Burnt	Priests	People	Outside
'*āšām*	fat, etc. 7.3-5	flesh, skin? 5.13; 7.6	–	(entrails, legs)
šelāmîm	fat, etc. 3.3-5, 9-11, 14-16; 7.30-31	breast and right thigh 7.32-34; Num. 18.18	flesh 7.11-21	(entrails, legs)

The distinction between major and minor blood ritual is significant here, too. If Lev. 6.26-30 [H 19-23] (cf. Lev. 10.16-18; Num. 18.9) is compared with Leviticus 4, it appears that the *ḥaṭṭā't* flesh could be eaten only if it the ritual took place outside the central sanctuary.

Reference	Spatial Dimension	Flesh	Where Eaten	Who Eats
Lev. 6.30 [H 23]	blood brought into the Tent of Meeting (i.e. major blood rite)	burnt	–	no one
Lev. 6.25-29 [H 18-22]	blood remains outside (i.e. minor blood rite)	most holy (v. 26; cf. v. 27)	in a holy place (v. 26)	priest (v. 26; male v. 29)

The similarity between the *ḥaṭṭā't*, the '*āšām* and the *minḥâ* (e.g. Lev. 7.7-10) implies that a similar pattern would be followed for these sacrifices. It is understandable that the priests do not benefit from the sacrifices occasioned by their own sins. But sacrifices offered by others belonged to God, and P considered that the flesh had been given to the priests as a contribution to their maintenance (Num. 18.9). The priestly portions were most holy (§6.4.3) and their holiness was com-municable (Lev. 6.18, 27 [11, 20]),[1] so only priests could eat them and they had to remain in a holy place in the court (6.16, 26 [H 9, 19]; 7.6). Further, any vessel used in connection with their cooking had to be broken (if earthenware) or scoured (if copper, 6.28 [H 21]).

The *šelāmîm*, on the other hand, could be eaten in the camp by any-one, provided he or she was clean (Lev. 7.11-21; Num. 18.19) and was in a clean place (Lev. 10.14).[2] The lay people were allowed to eat

---

1. Levine (1987: 246) translates כל אשר־יגע בהם יקדש here (and also in Exod. 29.37; 30.29) by 'Whoever would come in contact with them must be in a holy state', but this appears to be a forced interpretation of the verb.

2. Haran (1962: 39-45), Wright (1987: 235 n. 5).

all the flesh except the breast (חזה) and the right thigh (שׁוק הימין),[1] which could be eaten by the priestly family (Num. 18.11; see also Lev. 10.14; 22.12-13).[2] This could reflect the common grading where the right is superior to the left. The right hand is generally used for holy gestures (e.g. sprinkling by the priests Lev. 14.16, 27), and blood is applied to the right extremities (Lev. 8.23-24; 14.17, 25). The priests thus receive superior symbolic as well as culinary portions. The portions for the non-priests are simply holy (cf. תרומת הקדשׁים,[3] Lev. 22.12; Num. 18.19; קדשׁ יהוה, Lev. 19.8). Only priests are allowed to eat these meat classified as most holy (קדשׁ הקדשׁים, e.g. the atoning sacrifices §6.4.3).

6.5 *Conclusion*

The chapter has shown how grading can demonstrate the coherence of a great number of Priestly institutions and rituals, without loss of flexibility and specificity. A number of models for understanding sacrifice were briefly developed, and each was shown to incorporate various kinds of grading (§6.2). Purification is a particularly prominent model of sacrifice in P, and other purification rituals shed light on sacrificial purification (§6.3). They were of great importance in P because of the incompatibility of impurity and holiness, and great care was taken to ensure that major impurities were dealt with, particularly corpse impurity (§6.3.2) and skin disorder (§6.3.3). The rituals reinforce the association of impurity with death which has been found elsewhere (§§3.4.3, 5.4.2), and they make use of various symbols of life (cf. §4.6.1).

---

1. On the right thigh (Exod. 29.22; Lev. 7.32, 33; 8.25, 26; 9.21; Num. 18.18), see Milgrom (1983: 159-70). For the significance of the right–left polarity, see Needham (1973).

2. Num. 18.8-20 describes the gifts (מתנות) that are the due of the priests (18.1-10) and the priestly family (vv. 11-19). The first section describes the special sacrificial offerings that may be eaten only by the priests, and then other gifts, including the portions of the זבח שׁלמים (18.18). In Exod. 29.28 = Lev. 7.34, only the priest is mentioned with regard to the שׁלמים. This may be a development in Numbers towards greater liberality (Budd 1984: 202-203), but this is not necessary. The focus in Lev. 7 is on the cult rather than the wider social circle, and the text does not specify that the food be eaten in a holy place (contrast the instructions for the other sacrifices).

3. On the תרומה and its relation to the תנופה, see Milgrom (1983a: 159-70).

The final section of the chapter discussed in more detail the various kinds of grading which the sacrifices displayed. These could involve the spatial dimension (§6.4.3), the personal dimension (§6.4.2), and a graded choice of animals and other materials for sacrifice (§6.4.4). Although subsequent to the sacrifice proper, the distribution of the sacrificial portions (§6.4.5) also points to the different gradings in the personal dimension, particularly between the priests, the priestly family, and the rest of the Israelites.

Chapter 7

THE DIMENSION OF TIME

7.1 *The Holiness Spectrum and Time*

7.1.1 *Introduction*

In the Priestly conception time, as well as space and society, was structured and graded.[1] Natural rhythms, such as the day, the lunar month and the agricultural year determined many of the rituals of the cult (§7.1.2).[2] In Israel, as in other nations, important points in these cycles (e.g. harvest and new moon) marked the passage of significant units of time, and were celebrated by popular festivals (§7.2).

In addition to this general calendrical system, a second type of time reckoning existed in Israel which has not been found in the same form elsewhere in the ancient world. It comprised the regular seven-day cycle of the week, culminating in the Sabbath or the seventh day (§7.3.2). This was independent of any natural cycle, and the sabbatical principle affected the way in which the festivals were celebrated to a remarkable degree (§7.3.1).

The sacrificial system of the Priestly public cult provides an important criterion for grading and distinguishing the various appointed times (§7.2.1). In Chapter 6, various aspects of sacrifice were discussed in a general manner, but the introduction of the dimension of time into the discussion allows further insight into the influence of the Holiness Spectrum and the principle of grading in the Priestly cult.

The year is the basic unit for the longer passage of time, and the cultic calendar is organized on that basis. But Priestly texts occasion-

---

1. Time may be classified in various ways. For example, Navone (1971) analyses time as circular (agricultural, cultic), horizontal (annalic, synchronic), and vertical (salvation history).

2. Natural cycles are reviewed by Lamberty (1986), who takes up many of the insights of Knierim (1981).

ally refer to significant periodic events longer than the year. As with shorter measures of time, these could be determined by natural features, such as the life cycle (e.g. birth and death), or by the sabbatical principle (every 7 or 49 years, §7.3.2).[1]

7.1.2 *The Calendar*

The most important units of regularly repeated time in P were the day, the week and the lunar month.[2] The first part of the sacrificial calendar in Numbers 28–29 describes the sacrifices offered at the turning points of these cycles (28.4-8 dawn and twilight, 28.9-10 the Sabbath, 28.11-15 the New Moon). The performance of sacrifices did not necessarily indicate a holy day, and of these only the Sabbath is called holy in an unqualified sense (see §7.3).

Each day two lambs were offered as an 'ōlâ (Exod. 29.39-42; Num. 28.3-8), one in the morning (בבקר) and one at twilight (בין הערבים, Exod. 29.38).[3] The sacrifices offered on special occasions were additional to these regular (tāmîd, תמיד) offerings (על עלת התמיד, Num. 28.10, etc.). But the daily sacrifices were only part of a set of rituals that took place in the sanctuary and that comprised an important priestly responsibility. These took place in the holy place (הקדש, Exod. 28.29, 35) and thus before Yahweh (לפני יהוה, Exod. 28.29, 35; 38; 29.42; 30.8).[4]

---

1. The law stated that one who had committed an accidental homicide could return home after the death of the high priest (Num. 35.25, 28, 32). Relating the pollution (חנף hiph., v. 33; טמא piel v. 34), ransom (כפר v. 32) and atonement (כפר pual, v. 33) references in this passage to the rest of the priestly system is difficult. Although this may indicate that the death of the high priest was atoning (Greenberg 1959), the sacral conception has been modified (McKeating 1975). The ethical context indicates that the pollution refers to Israel's danger beliefs (Frymer-Kensky 1983: 404, 407), rather than having any specifically cultic implications. Dillmann (1886: 219-20) considers the law to be a simple limitation of a blood feud. Janowski (1982: 160) stresses the legal framework for the ideas behind כפר.

2. On the calendar see Segal (1957), Goudoever (1959), De Vries (1961) and de Vaux (1961: 178-94). The history of the calendar is complex and uncertain, and fortunately, largely peripheral to the present study.

3. The popular and practical reckoning of the day was from dawn to dusk, but for precise religious and calendrical purposes, the day began in the evening (Lev. 23.27, 32; Finegan 1964: 8-9; Baumgarten 1958: 360; Stroes 1966; Beckwith 1971). Smaller divisions (e.g. hours and watches) appear to have been of negligible cultic importance in P.

4. The following table is based on Haran (1978: 205-21). The number of senses engaged stresses the range of cultic expression (cf. §§4.5, 6.2).

Ritual	Frequency	Description (tāmîd)	Sense	References
Regular sacrifices (Aaron)	twice daily	עלת תמיד (מנחה תמיד+ Lev. 6.13) (cf. Lev. 6.6; אש תמיד)	smell[1]	Exod. 29.42 Num. 28.3
Offering incense (Aaron)		קטרת התמיד	smell	Exod. 30.8
Tending lamps (Aaron and sons)	twice daily	נר תמיד (תמיד ;Lev. 24.3, 4)	sight	Exod. 27.20 Lev. 24.2
Carrying 12 names into sanctuary (Aaron)	twice daily	לזכרן לפני יהוה תמיד (תמיד ;Exod. 28.30)	memory	Exod. 28.29
Jingling bells (Aaron)	twice daily	(תמיד missing)	hearing	Exod. 28.35
Carrying diadem (Aaron)	twice daily	והיה על־מצחו תמיד רצון להם לפני יהוה	grace?	Exod. 28.38
Setting out bread	once a week	לחם פנים לפני תמיד יערכנו לפני יהוה תמיד לחם התמיד	taste	Exod. 25.30 Lev. 24.8 Num. 4.7

These were events that concerned only the sanctuary and had no special association with the holy times which all Israel was required to honour.

The significance of the Sabbath, marking the week, is primarily independent of the cult, but is acknowledged in two ways. On the Sabbath the number of sacrifices for a day is doubled by the offering of an additional two lambs as an 'ōlâ (Num. 28.9-10). The Sabbath was also the occasion for the replacement of the loaves of bread placed on the table in the sanctuary (Lev. 24.8). The description of this bread as *leḥem hattāmîd* (Num. 4.7; Exod. 25.30) perhaps allows the sense of taste to be added to the list above. It is uncertain how the weekly cycle was connected with the calendrical system and its festival calendar.[2]

There is good evidence that the Priestly calendar was based on the lunar month.[3] From texts outside P (e.g. Isa. 1.13; Hos. 2.13) it is

1. Cf. the pleasing odour (לריח ניחח, Exod. 29.41; Num. 28.6, 8)

2. There are various interpretations of the phrase 'the day after the Sabbath' (ממחרת השבת, Lev. 23.15-16) occurring in relation to the Feast of Unleavened Bread. The 'Sabbath' here could refer to the weekly cycle or a day of rest, and it can be related more or less strictly to the festival week; see Haran (1976) for a discussion.

3. Kutsch (1961). Some have thought that the later Jubilees calendar was also the Priestly one (Jaubert 1957; followed by Wenham 1979b: 302). In this calendar

known that the beginning of the month at the new moon was marked by extensive celebrations.[1] Although they were acknowledged in the cult by a full complement of additional sacrifices (Appendix 4), there were no special rituals, with the exception of the seventh month (§7.2.2). It is likely that they were primarily popular festivals rather than priestly cultic ones.

In P, the months are usually identified by number counting from the beginning of the year in the spring (as in Lev. 23; Num. 28–29).[2] The large-scale structure of the biblical calendars was based on the solar year, since the celebration of many of the festivals was linked to seasonal factors.[3] In P, there are few hints that the lunar and solar calendars did not coincide. The lunar year of twelve months (354 days) is shorter than the solar year (365 days), so that the two systems had to be aligned at frequent intervals, if the months and the seasons were to correspond.[4] It is likely that there was a system of intercalation, as in the later Jewish luni-solar calendar.[5] By inserting an extra month

the year always begins on the same day. Jaubert and others think this is Wednesday, but Hoenig (1979) argues for Thursday (counting could begin once the sun was created on the fourth day, Gen. 1.14). In Hoenig's reckoning, the Day of Atonement takes place on a Saturday, agreeing with its description as a שבת שבתון (Lev. 16.31; 23.32). However, Trumpets is described similarly, and it would begin on a Thursday.

1. Snaith (1947: 85-103) argues unconvincingly that the months were counted originally from the full moon, which is considered to be the beginning of Unleavened Bread and Booths. However, the fifteenth of the month has no connection with the full moon (McKay 1972).

2. The usual critical view is that the pre-exilic year began in the autumn, in Tishri. This became the seventh month when the Babylonian calendar was adopted in the exile (e.g. Snaith 1947; de Vaux 1961: 190-93). However, this is uncertain (e.g. Clines 1974; Hoenig 1979: 197 n. 53), and the Priestly texts will be interpreted on their own terms.

3. In other sources, the main festivals are closely linked to the seasons of the year, as is indicated by their alternative names (see Appendix 5). Hoenig (1979: 197 n. 53) sets out the possible biblical allusions to a solar calendar.

4. For discussions see De Vries (1961: 486-87), Wacholder and Weisberg (1971), Segal (1957), Talmon (1958).

5. There are references in P both to the lunar calendar (the first day of the month Num. 29.11-15) and to the seasons controlled by the movement of the sun. Both sun and moon are referred to as determining appointed times (מועדים) in Gen. 1.14.

every two or three years, the lunar and solar calendars could be kept in step.[1]

The beginning of the year takes on a special historical and theological significance, according to the Priestly tradition in Exodus 12. The exodus was such a crucial event for Israel that the month in which the Passover took place was to be the first month of the year (Exod. 12.2). A link between the cultic calendar and the Priestly narrative is thereby made.

7.2 The Festivals

7.2.1 The Appointed Times

The Priestly conception of Israel's regular cultic celebrations is found primarily in two texts, a festal calendar (Lev. 23), and a sacrificial calendar (Num. 28–29).[2] The former is directed to lay Israelites, and records details of their responsibilities in the cult.[3] Numbers 28–29, on the other hand, provides the priests with details about sacrifices, and omits popular rituals such as the waving of the sheaf. The two texts therefore complement one another and may be read together.

Several terms are used to describe the festivals in the two calendars. The most general term is *mô'ēd* (cf. מועדי יהוה, Lev. 23.2, 4; במועדו, Num. 28.2).[4] The 'appointed time'[5] is probably a wider category than

---

1. The later Jewish calendar inserted an extra thirteenth month before the first month in years 3, 6, 8, 11, 14, 17, 19 of a 19 year cycle. Some of the dates of the festivals have been explained by postulating problems of intercalation, but none of these is certain (cf. §7.4.2).

2. The form and genre are discussed by Morgan (1974). The former is usually regarded as a Priestly reworking of a briefer list of festivals in the Holiness Code (e.g. Porter 1976: 179), and the latter as a late composition from the Priestly circle (e.g. Budd 1984: 312-15), but both reflect Priestly concerns. Some of their features are compared in Appendix 3.

3. The New Moon festivals are absent from Lev. 23, probably because there was no special lay involvement in its cultic celebration (Milgrom 1971c: 81).

4. The present text implies that these include the Sabbath (Lev. 23.2-3), but the festivals and the Sabbath were celebrated in different senses, and the repeated introduction in v. 4 implies that v. 3 was an addition intended to raise the dignity of the Sabbath in a general sense (Elliger 1966: 312).

5. Morgan (1974: 182 n. 44). Koch (1984: 750) translates מועד as 'festgelegte Zeitpunkt'. Most Israelites would come into contact with the sanctuary and the sacrifices only at the festivals.

the term *miqrā qōdeš* ('holy proclamation') with which it is closely associated.[1] Lev. 23.4 may be translated (NRSV) 'these are the appointed festivals of the LORD (מועדי יהוה), the holy convocations (מקראי קדש), which you shall celebrate at the time apointed for them (אשר תקראו אתם)'. The use of *qōdeš* implies that the festivals were holy occasions, but the concept of holy time is not simple or homogeneous. The holy proclamations are distinguished from the middle days of the seven-day festivals, which are not described in this way. The lesser sanctity of the latter is implied by the fact that work was allowed during them, as on ordinary days.[2] However, they are still appointed times (מועדים) and can be subject to ritual injunctions, such as the prohibition of eating leavened bread during the festival of Unleavened Bread.

All the one-day festivals, the first and seventh days of Unleavened Bread, and the first and eighth days of Booths are called holy proclamations (Lev. 23.2, 4, 37). On these days it was forbidden to work, a law shared with the Sabbath. This law served to heighten the distinction between a day devoted to God, and ordinary days which could be used to satisfy the needs of men. The comparison to the Sabbath is reinforced by the way the festivals are repeatedly called times of 'complete rest' (see Appendix 3) and by the prevalence of the number seven (§7.3.1). The holiness of the Sabbath and the holiness of the festivals is closely linked by these means, though they remain distinct.

The major popular festivals were the three pilgrimage festivals (*hag*, חג),[3] *maṣṣôt* or Unleavened Bread (חג המצות, Exod. 23.15; 34.18; Lev. 23.6), *šābŭôt* or Weeks (חג השבעות, Exod. 23.16; 34.18;

---

1. קרא normally means call, but מקרא could refer to the *day* called out ('sacred occasion', NJPSV), the *people* called together ('holy convocation', NRSV, RSV, RV) or the *event* of calling out ('holy proclamation'; Haran 1978: 291, 298; cf. Hoffmann 1906: 136-37; Noordtzij 1982: 228). Kutsch has argued persuasively that מקרא קדש probably means 'heiliger Festtag' (1953: 250), but the close association with קרא (Lev. 23.2, 24; Num. 10.2) may reflect the problem of determining the date of a festival, since it was difficult to keep track of longer periods of time in a traditional society. Timekeeping and the organization of the calendar were aspects of priestly expertise, and priests would be in charge of determining significant times.

2. In the Mishnah, a normal day (יום חול) is distinguished linguistically from a festival day (יום טוב), and from the mid-festival days (a minor feast, מועד קטן, or a non-sacred day חול המועד). See Danby (1933: 181 n. 11, 207 n. 19).

3. Haran (1978: 289-303), Kedar-Kopfstein (1977c: 730-44).

Deut. 16.16; cf. Lev. 23.15-16), and *sŭkkôt* or Booths (חג הסכות,
Exod. 34.22; Lev. 23.39). On these three occasions, every male Israelite
was obliged to visit the sanctuary and take part in the celebrations
there (Exod. 23.17; 34.23; Deut. 16.16). The other festivals in the
year were general ones, not requiring a journey or extending beyond
one day. Despite its status as a *ḥag*, Weeks appears to be the least
important festival, a purely agricultural occasion lasting only one day,
largely unrelated to the major festival seasons or to significant historical events in Israel's history and with a standard number of sacrifices
(see Appendix 4).

The holiness of the *miqrā' qōdeš* can be linked to an increased
activity around the sanctuary on such a occasion.[1] Most of the additional sacrifices were burnt offerings, the sacrifice particularly associated with God (§6.2.1) and thus an appropriate offering for a holy day.
Even when the occasion was not a pilgrimage feast, there were a
significant number of public sacrifices. Since no work was allowed,
many could come from the immediate surroundings to take part in the
celebrations. The *ḥaṭṭā't* sacrifice probably guaranteed that a degree of
purity appropriate for the holiness of the day was attained at the
sanctuary (cf. §§6.2.2, 7.4.1). It is likely that special care was taken to
attain a high degree of purity on these occasions, both by priests and
non-priests. Those who wished to eat meat would certainly have to
ensure that they were clean. Only at the sanctuary could animals be
slaughtered for food (Lev. 17), and a festival would be an ideal occasion for offering and eating *šĕlāmîm*. A state of purity was necessary
to eat from these sacrifices (§6.2.4), but clearly, purity could not a
universal or essential requirement otherwise.

7.2.2 *The Sacrificial Code*

The varying number of public sacrifices offered on different days
constituted a sacrificial code which unified the festival system, as well
as grading the festal days in importance. The official sacrifices
consisted of various *'ōlôt* and a *ḥaṭṭā't*, since the *šĕlāmîm* and the
'āšām were usually responses to the particular desires or needs of
individuals and families.[2] Special rituals further distinguished days

---

1. The festivals were also the occasion for handing over the compulsory
offerings (first-fruits, tithes).
2. At the Festival of Weeks, two lambs a year old were offered as זבחי שלמים
(Lev. 23.19; Num. 29.1).

such as Passover and the Day of Atonement (§7.4).

The animal most frequently sacrificed is the lamb. Because of the relatively small cost (compared to a bull or ram), it was possible to vary the number of sacrifices over a wide range. Only lambs were sacrificed in the most frequently repeated rituals (the daily offerings and those for the Sabbath). The prominence of the two extended pilgrimage feasts is acknowledged by the large number of sacrifices offered. Usually seven lambs were sacrificed at a feast, but fourteen were offered at Booths. The number of rams was also doubled, to express its importance. The single goat offered as a *ḥaṭṭā't* at each festival is a striking contrast to this, and suggests that it represents a cultic principle which is independent of the agricultural year. Since no specific impurity is mentioned, it is also possible that the purpose of this sacrifice was positive or precautionary, serving to heighten the purity of the sanctuary on that day. However, impurity could characterize any season, and a purification sacrifice would remove any unforeseen threat from this source to the holiness of the sanctuary on a festival day.

Both seven-day festivals occurred at strategic points in the year, forming the centre of two series of festivals, one in the spring (the first month) and the other in the autumn (the seventh month). The intensity of the celebrations at the sanctuary can be linked to the date of the festivals and their place in the agricultural year. Unleavened Bread occurred at the start of the barley harvest, and Booths after the fruit harvest had been gathered in (cf. Deut. 16.13). There was therefore sufficient leisure and provision for the appointed sacrifices and the accompanying celebrations.

In P, the two great pilgrimage feasts have taken on a memorial character, even though they may originally have been agricultural festivals.[1] Unleavened Bread is inseparable from Passover, and both of their names were derived from the Exodus events (Exod. 12, P). Their importance is seen not only in the way that the Passover determined the beginning of the year (Exod. 12.2), but also in the unusual

---

1. In later times, Weeks became a remembrance of the giving of the Law (Bloch 1978: 185-89). Some have detected this theme in P's dating of the arrival at Sinai to the third month (Exod. 19.1; Hyatt 1971: 200). However, the connection is not explicit, and it is more probable that it inspired the later historicization of the festival.

measures taken to ensure that someone who was impure or far away could celebrate it a month later (Num. 9.1-14). Further, the celebration of this festival concluded the Sinai revelation (Num. 9.1-14 with 10.11).[1]

Similarly, Booths refers to the time when Israel had to live in temporary shelters during their wilderness wanderings. While the festival was in progress, the people had to build booths and live in them (Lev. 23.43). Besides the names, the two extended festivals are linked by beginning on the same day of the month (the 15th).[2] The travel necessary for a pilgrimage feast no doubt reinforced the journey theme which is prominent in the Exodus narratives.

The two major festivals split the year into two, and the third pilgrimage festival, Weeks, can be regarded as concluding the spring series of festivals.[3] It is closely related to the the offering of the first sheaf (עמר התנופה, Lev. 23.15). It occurs a symbolic seven weeks after this minor ceremony, and the two loaves presented are first fruits (לחם הבכורים, v. 20; cf. ראשית קצירכם, v. 11) and are offered in the same way as the sheaf (לחם תנופה, v. 17, cf. v. 20). The injunction that these two loaves must be baked with yeast (v. 17) suggests a deliberate structural contrast to the unleavened bread which must be eaten at the festival of Unleavened Bread.[4] Coming at the end of the harvest, it suitably frames the opening season of the year.

The first day of the seventh month is singled out for mention (Lev. 23.23-25; Num. 29.1-6). It has an additional set of sacrifices, it is a holy proclamation and it is a *yôm t ᵉrû'â*, a day for blowing the trumpets (v. 1; cf. Lev. 23.24).[5] It appropriately introduces the month

---

1.   Fishbane (1975: 17-18) also links this with the completion of the Tabernacle.

2.   The theory that these were closely related to the full moon can no longer be held in a strict sense (McKay 1972). However, there were no doubt practical advantages to having an extended festival at around this time of the month during full moon. The alignment of the two series of festivals is even closer if the choice of the Passover lamb on the tenth of the month is significant (Exod. 12.3), though later tradition interpreted this as limited to the Exodus event (*m. Pes.* 9.5). It is interesting to note that the eight-day structure of the first festival (1 day Passover, 7 days Unleavened Bread) is reversed in the last (7 days Booths, 1 day closing feast).

3.   De Vaux (1961: 494), Bloch (1978: 179-82).

4.   The structural contrast is emphasized by the absence of leaven in other ritual preparations (de Vaux 1961: 493).

5.   Following Milgrom (1990b: 246, 372-73), who argues that תרועה indicates

with the most important festivals, both popular (Booths) and priestly (the Day of Atonement). During the festival of Booths, the number of animals sacrificed is almost twice as many as at any other festival, indicating that it was the climax of the liturgical year.[1]

There were a few sacrifices which stood outside the normal system.[2] The Passover lamb was not a public sacrifice, since the ritual focuses on the home, where each family was required to eat it.[3] It is therefore understandable that there is no detailed legislation for it in the calendars.[4] Leviticus 23 states that an additional *'ōlâ* lamb is to be offered at the waving of the sheaf, but again this is not a public sacrifice and is omitted from Numbers 28–29. The sacrifice is also exceptional in that twice the normal *minḥâ* associated with an *'ōlâ* is offered (i.e. 2/10 ephah, Lev. 23.13). This anomaly may be due to its dating at the beginning of the barley harvest.[5]

Another unusual feature is the way that the number of bulls offered as *'ōlâ* sacrifices gradually decreases from thirteen to seven during the seven days of Booths, while the number of rams and lambs remains constant. The reason for the decrease is obscure, although it may refer to a gradual decrease of joy at the end of the year.[6] The last day of

long blasts on animal horns by non-priests, thus distinguishing it further from ordinary new moons, when metal trumpets are played with short blasts by priests (cf. *m. Roš. Haš.* 3.3-4; 4.9). Gray (1903: 411) comments, 'the seventh new moon stands to ordinary new moons much as the seventh day to ordinary days.'

1. Despite the significance of the Day of Atonement (§7.4), Booths was not a subordinate feast (Kurtz 1863: 336), but the major popular festival, often called simply 'the festival', החג (de Vaux 1961: 495 quotes Josephus, who describes the feast as ἁγιωτάτης καὶ μεγίστης [*Ant.* 8.100]).

2. For the additional goat on the Day of Atonement (Num. 29.11), see §7.4.

3. The Priestly theology requires that it be sacrificed at the sanctuary (Haran 1978: 342-43). According to later Jewish tradition, all are priests at Passover because they officiate at the sacrifice (Philo, *Vit. Mos.* 2.224 τὸ ἔθνος ἱερᾶτει; quoted by Gray 1925: 179 n. 1).

4. Lev. 23.5 and Num. 28.16 probably have a passing reference to the sacrifice (if פסח ליהוה is translated 'a passover sacrifice to the LORD' [NJPSV]; Hoffmann 1906: 142-43). Most modern translations consider that it refers to the day of the Passover festival.

5. Wenham (1979b: 303).

6. Dillmann (1886: 297), Budd (1984: 318). Ehrlich (1969: 297) suggests that people cannot rejoice at the same level, but the explanation should also apply to the other extended feast, Unleavened Bread.

Booths is called an *'aseret* (עצרת, Lev. 23.36; Num. 29.35),[1] and the number of sacrifices on this day is different from other days in Booths. It may have been reckoned as a seventh festival in the calendar of Numbers 28–29.[2]

7.3 *The Sabbath*

7.3.1 *The Sabbatical Principle*

The festivals and other rituals are marked by the repeated appearance of the number seven. When the number itself does not occur, it is implied by the Sabbath root (שבת), or by a sevenfold pattern or literary structure. Its recurrence in a wide variety of different contexts helps to unify the Priestly system of rituals and festivals, as is illustrated by the following list.[3]

Day

 a. The 7th day (היום השביעי, Gen. 2.2-3; Exod. 31.15, 17; Lev. 23.3) was a special day of rest. Also known as the Sabbath (שבת, Exod. 31.16; Lev. 24.8).

 b. The 7th day was marked by additional sacrifices (Num. 28.9-10).

 c. 7 days were marked by compulsory cessation from work (Lev. 23.7, 8, 21, 25, 28-31, 35, 36; see Appendix 3).

 d. The two most important festivals were 7 days long (Unleavened Bread Lev. 23.6-8; Booths v. 36).

 e. The 7th day of the festival of Unleavened Bread was a special festival day (Lev. 23.8; cf. Deut. 16.8, where it is called an עצרת).

 f. The 6×2 (= 12) loaves on the Table were replaced every Sabbath (Lev. 24.8).

Month

 a. The 7th month had the greatest number of festivals, as well as the most important ones (Appendix 5; §§7.2, 7.4).

 1. Kutsch (1952: 65-67) argues that עצרת has a basic meaning of 'Zurück-haltung vom Arbeit', and in this context indicates a festal day rather than an assembly.

 2. Wenham (1979b: 301). In Deut. 16.8 it describes the seventh day of Unleavened Bread. Ehrlich (1959: 297), on the other hand, considered it to be distinct from Booths. In accord with the length of other extended festivals (§7.3), we would expect a seven day festival, and the number of sacrifices is quite different on the eighth day. In Lev. 23 it could well have been reckoned with Booths in order to retain the sevenfold pattern.

 3. Keil (1887: 469-82). Sometimes it is uncertain whether an implicit seven is accidental or intended. However, there is little doubt that 'the calendar was progressively adjusted to the sabbatical conception' (Hallo 1977: 10-11).

b. The first day of the 7th month was the only New Moon festival with a special ritual (Lev. 23.23-25) and additional sacrifices (Num. 29.1-6).[1]

Year

a. There were 7 major festivals in the year (Lev. 23; Num. 28–29).[2]

b. 7 weeks (beginning the day after the Sabbath) separated the waving of the sheaf from the festival of Weeks (Lev. 23.15-16).

c. 7 lambs were frequently sacrificed at a festival.

d. At Booths 14 (twice 7) bulls were sacrificed, diminishing to 7 on the seventh day (Num. 29.12-34), and the total number of bulls sacrificed over the 7 days was 70.

Longer Periods

The 7th year had a special festival character (Lev. 25.2-7; cf. Exod. 21.2-6; Deut. 15.1-18).

The 49th year (7×7; '7 sabbaths of years' Lev. 25.8) had a special name (the Jubilee), was an important social and cultic event, and began in the 7th month (Lev. 25.8-55).

Occasional and Other Rituals

a. The time for testing whether a person, a garment or a house was diseased was 7 days (Lev. 13.5, etc.; 14.38).

b. A person healed from skin disease was sprinkled 7 times with blood (Lev. 14.7; also for a house v. 51), waited 7 days (v. 8), and was then sprinkled 7 times with oil (vv. 16, 27).

c. Purification from a major impurity took 7 days (§§5.4.2, 6.3, Appendix 2).

d. There was a 7 day wait before circumcision on the 8th day (Lev. 12.2).

e. The ordination of the priests took 7 days (Exod. 29.35, 37 = Lev. 8.33-35).

f. The rite for the major bood ritual (§6.4.3) included a 7 fold sprinkling of blood before the veil (Lev. 4.6, 17).

g. The altar was consecrated by sprinkling it 7 times with the anointing oil (Lev. 8.11).

The seventh day of the week, the Sabbath,[3] had a special importance,

1. From texts outside P (cf. §7.1.2), it is clear that the other new moons were also celebrated, but the one for the seventh month had a special character, being proclaimed by trumpet blasts (Lev. 23.24). Keil (1887: 470) compares the rest from work on the seventh month to the rest on the seventh day. It is probable that work was forbidden on any new moon (1 Sam. 20.5; 2 Kgs 4.23; Isa. 1.13; Hos. 2.13; Amos 8.5).

2. See Appendix 3. This assumes that the waving of the sheaf is counted as a separate festival in Lev. 23, but in Num. 28–29 this ceremony is not mentioned, and the eighth day of Booths might be counted as a separate festival (§7.2.2).

3. The semantic link between seven (שבע) and Sabbath (שבת) is much clearer

and was the holy day *par excellence*. In Israel the regular repetition of the seven day cycle of the week,[1] independent of any natural periodic cycle, was a central feature of its perception of time.[2] It headed the list of appointed times in Leviticus 23 (v. 3), and was the only law concerning the dimension of time in the decalogue (Exod. 20.8-11).[3] In the Priestly tradition, the motive for keeping the Sabbath is traced back to the rest of God at the conclusion of creation (Exod. 20.11; 31.17; Gen. 2.1-3). It thus stands outside the ordering of time based on the sun and moon (Gen. 1.14).

Although a regular seven day cycle was specific to Israel,[4] the seven day period for a festival or other ritual was common in the Semitic world. It is attractive to suggest that seven has become the symbol of holiness in the dimension of time (cf. §4.3.2). The special significance of the Sabbath as a holy seventh day in Israel reinforces this association, and the number seven unifies the occasional rituals and the regular ones. It is appropriate that the liturgical calendar in Leviticus 23 is headed by the Sabbath, which is described in the same way as the other festivals as a holy proclamation (מקרא קדש, Lev. 23.3).[5] The major festival days are also called *šabbatôn* (שבתון), probably a derived form of 'Sabbath', which is further strengthened by the double appearance of the root in the phrase *šabbat šabbatôn* (שבת שבתון).[6]

The Sabbath was perceived to be a crucial feature of God's special

---

than any etymological link (North 1955). Scholars disagree how early (Jenni 1956: 11) or late (postexilic, Lemaire 1973) the Sabbath was kept.

1. The name of Weeks (שבעות) derives from the number of days it occurs after the waving of the sheaf. The interval, known as 'seven full Sabbaths' (שבע שבתות תמימה, Lev. 23.15), is also defined in Lev. 23.16 as 'the day after the seventh sabbath, fifty days' (NRSV).

2. 'The sabbatical cycle is indifferent to the harmony of the universe. It represents a neutral structuring of empty time' (Tsevat 1972: 457). However, the tracing of the Sabbath to creation is important for P (Gen. 2.1-3; Exod. 31.17), and a sharp nature/culture distinction cannot be maintained. Israel knows by revelation that keeping the Sabbath is a fundamental aspect of the world as God created it.

3. Although the decalogue is not Priestly, the motive reflects a Priestly theology (Jenni 1956: 19-20).

4. Hallo (1977).

5. This is likely to be deliberate, since nowhere else is the Sabbath called this, and in Num. 28.28 the term is reserved for the annual festivals.

6. Briend (1984: 1159-60).

covenant with Israel, and the sabbatarian pattern is integrated into the Priestly understanding of the calendar and society to a remarkable degree. The importance of the Sabbath is such that it is possible to speak of a 'sabbatical principle'.

7.3.2 *The Sabbath*

The Sabbath[1] does not have the significance in the cult that might be expected for a holy day.[2] While the additional sacrifices acknowledge the Sabbath's distinctiveness, they are relatively small (two lambs as an *'ōlâ*) compared to those on the New Moon (a bull, a ram, and seven lambs), which was also marked by a refrain from work.[3] Yet the Sabbath is frequently called holy (קדש, Exod. 16.23; 31.14, 15; 35.2) and was to be sanctified (*piel* of קדש; by God: Gen. 2.3; Exod. 20.11; 31.13; Lev. 23.2; by Israel: Exod. 20.8 = Deut. 5.12; cf. Lev. 25.10 of the Jubilee), whereas the New Moon is not.[4] In the other Sabbath ritual recorded, the replacement of the loaves of bread in the sanctuary every week (Lev. 24.8; cf. §7.1.2), the Sabbath is primarily a time marker.

This suggests that the holiness is of a general kind, not dependent on specific cultic actions or personnel (cf. §2.2.3). The redactional insertion of the Sabbath commandment in Exod. 31.12-17 stresses that the observance of the Sabbath takes precedence even over building the Tabernacle. In accord with this, it is traced back to creation, when God sanctified the seventh day (Gen. 2.3).

It was also, like the Passover, an institution rooted in the events before Sinai (Exod. 16).[5] Both were celebrated by Israel in their

1. For recent surveys see Andreasen (1972, 1974, 1978), Bacchiocchi (1980), Dressler (1982), Briend (1984).

2. Schmidt (1983: 90-91). Only in Lev. 23.3 is the Sabbath called a מקרא קדש, but this section (vv . 2b-3) may be a later systematization (Elliger 1966: 310-11), and should not be stressed.

3. Greenberg (1971: 558). In Amos 8.5, Isa. 1.13 and Hos. 2.13, the New Moon and Sabbath are juxtaposed, probably because they were the two most frequent festival days. In Num. 28.3-15 the sacrifices for the day, Sabbath and New Moon are described in accordance with their frequency of occurrence (Morgan 1974: 205-206). The remaining sections are organized according to the passage of the year.

4. If the New Moon was holy, then a note to this effect would be expected in the systematic record of the Priestly calendars.

5. Bacchiocchi (1980: 61-66, 80-83).

homes, and were essential aspects of being the people of God. The Sabbath was hence appropriately called the sign of the (Sinaitic) covenant.[1] Any desecration (*piel* of חלל) of its holiness resulted in the death penalty (Exod. 31.14; cf. Num. 15.32-36; cf. Ezek. 20.16, 24). The Sabbath could be kept at home, even by those who were cultically unclean. Although little information is given about how the Sabbath was to be observed positively, its most important feature was that no work is to be carried out during it, a secular rather than a cultic criterion.[2]

The general and non-cultic character of holy time arises perhaps because time cannot be easily aligned with a grade in the spatial or personal dimension. Every Israelite and every place experienced the same passing of time, and a holy occasion would be holy for all, not just the priests and the sanctuary. If holiness is a mark of the presence of God, then the general character of the Sabbath indicates that God dwells in the midst of his people on this day to a special degree. The command not to work stressed that Yahweh and not the earth or Israel's efforts is the source of blessing and joy.[3]

These themes recur in the laws for the sabbatical year (Lev. 25.1-7) and the Jubilee (Lev. 25.8-55; 27.16-25; Num. 36.4). No work was to be performed, and the enjoyment of the Sabbath by the people of God without distinction was mirrored in the proclamation of freedom to Hebrew debtors and slaves in the Sabbath year.[4] At the Jubilee the

1. Some consider this to be the climax of the sequence of covenants found in P. Wellhausen (1885: 338-40) recognized four covenants (ברית) with their signs (אות): (1) Adam and the Sabbath (cf. Gen. 1.26-31; Exod. 31.13), (2) Noah and the rainbow (Gen. 9.9, 12, 17), (3) Abraham and circumcision (Gen. 17.2, 11), (4) Israel (the Mosaic covenant) and the Sabbath (Exod. 31.16, 13, 17). The covenant with the priests (Num. 25.12) is of secondary importance, and does not affect the Sinai covenant. See Fox (1974).

2. The manna cannot be gathered (Exod. 16.5), houses cannot be built (Exod. 31.12-17; 35.2), a fire cannot be lit (Num. 15.32-36), the crop cannot be harvested (Exod. 34.21—outside P), and any agricultural work is disallowed in a sabbatical year or Jubilee (Lev. 25). Clearly, offering sacrifices and performing other cultic actions on the Sabbath did not count as work.

3. Bacciocchi (1980: 84-91); Westermann (1984: 172) comments, 'God's blessing bestows on this special, holy, solemn day a power which makes it fruitful for human existence'.

4. Cf. Deut. 15.1-11. In Lev. 25.10, this is the law of the Jubilee year, but the laws for the sabbatical and Jubilee years were probably combined (de Vaux 1961: 175).

land returned to the original owner and no work was performed for an additional period.[1] The demands of these years developed the economic implications already present in the command not to work on the Sabbath.[2] The leveling of economic and hierarchical inequalities stressed the unity of Israel and the absolute sovereignty of Yahweh over all.

7.4 *The Day of Atonement*

7.4.1 *Introduction*

In comparison to the other festivals and the standard sacrificial rituals, the Day of Atonement exhibits a number of unique features. This has given rise to a great deal of discussion and numerous conflicting interpretations. The most evident problem is how to relate the unique scapegoat ritual to the blood sacrifices which are similar to those known from elsewhere in P (§6.2).[3]

It is evident that the text of Leviticus 16, the main source of our knowledge of the ritual, reflects a complex history. The scapegoat ritual has frequently been isolated from the rest of the ritual and given a separate interpretation.[4] However, the concern in this study is with the final text and the possibility of a unitary interpretation should be taken seriously. Some of the difficulties in the text may have arisen because of its historical evolution, but it will be argued that many of

1. There is extensive debate about the character of the 49 extra days (Hoenig 1968), and whether the Jubilee was ever practised, but this is only one aspect to its theological significance (North 1954; Gnuse 1985).

2. Epsztein (1986: 132).

3. Although there is one other elimination ritual in P (Lev. 14.4-7), it is only superficially similar, and does not have the scapegoat's central significance.

4. De Vaux (1961: 507-10), Aartun (1980: 85). The scapegoat ritual is often considered to represent primitive thought (e.g. Hooke 1952: 9, Auerbach 1958b: 343), or foreign influence, since scapegoat rituals are widespread (e.g. Hittite [Gurney 1976: 47-52; Wright 1987: 45-72], ancient Greece [Parker 1983: 258-64], Ugarit [Aartun 1976]). Whatever the correctness of these explanations, they leave open the possibility that the ritual also has a role in the Priestly system of purifications, sacrifices and festivals. Further, the Priestly ritual exhibits contrasts as well as comparisons vis-à-vis other scapegoat rituals (Weinfeld 1983: 112-13). The basic ideas of transfer and elimination are simple and general enough but take on varying significance depending on the cultural framework.

the details make sense in the light of the Holiness Spectrum. The two parts complement one another, and the unique aspects of the ritual can be understood as consequences of its unusually comprehensive goals. This perspective can be explored in all four dimensions of the Holiness Spectrum.

7.4.2 *The Dimension of Time*

There are several indications that the Day of Atonement had a special place in the annual cycle of festivals.[1] It occurs in the important seventh month, and the special scapegoat ritual is specifically noted in the sacrificial calendar (חטאת הכפרים, Num. 29.11).[2] It was considered the appropriate time to begin the Jubilee year (Lev. 25.9). Above all, its striking rituals are described in detail in Leviticus 16, where its timing is stressed (v. 29). It is therefore likely that it was the most important day of the year from a priestly point of view.[3]

However, its focus on the sanctuary and the actions of the high priest suggest that it was not necessarily the high point of the festival year for the rest of the people. Although a *ḥaṭṭā't* was offered at festivals, its role is not emphasized or explained in any way, and the significance of the festivals lies principally outside the cult. The regular offering of a single *ḥaṭṭā't* probably reflected a concern to ensure that the sanctuary had a special purity consistent with a holy day, but the festivals were primarily for all Israel.[4]

On the other hand, the general festal character of the Day of Atonement is not stressed. It was not a pilgrimage feast, and the number of sacrifices only put it on a par with the other minor

---

1. Médébielle (1938: 63) call it 'la clef du voûte'.

2. Most of the versions translate this as 'the sin offering of atonement' (e.g. NRSV). However, NJB ('a victim for sin on the feast of Expiation') considers כפרים to refer to the occasion rather than the purpose. This would make good sense if (as is proposed below) the scapegoat has little to do with atonement.

3. Kaufmann (1960: 305). It is possible that ראש השנה in Ezek. 40.1 refers to the Day of Atonement as 'the climax of the year', in accord with Ezekiel's priestly perspective, rather than 'the beginning of the year', although other interpretations are possible (e.g. Kutsch 1985: 33-36).

4. While ensuring the purity of the sanctuary for the sacrifices offered during the festival, it was only directed towards that one day, and left unresolved any problems from the point of view of the whole year.

festivals.[1] Instead, its special rituals dealt with matters central to the cult, and the high priest, not the people, played a central role. The same contrast between priestly and popular festivals can be found when the principle of grading is considered. Grading is largely absent from the other festivals, perhaps since they are associated with the annual cycle, which is relatively independent of the cult. On the Day of Atonement, however, cultic matters of defilement and atonement are foremost, and these are graded concerns in the Priestly world view.[2]

The Day of Atonement took place on the tenth day[3] of the seventh month (Lev. 16.29; 23.27).[4] The series of festivals in the seventh month culminating in Booths marked the climax for both the cultic and the agricultural year (§7.2.2).[5] One consequence of the Day's dating was that a successful atonement removed any fault that might mar the fitness of the sanctuary and the people, and ensured that the large number of sacrifices offered at the pilgrimage feast would be accepted.

7.4.3 *The Personal Dimension*
Although the Day of Atonement benefited the people, the central figure in the ritual was the High Priest. He was the person supremely qualified to represent the people in the most solemn cultic act of the

---

1.   There may have been for practical reasons. A complex sanctuary ritual would reduce the time available for a large number of sacrifices.

2.   Van Baal (1976) distinguishes between normal festivals and rituals, which are of 'low intensity' and relatively routine, and 'high intensity' occasions. The foremost example of the latter in P is the Day of Atonement.

3.   The tenth day is often traced (e.g. by Snaith 1947: 131-41) to the difference between the lunar year (354 days) and the solar (considered to be 364 days; cf. *Jub.* 6.36-38). However, an important consideration may have been to avoid a clash with the New Moon celebrations, which exhibited a very different mood from that of the Day of Atonement.

4.   The date in Tishri has been used in arguments for an Autumn New Year (Landersdorfer 1924: 47-54; Aartun 1980: 102). The beginning of the year has been assumed to be the best time to perform an annual purification ceremony (cf. ראש השנה, Ezek. 40.1). However, the Autumn New Year theory remains unproved (§7.1.2), and the current Priestly dating also makes sense. The phrases describing booths in Exod. 23.14 (בצאת השנה) and Exod. 34.21 (תקופת השנה) need not refer to an Autumn New Year (Cassuto 1967: 303, 445).

5.   The great significance of these events allows this time to be thought of as the end of the year, although several months remained chronologically.

year. Yet the character of his role in the ritual was significantly different from his normal function. The uniqueness of the Day of Atonement is mirrored in the unparalleled role of the high priest.

This is illustrated by his clothing. Instead of the resplendent high priestly garments (§5.2.3), he wore a set of four garments of white linen (Lev. 16.4). The contrast with the normal state of affairs implies that he takes on a special status. While he still offers sacrifices for himself, the hierarchical distinctions of the personal dimension are modified in line with the primary purpose of the ritual.[1] The simple set of clothing on this occasion did not manifest the holy mixed character (§3.5.2) of the normal garments, and so reduced the emphasis on his special high-priestly grade of holiness.[2] Whereas at other times the graded hierarchy was reflected in the ritual symbolism,[3] on the Day of Atonement the high priest is closely identified with the rest of Israel.[4]

This solidarity distinguishes the role of the high priest from the times when he offered sacrifices to deal with specific sins and impurities (§§6.2.2, 6.2.3). P normally assumes that the priest is in a state of purity, and thus able to minister in the sanctuary and offer the sacrifice (§6.4.5). On the Day of Atonement this is not taken for granted, and the high priest has to take every precaution to ensure his purity, especially since he had to enter the Holy of Holies.[5] Instead of simply

---

1.   Haran (1978: 174) thinks that the white clothes represent an even higher level of holiness, akin to that of the angels. But angels are not prominent in P, and white more probably indicates the high degree of purity necessary on the day (cf. Isa. 1.18).

2.   The contrast of high priest–ordinary Israelite is more likely than that of holy–sinful (as suggested by D. Davies 1977: 394).

3.   The breastplate, for example, contained the names of the twelve tribes and the appearance of the high priest as their representative in the holy place was a reminder to God (cf. §§5.2.3, 7.1.2).

4.   Like any other human being, the high priest could not see God and live. Thus an incense barrier must be set between him and the presence of God (over the כפרת, Lev. 16.2) when he is performing the atonement ritual in the Holy of Holies (vv. 12-13). It is unlikely that the incense was associated with human sinfulness in this context (as in Num. 17.11: cf. §4.5.3). Instead, there may be a contrast between his censing and the illegitimate incense offered by Nadab and Abihu, whose sin is mentioned in the redactional introduction to the chapter (vv. 1-2).

5.   Later Judaism elaborated on the precautions that the high priest had to take (*m. Yom.* 1–3; Horbury 1983: 51-52). *m. Par.* 3.1 indicates that he was sprinkled

washing his hands and feet in the laver (Exod. 30.19-21), he had to bathe himself (Lev. 16.4), and he had to offer a special sacrifice for himself and his household.

While the high priest was assimilated in some measure to the people, they in turn were subject to unusual restrictions. On this one day in the year the Israelites were commanded to 'afflict themselves' (תעַנּוּ אֶת־נַפְשׁתֵיכֶם, Lev. 16.29; cf. v. 31; 23.27, 32; Num. 29.7; 30.14).[1] The comprehensive character of the day made such a requirement very appropriate.[2] The people were associated in this way with the negative role of the sanctuary ritual which was being carried out on their behalf.

Only when atonement had been successfully accomplished was the normal hierarchical order re-established, and the distinctive high priestly garments once again donned (Lev. 16.24). For the people, a successful atonement opened the way for the general rejoicing at Booths (וּשְׂמַחְתֶּם לִפְנֵי יהוה, Lev. 23.3), and the enjoyment of the feasting on that occasion would be heightened by the affliction which the people had endured on the Day of Atonement.[3]

7.4.4 *The Spatial Dimension*

The two parts of the ritual on the Day of Atonement introduced two unique movements in space. Only once in the year was the blood of the *ḥaṭṭā't* (a goat) brought into the heart of the Tabernacle, the Holy of Holies, and sprinkled on the cover (כפרת) of the ark (Lev. 16.14-15). The second movement was equally infrequent, and even more unusual. A second goat was presented at the sanctuary, but instead of

---

with the water mingled with the ashes of the red cow (§6.2.3) prior to the Day of Atonement.

1. This included fasting and probably other abstinences (*m. Yom.* 8.1; Brongers 1977: 2; Milgrom 1971a: 1189-91). Although the Day of Atonement was a fast, not a festival, the distinction is not made in P. In postexilic times, the tenth day of the seventh month is one of the four fasts (צום) in the year (Zech. 8.19). Since fasting is a mourning custom (e.g. 1 Sam. 31.13; 2 Sam. 1.12), the day may have overtones of a day of mourning (Brongers 1977: 15), appropriate for the day's focus on sin and impurity.

2. Lev. 16.29-34 and 23.26-32 are generally regarded as later passages (Elliger 1966: 207; Noth 1982: 126), but the development is consistent with the significance of the Day of Atonement.

3. Kurtz (1862: 336).

being sacrificed, it was driven out into the wilderness. At no other time of the year were these two extreme poles of the spatial dimension of the Holiness Spectrum employed in Priestly rituals.[1]

The close juxtaposition of the two parts of the Day of Atonement can be understood as a significant structural contrast between the ritual movements in the spatial dimension. In the text the two goats begin by being indistinguishable,[2] and are both initially designated 'for the *ḥaṭṭā't*' (לחטאת, Lev. 16.5), before being distinguished by the casting of lots. But by the end of the day they have embraced the extreme reaches of significant space.

This may be restated in terms of holiness and impurity, since in P space can have quality as well as quantity. Near to the sanctuary, the ground and the buildings on it are holy, while major impurities have their proper place outside the camp (Num. 5.1-3), and a person who commits a serious sin is taken outside the camp to be stoned (e.g., Lev. 24.14-15). On the Day of Atonement, the blood is brought into the holiest place (zone I), but the scapegoat is driven in the opposite direction, into the wilderness (zone V).

This extreme polarization in the spatial dimension is closely aligned with a similar one in the personal dimension. The identity and etymology of Azazel have been disputed, but the weight of the evidence seems to point to its identification with a demonic being which dwelt in the wilderness.[3] From an equivalence at the beginning of the ritual, the two goats end up at opposite poles of the Holiness Spectrum, both in the spatial (Holy of Holies–wilderness) and in the personal dimension (Yahweh–the impure, the sinful and the demonic).

This did not mean that Azazel was regarded as an active participant in the ritual. The wider context of P and the specific details of

---

1. The ritual of Lev. 14.9 had to be performed in the wilderness because of the incompatibility of impurity with the holiness of the sanctuary, but it is closely associated with the sanctuary (על פני הקדש).

2. Stressed in *m. Yom.* 6.1.

3. When lots are cast over the two goats, the one designated for Yahweh (v. 9) is parallel to the one 'for Azazel' (v. 6, לעזאזל), implying that it too was a personal being. Tawil (1980) has convincingly argued for the demonic character of Azazel. However, the significance of this is strongly qualified by the larger Priestly context. Azazel has a symbolic role within a carefully defined ritual context, and thereby does not compromise Israel's absolute allegiance to Yahweh and confession of his sovereignty.

Leviticus 16 make this unlikely.[1] Azazel is so reduced in substance that the text calls primarily for a symbolic reading.[2] Yet the unique reference to a demon in a legitimate ritual context could be because Azazel represented the extreme opposite of God's holy presence in the Holy of Holies. The domain of Azazel is not neutral or undefined space, but imbued with a personal quality which is the mirror opposite to God's presence in his holy sanctuary. Given the ambiguities of the allusion, it is perhaps possible to regard Azazel's domain as a coalescence of the demonic, the impure, and the sinful.

In terms of the dynamics of the ritual, it seems that in some way harmony between God and Israel was restored by means of an extreme and complementary movement in the spatial dimension. During the year various faults (sins and impurities) had compromised the ordered life of Israel. These tensions were represented and eventually resolved in terms of the spatial movement as well as the normal sacrificial action. The normative state of affairs in the Priestly conception was that there should be a clear separation between the spheres of holiness, purity and impurity. Impurity properly belonged to regions outside the camp, but Israel's impurities defiled the inner sanctuary, and its sins threatened to separate God from his people. If unchecked, these tensions could grow and threaten the validity of the cult, and endanger God's continued presence in Israel. The ritual on the Day of Atonement was intended to deal with these problems, freeing the sanctuary from impurity, and the community from sin. In the double movement of the ritual on the Day of Atonement, all the tensions were gathered up and dealt with by a decisive purification and elimination.

In spatial terms, the blood manipulation was comprehensive.[3]

---

1. Kaufmann (1960: 114-15). The subsequent uncertainty about the meaning of the word illustrates this point. However, it is less certain that the meaning of Azazel should be reduced to a mere indication of where the scapegoat is to be sent (Wright 1987: 24).

2. We might compare the way that death can be personified in poetic texts. Although this is the opposite process, it illustrates the way in which a poetic or cultic context encourages such metaphoric and symbolic associations. Even when opposed to Yahweh, death is under his authority and control. While it is not explicitly stated that the scapegoat is to die in Lev. 16, this is strongly implied, and the later ritual ensured it (*m. Yom.* 6.6).

3. Gese (1977: 103) suggests that the doubling of rites (the two goats, atonement for priests and people) reflects completeness.

Generally the blood was only sprinkled in the inner sanctum (zone II) or applied to the altar (zones II and III; §6.4.1), but on the Day of Atonement it was applied to all the holy objects.[1] The purification began at the Holy of Holies (zone I, here called קדש in Lev. 16.16), moved on to the Tent of Meeting (zone II, v. 16; including the incense altar of Exod. 30.10), and finally encompassed the altar of Burnt Offering (zone IIIa, vv. 18-19), the most holy object in the court. The threefold purification was therefore performed in accordance with the order of holiness in the spatial dimension.[2]

The ritual ends with the re-establishment of the normative world order and the resumption of the normal offerings, performed by the high priest in his normal clothes (§7.4.3).

7.4.5 *Sin and Impurity*

The Day of Atonement illustrates well the difficulty of relating the sin and impurity models (§6.2). The most important statements are set out below (italics for words normally associated with the *purification* model, including *kpr*, and underlining for the <u>sin</u> model):

a. The *ḥaṭṭāʾt* for the people

v. 16   וכפר על־הקדש   thus he shall *make atonement* for the holy place,

מטמאת בני ישראל   because of the *impurities* of the people of Israel

ומפשעיהם לכל־חטאתם   and because of their <u>transgressions</u>, all their <u>sins</u>

v. 30   כי ביום הזה יכפר   for on this day shall *atonement be made*[3]

עליכם לטהר אתכם   for you to *purify* you;

מכל חטאתיכם   from all your <u>sins</u>[4]

לפני יהוה תטהרו   you shall be *clean* before Yahweh.

b. The Scapegoat   [the goat]

v. 10   יעמד־חי לפני יהוה   shall be presented alive before Yahweh

לכפר עליו   to make *atonement* over it. . .

---

1. The prohibition of people from the Tabernacle (v. 17) could be because the sprinkling was subject to a sight prohibition (§4.5.2).

2. Finn (1916: 473) notes the threefold purification. Most Jewish exegesis (Ibn Ezra is an exception) mistakenly identified the altar of v. 18 with the golden altar (Hoffmann 1905: 450; Kiuchi 1987: 128).

3. NRSV has followed the Syriac in reading the passive יְכֻפַּר (cf. *BHS*).

4. The context suggests the the purification idea is primary, and the word should be translated 'impurities'.

v. 21   והתודה עליו   and he [Aaron] shall <u>confess</u> over it

               את־כל־עונת בני ישראל   all the <u>iniquities</u> of the people of Israel,

      ואת־כל־פשעיהם לכל־חטאתם   and all their transgressions, all their sins. . .

From this it appears that the sin and purification terms are mixed, or even confused. Further, the statements are so general that it is difficult to define what kinds of sin and impurity are intended. The interpretation of these statements depends to a large extent on how the two parts of the ritual are related to one another and to the rest of the priestly system.[1]

1. The rites deal with the same faults. There is a significant overlap of language used of the two rituals,[2] but although this may be true at a certain level (§6.2.6), there are significant differences in the language and the two parts should not be coalesced prematurely.

2. The rites are continuous in their action. One version of this view is that the blood ritual removes the sins, and the goat then carries these away from the sanctuary. Another view has recently been proposed by Kiuchi, for whom the scapegoat atones for priestly sin in a way which is not possible in the regular cultic ritual.[3] The priest atones by substitutionally bearing the guilt of the people, and by purifying the sanctuary (*kpr* deals with both sin and impurity). The first is confirmed when the priests eat the *ḥaṭṭā't* (when it is offered for the people), and is symbolized when it is burnt outside the camp (when it is offered for the priests). No forgiveness for the priest is recorded in Leviticus 4, indicating that the high priest cannot bear his own guilt. This is performed by the special *ḥaṭṭā't*, the scapegoat.[4] The scapegoat's destination in the wilderness is the symbolic equivalent of burning the *ḥaṭṭā't* outside the camp.

This is a persuasive account, but there are difficulties with some aspects. It is uncertain that the burning of the *ḥaṭṭā't* outside the camp has the significance Kiuchi imputes. The priestly bearing of guilt appears to be an aspect for maintaining the proper cultic order

1. This largely follows Kiuchi (1987: 145-47), who cites representatives of the various positions.

2. E.g. Rodriguez (1979: 117): 'the ritual as a whole cleanses the sanctuary. Sin/impurity is here the totality of the individual's sins which throughout the year contaminated the sanctuary.'

3. Kiuchi (1987: 49-88).

4. This part of Kiuchi's argument is accepted by Rendtorff (1990a: 160).

(Num. 18.1). Nor should too much stress be placed on the relation of Leviticus 4 and 16, since the sins and impurities of ch. 16 appear to be primarily those of the people of Israel, and confession is not mentioned at all in Leviticus 4. It seems best to attempt to make sense of the references to sin and impurity, and continue to maintain their distinctiveness. The two rituals are for the most part distinct, and the chronological order of their performance may not be of great significance.

3. The rites deal with two kinds of fault. Milgrom proposes that the scapegoat deals with sins in general, and atonement in the Holy of Holies with the extreme polluting power of deliberate sin (cf. §6.2.2). A valuable aspect of his theory is the attention he draws to the way that the blood ritual on the Day of Atonement is the highest grade of atonement possible through a *ḥaṭṭā't* ritual (cf. §6.4.3).[1]

Zone		Sins	Purification (*ḥaṭā't*)
I	Holy of Holies	deliberate	Day of Atonement (Lev. 16)
II	Shrine	inadvertent—communal	major blood rite (Lev. 4.5-7, 16-18)
III	Altar	inadvertent—individual	minor blood rite (Lev. 4.25, 30; 9.9, 13)

However, Milgrom's distinctions are probably too precise for the Priestly system, and his understanding of impurity and sin has already been questioned (§6.2.2).[2]

4. The rites are complementary. In the light of the priestly conception as a whole, it would seem advisable to maintain the distinction between the sin and purification models, at least to begin with. The blood rituals belong more to the purification model, as suggested by the use of *kpr* (for the sanctuary and people),[3] and the normal func-

---

1. Milgrom (1983a: 81; cf. 1976b: 82-83). Compare the Mishnah, 'For uncleanness that befalls the Temple and its Hallowed Things through wantonness (זדון), atonement is made by the goat whose blood is sprinkled within [the Holy of Holies] and by the Day of Atonement; for all other transgressions spoken of in the Law, venial or grave, wanton or unwitting, conscious or unconscious, sins of omission and sins of commission, sins punishable by Extirpation or by death at the hands of the court, the scapegoat makes atonement' (*m. Šebu.* 1.6; translation from Danby 1933: 410).

2. The Mishnaic distinctions also probably desires too much precision, and the ethical basis of impurity is more prominent than in P (Eilberg-Schwartz 1990: 195-216).

3. The object of the כפר can be either the sanctuary (כפר + accusative, Lev. 16.20, 33; כפר + על, vv. 16, 18), or people (בעד + כפר, vv. 6, 11, 17, 24,

tion of the *ḥaṭṭā't* (§6.2.2). In contrast, the scapegoat ritual deals with sins, which the high priest confesses. Lev. 16.21 includes the three major words for sin, implying comprehensiveness.[1]

The difficulties facing this interpretation are serious but not insuperable. Lev. 16.10 refers to *kpr* in the context of the scapegoat, but the meaning is obscure and it could (1) have a special non-purificatory meaning,[2] (2) reflect the Priestly tendency to make all rituals atoning ones,[3] or (3) be a textual error.[4] Similarly, the reference to sins and rebellions with reference to the blood manipulations could (1) be subsequent harmonizations,[5] or (2) indicate in a general manner that the impurities which are being cleansed can result from sin (§6.2.3).

7.4.6 *The Source of Impurity*

There are several possible sources for the impurities which were cleansed by the blood ritual on the Day of Atonement. They could derive from (1) the direct contact of an unclean object or person with the sanctuary (whether accidental or deliberate), (2) the neglect of purification of a major impurity,[6] (3) deliberate sins, for which no atonement is possible (Num. 15.30; cf. vv. 25, 28).

However, it is not clear that these actions defiled the sanctuary and compromised its holiness in any substantial way.[7] It is assumed that

---

30, 33, 34; כפר + על, vv. 18, 30). The occurrences are analysed and discussed in Janowski (1982: 186-87) and Kiuchi (1987: 88).

1. Knierim (1967: 229-35). Note the qualifier, 'all' (כל).

2. Milgrom (1983a: 76 n. 10, 80-81) understands confession as the way in which a non-expiable wanton sin is reduced to an inadvertent sin, and so the verse refers to a transfer of sins onto the scapegoat, and כפר has a ransom/substitute meaning (1976b: 80).

3. Porter (1976: 127-28).

4. Elliger (1966: 201); Janowski (1983: 182 n. 5); cf. Lang (1984: 312-13). Kiuchi (1987: 149-51) reviews the interpretations of the verse and argues that the scapegoat atones for Aaron.

5. Wright (1987: 18-21) suggests that an earlier form of the text was without the phrase referring to rebellions and sins in both v. 16 and v. 21.

6. Lev. 15.31, בטמאם את־משכני אשר בתוכם (leading to death); Num. 19.13, טמא את־משכן יהוה (leading to being cut off). According to *m. Yom.* 8.9, the Day of Atonement does not atone for deliberate sin, but death does.

7. Kiuchi (1987: 81) argues that the sanctuary came into contact with impurity only when the impure person presented him- or herself to be purified. However, there is no hint of this in the texts, and the contagious character of impurity should

the sacrificial system remains effective throughout the year. At this point it is necessary to widen the perspective and suggest that defilement was not so much a physical as a social and theological category, and often expressed tensions between the ideal divine order and its human expression. Deliberate defilement could therefore affect not just the individual involved, but also in some measure the community of which he was part. It would be appropriate for these tensions (and any others) to be dealt with in a decisive fashion. Otherwise they could accumulate and reach dangerous proportions. The unique and comprehensive form of the corrective measures applied on the Day of Atonement was appropriate for the general character of the impurities being cleansed, and their accumulation in the course of the year.

Although the texts dealing with purification dominate,[1] the scapegoat ritual deals primarily with sins.[2] The comprehensive phraseology suggests that the scope of the ceremony was intended to include every kind of sin. This could include even those which may already have been dealt with, from the human side by the civil law, or from the divine side by direct action. What happens outside the sanctuary affects in some way what goes on inside, since it is the same God who dwells in the sanctuary and who is sovereign over all that Israel does. It would be appropriate to have some sort of cultic ritual which acknowledges the implications for God of human sin.

7.5 Conclusion

The dimension of time is the least amenable of all to classification and integration with other dimensions. Nevertheless, it is possible to structure time by assigning different cultural and cultic values to units of time, particularly in the weekly and annual cycles. In the Priestly system, the number and character of public sacrifices play an important

---

not be regarded mechanically (§3.3.3). The ritual as a whole, including the fulfilment of the days of impurity, resulted in purification, and the status of the person during the ritual is ambiguous and undefined, as is often the case in the course of a ritual (cf. §3.2.4).

1. Although the scapegoat ritual is striking, more verses are devoted to the blood rituals and other actions which can be subsumed under this model.

2. The secondary application of the purification metaphor to the scapegoat (if this is the explanation of כפר in 16.10) could be a recognition that sin against God might involve impurity and defilement.

role in ordering and grading the days, particularly the Sabbath in the week, the New Moon in the month, and the festivals in the year (§7.3).

In the Priestly classification of time, there is a fundamental distinction between natural cycles, which determined the agricultural year and its festivals, and the regular weekly recurrence of the Sabbath independent of any natural period. The former were not specific to Israel and its cult. But in Israel the Sabbath is independent of any natural cycle and the sabbatical principle greatly affected the way in which the festivals were celebrated (§7.3).[1] The culturally specific link between Israel and the Sabbath made it an appropriate sign of the covenant, and the sanctification of the Sabbath was a fundamental criterion for belonging to Israel.

Although the Day of Atonement was a festival among the others, it had a very different character (§7.4). Whereas they were oriented more towards the people (notably the pilgrimage feasts), the Day of Atonement was the most important event in the year for the cult. The other festivals were times of rejoicing, but on the Day of Atonement the people afflicted themselves. The purpose of the day was not to celebrate a natural season, but to deal with the sins and impurities of Israel by cultic means.

Unlike the other festivals and the Sabbath, where the equality of all Israel was stressed, the Day of Atonement participated fully in the graded conception of the world at the heart of the Priestly world-view, and explored its boundaries to the furthest limits. The high priest enters the Holy of Holies 'to create a perfect and remarkable coalescence of the most sacred individual, the most sacred of space, the most sacred day of the year, and the most sacred rite'.[2] A successful conclusion to the highly charged ritual of this day enabled Israel to enjoy fully the pilgrimage festival of Booths, the greatest of the year.

---

1. Heschel (1957: 8) subsumes the spatial dimension under the structure of time but does not extend the idea to include the festival year (e.g. p. 8, the Sabbath enables 'a holy architecture of time'; p. 14, 'The seventh day is a *palace in time* which we build', author's italics).

2. Sarna (1986: 205).

Chapter 8

CONCLUSION

8.1 *A Theology of the Priestly Cultic Texts*

The argument of this book has not been to claim that the Holiness Spectrum is the sole key to the theology of the Priestly writing. Nevertheless, it has led to a wide-ranging and nuanced exploration of the Priestly cultic texts which, it has been shown, set out an orderly representation of the world in accord with four basic dimensions of human experience. The structuring and interpretation of these four dimensions is carried out in such a way as to reflect and convey Israel's understanding of God, society and the world. In particular, the principle of grading has a major role in the way that central concepts, institutions and rituals are presented. In this concluding chapter, the implications of the study for the theology of the Old Testament will be briefly developed in two directions.[1] These are the structure of a theology which would do justice to the Priestly conception of the world (§8.2), and the concept of order as a possible centre for a theology of the Old Testament (§8.3).

Before this, however, two limitations of the approach adopted here should be recalled. First, relatively little attention has been paid to the historical and social realities to which the texts bear witness. This bracketing has been defended as a useful measure in the light of present uncertainties in Pentateuchal studies and the special nature of the material. But it runs the danger of making the Priestly writing too abstract and intellectual, and postpones important questions regarding the function and role of the texts. Ideally, the observations made here

---

1. 'Old Testament' recognizes the predominantly Christian context of the discussion and my own commitment. There is lively debate whether parallel theological approaches to the 'Hebrew Bible' or 'Tanak' are possible.

need to be linked to a hypothesis about the setting and tradition-history of the priestly texts.

Second, the abstraction of the cultic material from its role in the larger Pentateuchal context is a serious weakness. Admittedly, the discussion is again hampered by the lack of consensus on crucial introductory issues, particularly the relation of P to the overall redaction of the Pentateuch (§1.3). Yet the Sinai revelation and the institution of the cult belong to a larger and longer story, encompassing the whole Pentateuch, or even the entire narrative from Genesis to Kings.[1]

Much effort has gone into elucidating the formulaic, lexical and theological links between creation, the flood, the patriarchal narratives, the institution of the cult at Sinai, the wilderness wanderings and (if thought to be part of the Priestly work) the conquest of the land.[2] The kerygmatic treatments of P seek to relate the narrative and the cult by means of key words or themes (§1.4). Other links have been traced with through the genealogies,[3] the chronologies,[4] the speech formulae,[5] the divine founding word,[6] the perception of time,[7] and the liking for sevenfold structures.[8] However, it has proved difficult to do justice to the discontinuity and change in P as well as the continuity.[9] There is a tendency to choose one aspect of P as primary and subordinate everything else to it. Yet it is also clear that, in P, institutions develop and change, and the role of each part in the whole story must be respected. Sinai marked an important new beginning and was in

1. Clines (1990: 93-98).

2. E.g. Elliger (1952), Blenkinsopp (1976).

3. Johnson (1988: 26-27) comments how the genealogies of the *Toledoth* book highlight Levi and Aaron, the seventh from Abraham. Num. 3.1 also links the Genesis traditions with the Sinai revelation.

4. Hughes (1990: 5-54).

5. Blenkinsopp (1976).

6. Gorman (1990).

7. On the fourth day the sun and moon were created, and ordained as 'signs for the set times' (לאתת ולמועדים, Gen. 1.14). Israel was to celebrate the מועדי יהוה (§7.2.1), and thus to acknowledge God's universal lordship over time.

8. There are narrative as well as cultic sevens (§7.3). Kearney (1977) detected a sevenfold pattern in the opening 'speech' of Exod. 25–31, and aligned their content with the seven creative acts of Gen. 1. The Sabbath has the significant seventh place in both (Exod. 31.10-14—Gen. 2.1-3; cf. §4.3.2), although other links are tenuous. See also Sarna (1986: 213-14), Gorman (1990: 45-50).

9. See now the careful comments by Blum (1990: 287-332).

some sense authoritative,[1] but it did not define a rigid eternal order and the legitimacy of further interpretation is witnessed to by later biblical writers.

8.2 *The Structure of an Old Testament Theology*

The difficulty of writing a theology of the cultic texts is well known. This has not led not so much to silence as to an embarrassing diversity of ways in which it has been done. It may be useful to list some of the possibilities, most of which have been touched upon in the course of this study:

> *a*. The lexical approach: via key theological words.
>
> *b*. The thematic approach: via a selection of important ideas.
>
> *c*. The comparative approach: the setting within an ancient Near Eastern context.
>
> *d*. The history of religions approach: the setting in a general history of Israelite religion.
>
> *e*. The kerygmatic approach: the message of the texts for a community in a particular historical context.
>
> *f*. The canonical approach: the theology of the final form of the text in the context of the community of faith.
>
> *g*. The apologetic approach: the relation of P to contemporary modes of thought.
>
> *h*. The dimensional approach: the ordering of the cult in terms of basic aspects of human experience (space, society, action, time).

Each of these is concerned to answer a particular kind of question, since no theological or historical study is disinterested. Correspondingly, each has its limitations, although some approaches will be more fruit-ful than others, depending on the nature of the material and the state of our knowledge. It has been argued that the dimensional approach is a particularly fruitful one, and deserves recognition within the wider debate about the method and content of an Old Testament theology.[2] It

---

1.   This may be the significance of the use of the term 'perpetual' or 'everlasting' (עולם) in the cultic texts (e.g. the Sabbath is to be kept לדרתם ברית עולם, Exod. 31.16; חק(ת) עולם occurs in Exod. 30.21; Lev. 6.11, 15, etc.). All dimen-sions of the cult are described in this way: the Tabernacle (e.g. Exod. 27.21), the sacrifices (e.g. Lev. 6.11), the priests (e.g. Exod. 29.28; Lev. 10.9) and the festi-vals (e.g. Lev. 23.14).

2.   For methodological surveys, see Reventlow (1985), Hayes and Prussner (1985) and Hasel (1982, 1985).

is striking that, although the Priestly cultic texts comprise a large proportion of the Pentateuch, the theology of the cult is often given a subordinate role within the whole.[1]

One way to approach this question is through a consideration of the way in which the theology treats the various parts of the Hebrew Bible. The unit chosen for discussion can vary from the level of a book, or section of a book, to the whole Bible. In practice, aspects of each level are employed in order to do justice to the diversity of the whole, but one usually predominates.

A theological discussion of a biblical book is normally found within the introduction to a commentary. Childs's high regard for the traditional canonical divisions between the books is one reason why he has chosen the genre of Introduction to expound his theological understanding of scripture.[2] There does, indeed, appear to be significance in the present divisions,[3] but studies oriented towards a book cannot easily expand to see the larger picture. The Priestly cultic material (spanning Exodus, Leviticus and Numbers) is so closely linked that fragmentation into books reduces and distorts the theology of the whole.[4] In practice, the results of a book-oriented reading are meagre in comparison to discussions which range further afield.[5]

Recently, there has been renewed interest in the larger units of the Bible, particularly the traditional division of the Hebrew Bible into Torah, Prophets and Writings, the three parts of the Hebrew canon.[6] For example, Brueggemann has sought to explore their complementary functions. He assigns to the Torah a special role as 'a statement of community ethos, a definitional statement of the character of the

1. McKenzie (1974) is a notable exception among the smaller theologies. Saebø (1980: 373) distinguishes three principal types of OT theology, orientated towards: (1) salvation-history (*geschichtsbezogenen Heilstheologie*), (2) order or creation (*Ordnungstheologie bzw. Schöpfungstheologie der Weisen*), (3) cult (*Kulttheologie* [*bzw. kultbezogenen Heilstheologie*]). Levenson (1985: 36-45) might be aligned with the third, since he argues that history prepares for the giving of the law.

2. Childs (1979).

3. For example, the integrity of Numbers is defended in the recent works by Durham (1987: xix-xxi) and Olson (1985: 1-2).

4. Wenham (1979b: 16; 1982: 39) asserts the 'impossibility' of discussing the theology of the books separately.

5. Childs (1985) is theologically richer at the cost of abandoning the focus on book and section.

6. Earlier critics preferred to consider the Hexateuch as a unit.

community which is a given and is not negotiable among the new generation'.[1] His exposition of the Torah is drawn primarily from the Pentateuchal narratives, but the extent of Priestly cultic texts needs to be acknowledged in a theology of the Torah which does justice to both narrative and law.[2] Indeed, the theology developed here complements his observations. The cult, as much as stories of origins, conveys an all-embracing world order that provides a firm basis for social and religious life.

A third alternative is that taken by the cross-sectional theologies, which attempt to draw from relevant parts of the whole Bible to illustrate the points being made. The major problem for this approach is that it is difficult to find a structure which will do justice to the diversity of the Bible.[3] Thus, in Eichrodt's theology, aspects of the Priestly cult are dispersed in various sections of his work and juxtaposed with quite different conceptions. The freedom to draw from texts of the most diverse kind is often of great value, but it can obscure the unity and distinctiveness of the Priestly writing. In practice, Eichrodt partly overcomes the constraints of his structure by discussing more restricted sections of the Bible.

Rather than any of these approaches, the present study has suggested the validity of a fourth alternative, which might be termed the conceptual approach. In the Bible it is possible to find groups of texts which reflect a distinctive set of concerns and a relatively unified outlook (e.g. the prophets, the Deuteronomic history, the Priestly writing, the wisdom writings). These tend to reflect the predominance of a certain style of writing or genre (e.g. cultic law), and a particular social setting (e.g. the priesthood). The relative unity of such a conception need not be compromised by minor inconsistencies and indications of historical development within the overall perspective.

This unit of investigation may provide the best starting point for a theology of the Old Testament which does full justice to the Priestly conception illuminated in the preceding pages. It supplies a unit of investigation intermediate between that of a book, and that of a larger

1. Brueggemann (1983: 12). This is not specifically a work of Old Testament theology (it is titled *The Creative Word: Canon as a Model for Biblical Education*), but its wider concerns enhance its theological value.

2. This point is reinforced from a historical point of view if the Priestly school is responsible for the redaction of the Pentateuch (§1.3.3).

3. Hasel (1985: 54), Gottwald (1970: 45-47).

canonical division (or the whole Bible). It is the level which von Rad chooses when he comes to discuss the cult.[1] Admittedly, there remains the larger task of relating the conceptions of the world to one another. Yet a clear understanding of the distinctive nature of the major conceptions is a good starting point in a synthetic and comparative enterprise.

There is a further diachronic aspect which should be mentioned. While the focus here has been on the Pentateuchal priestly texts, there are a number of other texts stemming from priestly circles which have strikingly similar interests. Different social and historical contexts ensure that there is considerable variation, but the ground base is similar. Such writings include Ezekiel 40–48 (a strand of exilic and post-exilic Judaism), the Temple Scroll (sectarian Judaism), the Epistle to the Hebrews (early Christianity), and the Mishnah (early rabbinic Judaism).[2] All these seek to develop a systematic world view in terms of the cult, with extensive use of the principle of graded holiness.

8.3 *Order in the Old Testament*

A recurring concept in the previous chapters has been that of order. Along with associated ideas of structure, classification and grading, it has proved a valuable guide for unlocking the Priestly theology of the cult. In the general discussion of holiness and purity, and in each of the four dimensions, there is an evident concern to create and sustain an ordered life and worship which will be consistent with the character of the God of Israel.

This has been recognized by a number of authors without detailed exposition, as in the following quotation.[3]

> Probably no major stream of tradition in the Old Testament is more theologically reflective and integrated than the P-source. This material is organized and structured so as to present a total worldview and a structure of time, geography, cultural roles, weekly, seasonal, and multiyear

1. Von Rad (1962: 232-79).
2. See Milgrom (1981a) on the history of contagion, or Schiffman (1985) on spheres of exclusion. One of Neusner's interests is the relation between the Mishnaic and Priestly conceptions (e.g. Neusner 1973, 1981).
3. Hayes and Prussner (1985: 275); cf. Eichrodt (1961: 433-36), Fretheim (1977: 317-19). The Priestly concern for order is central to the volume by Gorman (1990). See also the quotations in §6.2.6.

cycles, a view of the proper orders of life and how they interrelate, ritual and routine for overcoming the disruptions in life and for the restoration of proper relationships both between persons and between humans and the divine. It should be noted that the priests, not the prophets, were the real custodians of the care of souls in ancient Israel and priestly theology created a universe of meaning which could deal with the totality of life in its many dimensions and exigencies. There was certainly nothing less spiritual about cultic and legal piety than about prophetic proclamation; in fact, probably the opposite was the case.

The scope of the study has been deliberately restricted to the cultic texts. However, a number of scholars have suggested that order is an interpretative key for other parts of the Old Testament as well. Indeed, this is so to such an extent that 'order' promises to be as reasonable a centre to Old Testament Theology as any of the other suggestions which have been made.[1] We might test this by exploring briefly some of the other major genres in the Bible, and seeing whether scholars have found similar patterns to those in P, for which order is a useful mediating concept.

This is most clearly seen in the creation texts, as might be expected, since Genesis 1 is a paradigmatic Priestly text. It is not accidental that structural analyses have been especially illuminating.[2] The importance òf 'order' in these texts is such that Schmid has even argued that creation is the basis for other major aspects of Old Testament theology.[3] Thus the world is created in an orderly fashion which, along the way, sets up the basic four dimensions of the cult. While the spatial separation is vertical rather than horizontal, there is a similar concern to set boundaries and limits. The differentiation in the personal dimension is equally explicit, especially between humanity, the animal kingdom, and those further removed. The classification of animals has been closely linked with that found in the cultic texts.[4] The sevenfold

1. The debate about a centre is reviewed in Hasel (1982: 117-43).
2. E.g. Beauchamp (1969).
3. Schmid (1974); cf. Knierim (1981). See the qualifying remarks of Reventlow (1985: 179-82).
4. Eilberg-Schwartz (1990: 115-40). There is no distinction between clean and unclean animals in the creation narrative, and it is generally held that P deliberately excludes any mention of sacrifice or clean/unclean animals before Sinai (e.g. Westermann 1984: 599). However, it is also true that the purity laws are a 'natural' classification (Porter 1976: 11), and are not necessarily specifically Israelite.

ordering of the week, with the Sabbath at the conclusion, is crucial for Israel's festival and sacrificial calendar.

There is less to say about the ritual dimension in Genesis 1, although this might be expected if most of the rituals concern the restoration of order, and the ongoing life which is merely initiated at creation. However, ritual concerns are paramount in the the instructions to Noah following the flood. This was required to purify the earth from evil and pollution, and was followed by a change of dispensation which assured that similar measures would not be required again.[1] The permission to kill animals, and the special law about the shedding of blood, opens up the way for the sacrificial system and prepares for the symbolic significance of blood.

In the Pentateuch, creation and cult are linked by a narrative which records a gracious salvation-history.[2] Here, too, order can provide a valuable overview. Narrative brings order, plot and meaning to events which would otherwise be random chronicle. But the Pentateuch is also concerned to show how God's purpose with his people is to restore an order of righteousness, blessing and life that has been corrupted and perverted.[3] This is demonstrated in the civil law as well as the cultic law, and they share a common concern for boundaries, sanctions, maintenance and correction.[4] In both P and Deuteronomy, laws combining civil and ritual aspects are found, although ritual tends to predominate over the the civil aspects in P (cf. Lev. 5; Num. 35), whereas in Deuteronomy the priority is reversed (cf. Deut. 21.1-9).

Order also provides a way into the wisdom literature,[5] a genre which theologies of the Old Testament have often found difficult. A chief concern of the sages is to discern the regularities of life, physical, moral and religious. There is little mention of the cultic institutions, but similar patterns of act, consequence and restoration can be found. Similarly, there is no necessary mention of God in every

1. According to the interpretation of Frymer-Kensky (1977: 151-54; 1983: 409-12). However, it should be noted that cultic language is not used: the fault is not sin or impurity, but violence (חמס, Gen. 6.13).

2. In contrast to one traditional Protestant view (e.g. Köhler 1957: 181), God's initiative and grace is evident throughout the cult (Schenker 1981: 95-119; 1983: 202-204).

3. Westermann (1963). Much of Clines (1978) is relevant.

4. Cf. Patrick (1989).

5. E.g. Murphy (1990: 115-18).

phrase. This could be misinterpreted as an expression of secularity or magic, but it is more appropriate to speak in terms of a delegated autonomy. The underlying assumption of both cult and wisdom is that there is a regular and dependable framework for life and worship. There are parallel concerns to trace the origins of the God-given order with creation (Prov. 8.22-31). However, the primary orientation remains to the world as a stable and enduring sphere of ordered relations.

The history books and the prophets share many of the themes already mentioned. There is a recurring pattern of sin, consequence, and potential restoration, although the moral and religious rather than the cultic dimension is emphasized. As with cult and wisdom, there is a similar question as to how far God works directly in the world, and how far he has delegated a certain order of things which all the nations neglect at their peril. Koch has referred to a sphere where act and consequence correspond without necessarily referring to God,[1] and Barton suggests that the prophets are also concerned with a universal 'natural law'.[2]

When we turn to the Psalms, the perspectives of Brueggemann are particularly relevant.[3] He classifies the Psalter in terms of psalms of orientation, disorientation and new orientation. The function of the Psalms, like the cult, may be to affirm the present order or restore a situation which has been disrupted in some way. The orientation metaphor is primarily a spatial one, providing a helpful entry into the full range of human expression in other dimensions.

Finally, we may consider apocalyptic. In P, the earthly order and the divine order are closely identified (cf. the 'blueprint' of Exod. 25.9). In the course of time, the disorder and sinfulness of the present order becomes so prominent that the ideal of harmony is located in an order brought about by God at the end time. Indeed, the order and perfection of the cult is a powerful inspiration for expressing the eschatological order (Ezek. 40–48; Rev. 21). The apocalyptic writers also seek to discern the divine ordering of times and seasons, often in terms of repeated patterns (e.g. Dan. 2; 7–12).[4]

---

1. A 'schicksalwirkende Tatsphäre' (Koch 1972: 160) or 'Action–Consequences–Construct' (translation in Koch 1983: 68).
2. Barton (1979).
3. Brueggemann (1984).
4. Cf. Hanson (1979: 434) on the apocalyptic world-view: 'unless a new

Clearly, this approach could be explored in far greater detail. Order is one of the most promising categories through which the Old Testament can contribute towards the contemporary theological debate. If this work has contributed towards taking seriously the Priestly contribution to this larger task, then it will have achieved its purpose.

symbolic universe is constructed to replace the old, life will lapse into chaos. . . a vision of a "higher" order of reality'.

Appendix 1

THE PRIESTLY NARRATIVE (P_g)[1]

	Noth	Elliger	Lohfink	Weimar	Holzinger
Genesis					
1 (31)	1-31	1-31	1-31	1-10,11*,12*,13, 14*,15,16*, 17-19,20*,21*, 22-25, 26*,27, 28*,29,30b,31	1-31
2 (24)	1-4a	1-4a	1-4a	2-4a	1-3
3 (24)	x	x	x	x	x
4 (26)	x	x	x	x	x
5 (32)	1a,1b,2,3a,3b, 4-27,28a,*28b, 30-32	1-28,30-32	1-27,28*,30-32	1a,3*,4-27,28*, 30-32	1-3*, 4-19,2-24* 5-27,28*,30-32
6 (22)	9-22	9-22	9-22	9-11,12a,13*, 14*, 15,16*,17*, 18, 19*,20,22	9-22
7 (24)	6,11,13-16a,18-21,24	6,11,13-16a,17a, 18-20,24	6,11,13-16a,17a, 18-21,24	6,11,13,14a,15a, 16a*,17a,18-19, 21a,24	6,11,13-16a,17a? 18-21, 24?
8 (22)	1,2a,3b-5,7,13a, 14-19	1,2a,3b-5,13a, 14-19	1,2a,3b-5,13a, 14-19	1,2a,3b,4,5,13a, 14-16,17*,18,19*	1a,2a,1b,3b?,4f, 13a,14-19
9 (29)	1-17,28,29	1-17,28f	1-3,7-17,28f	1-3,7-9,10*,11, 12a,13-14,15*, 28,29	1-3,8-17,28f
10 (32)	1a,1b,2-7,20, 22,23,31,32a, 32b	1-4a,5ab-7, 20,22f,31f	1-7,20,22f,31f	1-3,4a,5*,6-7, 20*,22-23,31*, 32*	1a,2-7,20,22f,31f
11 (32)	10-26,27,31,32	10-27,31f	10-27,31f	10-26,27a,31*,32	10-26,27,31,32

1. The proposed narrative portions of the Priestly Writing according to Noth (1948: 17-19), Elliger (1952: 121-22), Lohfink (1977: 198 n. 29) and Weimar (1984: 85 n. 18). In addition, Holzinger's analysis is given as a representative from the older generation (taken from his commentaries on Genesis [1898], Exodus [1900], Leviticus [1922] and Numbers [1903]). Noth also includes a list of passages belonging to P_s, including (in Gen. and Exod. 1–25) Gen. 46.8-27; Exod. 6.13-30; 11.9, 10; 12.2, (42), 43-51; 16.8. The table does not include a number of important qualifications and explications in the original presentations (and in later works by the same author). The abbreviations in the table vary from author to author and have been only partly harmonized:

x	No P_g in this chapter
[ ]	The passage was originally in a different place
(), ?	The attribution to P_g is uncertain
*	Only partial P_g character in the verse
f	This verse and the next (e.g., 1f = 1-2)
. . .	The intervening verses originally contained some P_g

	Noth	Elliger	Lohfink	Weimar	Holzinger
Genesis					
12 (20)	4b,5	4b,5	4b,5	4b,5*	....4b,5
13 (18)	6,11b,12abα	6,11b,12abαβ	6,11,12*	6b*,12abα	6abα,11b,12abα
14 (24)	x	x	x	x	x
15 (21)	x	x	x	x	x
16 (16)	1a,3,15,16	1,3,15f	1,3,15f	1a,3*,15-16	1a,3,15,16
17 (27)	1-27	1-27	1-13,14*,15-27	1-6,7*,8*,9aα, 10*, 11,15,16*, 17a,18,19a,20a*, 22,24-26	1-27
18 (33)	x	x	x	x	x
19 (38)	[29]	[29]	29	x	29
20 (18)	x	x	x	x	x
21 (34)	1b-5	1b-5	1b-5	1b,2a*,3*,4a,5	1b,2b-5
22 (24)	x	x	x	x	x
23 (20)	1-20	1-20	1-20	1a,2*,19*	1-20
24 (67)	x	x	x	x	x
25 (34)	7-11a,12-17, 19,20...26b	7-11a,12-17, 19f...15b	7-11a,12- 17,...26b	7,8*,9*,10b,12*, 13-15,16aα*,17, 19,20*, ...26b	7-11a,12-17,19, 20....26b
26(35)	34,35	34f	34f	34*,35	34,35
27 (46)	46	46	46	x	x
28 (22)	1-9	1-9	1-9	1-3,5	1-9
29 (35)	x	x	x	x	24,28b,29
30 (43)	x	x	x	x	1aα?,4a?,9b?,22a ?
31 (54)	....18aβb	....18aβγδb	....18*	....18aβb	....18aβγδb
32 (33)	x	x	x	x	x
33 (20)	18a	18a	18a	x	18a
34 (31)	x	x	x	x	x
35 (29)	6,9-13a,15, 22b-29	6a,9-13,15, 22b-29	6a,9-15, 22b-29	6a*,9-13,15,22b, 23-26,27*,28-29	6a,9-13a*,15, 22b-29
36 (43)	1-8,9-14	1-14	1,2a...6-8,40-43	1a,2a,6*,8*, 10-11,12b,13, 14a*, 43bβ	6-8,9-14?,29?, 40-43
37 (36)	1,2aαb....	1f....	1f	1,2*	1,2*
38 (30)	x	x	x	x	x
39 (23)	x	x	x	x	x
40 (23)	x	x	x	x	x
41 (57)	....46a	....46a	46a	....46a	36?,46aβ?,47?
42 (38)	x	x	x	x	x
43 (34)	x	x	x	x	x
44 (34)	x	x	x	x	x
45 (28)	x	x	x	x	x
46 (34)	6,7	....6f	6f	6*	6f,8-27?
47 (31)	27b,28	27b,28	27b,28	27b,28	5b,6a,7-11,27b, 28
48 (22)	3-6	3-6	3-6	3,4*	3-6
49 (33)	1a,29-33	1a,28b-33	1a,28b-33	1a,28b*,29a,30a, 33*	1a,28bβ-32, 33aαb
50 (26)	12,13	12f	12f	12,13*	12f

	Noth	*Elliger*	*Lohfink*	*Weimar*	*Holzinger*
Exodus					
1 (22)	1-7,13,14	1-5,7,13f	1-5,7,13f	1*,2-4,5b,7*,13, 14aαb	1-5,7a(*?)b,13, 14bβ
2 (25)	23aβb-25	23aγb,24f	23*,24f	23aβb-25	23aβ-25
3 (22)	x	x	x	x	x
4 (31)	x	x	x	x	x
5 (23)	x	x	x	x	x
6 (30)	2-12	2-12	2-12	2-12	2-12
7 (29)	1-13,19,20aα, 21b,22	1-13,19,20aα, 21b, 22	1-13,19,20*,21b, 22	1-13,19,20aα, 21b, 22	1-5,(6:13),6-13, 19,20aα,21b,22
8 (28)	1-3...11aβb-15	1-3...11aδb,12-15	1-3,11*,12-15	1-3...11aβb,12-15	1-3,11aγb,12-15
9 (35)	8-12	8-12	8-12	8-12	8-10*,11,12aβb
10 (29)	x	x	x	x	x
11 (10)	x	x	9f	x	10?
12 (51)	1,3-20,28,40, 41	1,3-14,28,40f	37a,40-42	1aα*,3aα*,3b, 6b*,7a,8*,12*, 28, 40-41	1,3,5-14, ...28...40f,37a
13 (22)	x	x	20	x	20
14 (31)	1-4,8,9aβb, 10abβ,15-18, 21aαb,22,23, 26,27aα,28, 29	1-4,8a,10abγ,15-18,21aαb,22f,26, 27aα,28f	1-4,8f,10*,15-18, 21*,22f,26,27*, 28f	1,2a,4,8*,10a, 10bβ,15aαb,15-17a, 18a,21aα, 21b, 22, 23aα, 23b, 26aba, 27aα,28a, 29	1,2,4,5a,8,9*, 10bβ,15aαb,16a, 16b,17f,21aα, 21b?,22(?),23, 26?, 27aα?, 28a(b?), 29?
15 (27)	22aα,27	27	22*,27	x	x
16 (36)	1-3,6,7,9-27, 32-35a	1-3,6f,9-13a, ...14bα,.... 16abγ-20,22-26, 31a,35b	1-3,6f,9-12,13, ...14*,....16*,17, 18*,19-21a, 22*, 23-26,31a, 35b	1aβ,2-3,6,7abα, 8bβ,10aαb,11, 12	1f,3?,9-12*,13, 14*, 15b, 16f, 21a(b?), 31a, 32...34, 35aα?bβ
17 (16)	1abα	1abα	1*	x	1abα
18 (27)	x	x	x	x	x
19 (25)	2a,1	2a,1	1,2a	1	2aα,1,2aβ,3bα, 9a,8a
24 (14)	15b-18	15b-18a	15b-18a	15b,16,18a	15-18aα
25 (40)	1-40	1-40	1-2,8,9*	1a,2aα,8,9	x
26 (37)	1-37	1-37	1-30	1*,2a,6*,7,8a, 11a*,15a,16,18*, 20*,22*,23a,30	x
27 (21)	1-21	1-19	x	x	1-19*
28 (43)	1-43	1-41	x	x	x
29 (46)	1-46	1-37....42b-46	43-46	45,46	x
30 (30)	x	x	x	x	x
31 (18)	18	18	18	x	18a
32 (35)	x	x	x	x	x
33 (23)	x	x	x	x	x
34 (35)	x	x	29-32	x	29-32?
35 (35)	1a,4b,5-10, 20-27,29-31a,32, 33	1a,4b-10,20-29	4,5a,10,20-22a,29	x	4-7,9f....? 20ff*, 2f*,8....?
36 (38)	2-7,[8-38]	2, [(8-38)]	2-3a,8*	x	x
37 (29)	1-24	(1-24)	x	x	x
38 (31)	1-7,9-22,24-31	(1-7,9-20)	x	x	x
39 (43)	1-32,43,	(1-31),32,43	32-33a,42f	32b,43	32,43
40 (38)	1,2,9,17-25,28, 29a,33	17,33b,34,(35)	17,33b-35	17,34	1f,16f,33b,34, (35?)

	Noth	Elliger	Lohfink	Weimar	Holzinger
Leviticus					
8 (36)	1-6aα,7-10aα, 12-36	(1-10aα,12-36)	x	x	x
9 (24)	1-7a,8-14,15b-23	1-24	1*,2f,4b-7,8*, 12a, 15a,21b-24	1a*,2,3*,4b,5b, 7abα,8*,12a, 15a, 21b,23,24b	1-24
10 (20)	x	x	x	x	1-5,12-15
16 (34)	x	x	x	x	34b
Numbers					
1 (54)	1-47	1-3, (4-19a), 19b-43, (44), 45-47	1,2*,3*,19b,21*, 23*,25*,27*, 29*,31*,33*, 35*,37*,39*, 41*,43*, 46	x	1-3*,49,4-18*, 19bα,20-47*
2 (34)	1-34	(1-34)	1*,2,3*,5*,7a, 10a,12*,14a, 18a, 20a,22a, 25a, 27*, 29a, 34	x	1,(1:53), 3-31*, 34
3 (51)	14-32a,33-51	14-16, (17-38), 39, (40-51)	x	x	14-20,21f,27f, 33f, 39*,23f,29f, 35, 38aα...5-8aα 25f,31, 36f
4 (49)	1-10,12-15,21-28a,29-33a, 34-49	x	1*...2*,3,34*, 35f, 37*,38-40, 41*,42-44,45*, 46*,47f	x	x
5 (31)	x	x	x	x	x
6 (27)	x	x	x	x	x
7 (89)	x	x	x	x	....89....
8 (26)	5-22	(5-10,12-15a,20)	x	x	(1-3),5f,7*,8,9a, 12,13a,15a, 20a*bα,22*
9 (23)	15-23	(15-18)	x	x	....15b,17*,18
10 (36)	11,12	11f	11-13	11abα,12b	11,12a,13b,12b,
11 (35)	x	x	x	x	x
12 (16)	x	x	16b	x	x
13 (23)	1-3a,17aβ,21, 25,*26,32, 33aαb	1-3a,17aβ,21,25, 26a,32	1-3a,17*,21,25, 26*,32	1,2a,3aα,17aβ, 21,25,32a	1-16a*,17a,21, 25,26a*,32abα
14 (45)	1a,2,3,5-10, 26, 27a,28,29, 35-38	1a,2,5-7,10,26-29aα,35-38	1a,2,5-7,10, 26-28,29*,35-38	1a,2*,5-7,10, 26, 35b,37-38	1aα...2*,5-7, 10,26,27b,28*, 29,30,33,36-38
15 (41)	x	x	x	x	x
16 (35)	x	x	x	x	1a,2ab,2b,3a-7a*, 18,19*,35*
17 (28)	x	x	x	x	6-10...17,28... 11-26*
18 (32)	x	x	x	x	1,2a*,3a,5,20, 8-19**,21,23b, 24a

	Noth	Elliger	Lohfink	Weimar	Holzinger
Numbers					
19 (22)	x	x	x	x	x
20 (29)	1aαb,2,3bα,4, 6,7,8aβ,bβ,10, 11b,12,22b, 23aα, 25-29	1aα,2,3b,4,6f, 8aβγbβ,10,11b, 12,22,23aα, 25-29	....1*....2,3b-7, 8*,8a*,10,11b, 12*....22b, ...23*, 25-29	1aα,2,3aβb,6,7, 8a*,10,12,22b, 23a*,25-29	1aα*,2,3bα*b, 4abα*,6,....10a. .11b(a?)b*,12*, 13a*, 22-29
21 (35)	4aαℵ	4aα	4*,10f	x	10,11bα
22 (41)	1b	1b	1	x	1
. . .					
27 (23)	12-23	12-14a,15-23	12-14a,15-23	12,13,14a*,18*, 20, 22a,23	x
28 (31)	x	x	x	x	x
29 (39)	x	x	x	x	x
30 (17)	x	x	x	x	x
31 (54)	x	x	x	x	x
32 (42)	x	x	x	x	....2b....4aa....18 19....(28aα)
33 (56)	x	x	x	x	50f,54
34 (29)	x	x	1-18	x	2aβb, 13abαβ, 3-12*, 16-29
35 (34)	x	x	x	x	9-15*
36 (13)	x	x	x	x	13
Deuteronomy					
1 (46)	x	x	3	x	
32 (52)	x	x	48-52	x	
34 (12)	1aα....7-9	1a,7-9	1*....7-9	7-9*	
Joshua					
4	x	x	....19*	x	
5	x	x	10-12	x	
14	x	x	1,2*	x	
18	x	x	1	x	
19	x	x	51	x	

Appendix 2

GRADES OF IMPURITY[1]

a. Minor defilements

Impurity	Time	Contact	BW[2]	Reference
from carcass	1 day[3]	touching (v. 24, 27)	(B)[4]	Lev. 11.24-28
		carrying (v. 25, 28)	B (W)	
from clean carcass	1 day	touching (v. 39)	(B)	Lev. 11.39-40
		carrying (v. 40)	(B) W	
		eating (v. 40)	(B) W	
from carcass	1 day	eating	WB	Lev. 17.15
from carcass of a swarmer	1 day	touching (by priest)	(B)	Lev. 11.31; Lev. 22.5-6
from corpse defiled	1 day	touching	(B)	Nu 19.22
		touching (by priest)	B	Lev. 22.4,6
[from skin disease	1 day	touching	(B)	Lev. 13.45-46]
from diseased house	(1 day)[5]	entering, sleeping in, eating	(B) (B) W	Lev. 14.46-47
from discharge (m)	1 day	touching him/items	WB	Lev. 15.5-11
		in contact with him	(B)	Lev. 15.10
		touching saddle		
		carrying saddle	WB	Lev. 15.10
from discharge (f)	1 day	touching her/items in contact with her	WB	Lev. 15.26-7
from menstruant	1 day	touching	B	Lev. 15.19-23
		touching items of	WB	
semen	1 day	self	B	Lev. 15.16
		(by priest)	B	Lev. 22.4, 6
intercourse	1 day	man with woman	B	Lev. 15.18
new mother (m — after 7 days) (f — after 14 days)	33 days 66 days	self	(BW)	Lev. 12[6]

1. See also Wright (1987a: 179-219), Frymer-Kensky (1983: 404), Milgrom (1986: 118-19).
2. *Key:*   B = bathing body   W = washing clothes
              ( ) = assumed purification   [ ] = case is implied but not described.
3. I.e. 'until evening' (עד־הערב, Lev. 11.24, 25, 27, 28, 39, 40, etc.).
4. Some of the versions add bathing (e.g., Sam. in v. 25; some LXX mss. in v. 40; cf. *BHS*). Bertholet (1901: 36) suggests that both washing and bathing were involved, but clothes were mentioned specifically because they had been in direct contact with the carcass.
5. Assumed (with Frymer-Kensky 1983: 413 n. 2).
6. Purification from childbirth is unusual in that there were two stages, the first having a status of major impurity, the second of minor impurity (§6.3.3).

b. Major defilements

Impurity	Time	Sacrifices[1]		Reference
from corpse	7 days day 3, 7	a. *haṭṭāt* (red cow) b. sprinkling with waters of impurity	WB	Num. 19
skin disease	7 days	a. *'āšām* lamb (m) b. *haṭṭāt* lamb (m) c. *'ōlâ* sheep (f)	WSB	Lev. 13–14
new mother	7 - m 14 - f	a. *'ōlâ* year lamb b. *haṭṭāt* bird	(BW)	Lev. 12
menstruation (regular discharge)	7 days	none	(BW)	Lev. 15.19
man and woman with discharge	7 days	none	(WB)	Lev. 15.24
discharge — male	7 days	a. *'ōlâ* bird b. *haṭṭāt* bird	BW	Lev. 15.13-15
discharge — female	7 days	a. *'ōlâ* bird b. *haṭṭāt* bird	(BW)	Lev. 15.28-30

The preceding tables describe the source, duration and purification of the two main classes of impurity which affect people (§2.2). The major impurities are distinguished primarily by the length of time that purification requires (seven days rather than one), by the agent of purification (sacrifice rather than water), and whether the impurity is contagious or not. In most cases minor defilements are derived from a major source of impurity.[2] In the second group, the person who has had contact with a human corpse is the only example of a derived major defilement. It is sometimes difficult to know how complete or consistent the Levitical texts are. In the table it has been assumed that all minor impurity required bathing, but this ritual is not always mentioned.[3] Washing clothes and bathing may have been a more effective purification than washing alone.[4]

---

1. Key: bird = turtle dove (תר) or dove (יונה); S = shaving hair
2. Exceptions include emission of semen, the second stage of the impurity after childbirth, and intercourse.
3. With Wright (1987a: 185 n. 38). Washing probably comes second in the instructions for practical reasons.
4. In the preparation of the ashes of the red cow, the priest who casts cedarwood, hyssop and scarlet stuff into the fire, and the person who burns it must wash and bathe (Num. 19.7-8). But the person who gathers up the ashes (v. 10) and the one who sprinkles the water of purification (v. 21) need only wash (Kiuchi 1987: 139).

Appendix 3

THE PRIESTLY CALENDARS (Leviticus 23; Numbers 28–29)

Regular Periods	Reference[1]	Proclamation[2]	No Work[3]	Rest[4]
Daily	Num. 28.3-8			
	Exod. 29.38-42			
Sabbath	Lev. 23.3	23.3	23.3*	23.3
	Num. 28.9-10		Exod. 31.15*;	Exod. 31.15;
			35.2*	35.2[5]
New Moon	Num. 28.11-15			

Annual Festivals	Reference	Proclamation	No Work	Rest
1. Passover	Lev. 23.5	–	–	–
I.14	Num. 28.16			
2. Unleavened Bread				
I.15 Day 1	Lev. 23.6-7	23.7	23.7	–
	Num. 28.17-23	28.18;	28.18;	
		Exod. 12.16	Exod. 12.16*	
I.16-21 Days 2–6	Lev. 23.8	–	–	–
	Num. 28.24			
I.22 Day 7	Lev. 23.8	23.8	23.8	–
	Num. 28.25	28.25;	28.25;	
		Exod. 12.16	Exod. 12.16*	
3. Waving of the Sheaf	Lev. 23.9-14	–	–	–
4. Weeks	Lev. 23.15-21	23.21	23.21	–
III.x	Num. 28.26-31	28.26	28.26	
5. Trumpets	Lev. 23.23-25	23.24	23.25	23.24[†]
VII.1	Num. 29.1-6	29.1	29.1	
6. Day of Atonement	Lev. 23.26-32	23.27	23.28, 30, 31*;	23.32
VII.10	Num. 29.7-11	29.7	29.7*	
			Lev. 16.29*	Lev. 16.31
7. Booths				
VII.15 Day 1	Lev. 23.33-35	23.35	23.35	23.39[†]
	Num. 29.12-16	29.12	29.12	
VII 16-21 Days 2–7	Lev. 23.36-43	–	–	–
	Num. 29.17-34			
VII 22 Day 8	Lev. 23.36, 39	23.36	23.36	23.39
	Num. 29.35-38		29.35	

1.   Knohl (1987) discusses the differences between Lev. 23 and Num. 28–29.

2.   *miqrā' qōdeš* (מקרא קדש). See §7.2.1.

3.   'You shall not do no laborious work' (כל־מלאכת עבדה לא תעשׂו), but 'you shall do no work' (כל־מלאכה לא תעשׂו, marked by *) is also found.

4.   Either *šabbat šabbatôn* (שבת שבתון) or *šabbatôn* (שבתון) alone, marked by [†]. שבת שבתון can also describe the sabbatical year (Lev. 25.4-5).

5.   Cf. Exod. 16.23, שבתון שבת־קדש ליהוה.

Appendix 4

THE SACRIFICIAL CALENDAR (Numbers 28–29)

Regular Offerings

Occasion[1]	'ōlâ			minḥâ (bulls rams lambs)[2]			ḥaṭṭā't goats
	bulls	rams	lambs				
Daily (× 365) תמיד	–	–	2	–	–	0.2 (flour) 0.5 (oil) 0.5 (wine)	–
Sabbath (× 52) שבת	–	–	2	–	–	0.2 (flour) 0.5 (oil) 0.5 (wine)	–
New Moon (× 12) ראש חדש	2	1	7	0.6 (1.0) 1.0 0.2 (0.33) 0.33		0.7 (flour) (1.75) (oil) 1.75 (wine)	1

1. The list is for a solar year and assumes that the sacrifices are additive (totals exclude the Passover and sheaf lambs, and scapegoat). See similarly Rainey (1970: 492-93—who lists 32 rams) and Wenham (1982b: 197).

2. The *minḥâ* (flour, measured in ephahs) accompanies the *'olâ* and is mixed with oil (measured in hins). It is accompanied by a libation of wine (נסכה, in hins). See also the table in §6.4.4.

Annual Festivals

Occasion		'ōlâ			minhâ			ḥaṭṭā't
		bulls	rams	lambs	(bulls	rams	lambs)	goats
1. Passover פסח		–	–	(1)	–	–	–	–
		(Passover lamb)						
2. Unleavened Bread מצות Days 1–7		2	1	7	0.6	0.2	0.7	1
3. (Waving of Sheaf) ביום הניפכם את העמר		–	–	(1)[1]	–	0.2	–	–
4. Weeks[2] שבעות		2	1	7	0.6	0.2	0.7	1
5. Trumpets יום תרעות		1	1	7	0.3	0.2	0.7	1
6. Day of Atonement יום הכפרים		1	1	7	0.3	0.2	0.7	1 1[3]
7. Booths סכות	Day 1	13	2	14	3.9	0.4	1.4	1
	Day 2	12	2	14	3.6	0.4	1.4	1
	Day 3	11	2	14	3.3	0.4	1.4	1
	Day 4	10	2	14	3.0	0.4	1.4	1
	Day 5	9	2	14	2.7	0.4	1.4	1
	Day 6	8	2	14	2.4	0.4	1.4	1
	Day 7	7	2	14	2.1	0.4	1.4	1
8. Solemn Assembly עצרת	Day 8	1	1	7	0.3	0.2	0.7	1
TOTALS		113	37	1093				30

1. A private rather than a public sacrifice (Lev. 23.12). One burnt offering is offered on the waving of the sheaf (cf. Lev. 2.14-15), and two lambs as peace offerings seven weeks later at the first fruits proper (cf. Lev. 2.11-12).

2. According to Lev. 23.18 the offering is one bull and two rams.

3. חטאת הכפרים (Num. 29.11).

Appendix 5

THE CALENDAR AND THE FESTIVALS

Month		Season	Date	Festival	
I. Abib Exod. 23.15; 34.18; Deut. 16.1	אביב (PE)	March–April latter rains barley and flax harvests	I.14	1. Passover Exod. 34.25; Lev. 23.5; Num. 28.16	פסח
Nisan Neh. 2.1; Est .3.7	ניסן (E)	Spring vernal equinox	I.15–21	2. Unleavened Bread Exod. 23.15; 34.18; Lev. 23.6	חג המצות
				3. Waving of the sheaf Lev. 23.9-14	(עמר)
II. Ziv 1 Kgs. 6.1, 37	זו (PE)	April–May dry season begins	II.14	Second Passover Num. 9.6-13	
Iyyar m. Roš Haš. 1.3	איר (E)				
III. Sivan Est. 8.9	סיון (E)	May–June	III.x	4. Weeks Exod. 34.22; Deut. 16.10 or Harvest Exod. 23.16 or First Fruits Lev. 23.17; Num. 28.26	חג השבעות חג הקציר יום הבכרים
IV. Tammuz Ezek. 8.14; m. Taan. 4.5	תמז (E)	June–July			
V. Ab m. Pes. 4.5	אב (E)	July–August grape harvest			
VI. Elul Neh. 6.15	אלול (E)	August– September dates aummer figs			

Month		Season	Date	Festival
VII. Ethanim 1 Kgs. 8.2	אתנים (PE)	September– October early rains	VII.1	5. Trumpets יום תרועה Lev. 23.24; Num. 29.1; cf. 10.10
Tishri *m. Šeq.* 3.1	תשרי (E)	wheat harvest Autumn equinox		or New Year ראש השנה Ezek 40.1
			VII. 10	6. Day of יום הכפרים Atonement Lev. 23.27; 25.9-10
			VII. 15–22	7. Booths חג הסכות Lev. 23.34; Deut. 16.13; 31.10
VIII. Bul I Kgs 6.38	בול (PE)	October– November Ploughing		
Marcheshvan *m. Taan.* 1.3	מרחשון (E)	Winter figs		
IX . Chislev Zech. 7.1; Neh. 1.1	כסלו (E)	November– December Sowing		
X. Tebeth Est. 2.16	תבת (E)	December– January Rains/snow		
XI. Sebat Zech. 1.7	שבת (E)	January– February Almond Blossom		
XII. Adar Est. 3.7, 13; 8.12; 9.1	אדר (E)	February– March Citrus fruit		
XIII. *m. Meg.* 1.4	אדר שני (E)			(Second Adar is an intercalary month)

Key: E = Exilic name
      PE = Pre-Exilic name

BIBLIOGRAPHY

Aartun, K.

1976   'Eine weitere Parallele aus Ugarit zur kultischen Praxis in Israels Religion', *Bibliotheca Orientalis* 33: 285-89.

1980   'Studien zum Gesetz über den grossen Versöhnungtag Lv 16 mit Varianten: Ein ritualgeschichtlicher Beitrag', *ST* 34: 73-109.

Abrams, M.H.

1953   *The Mirror and the Lamp: Romantic Theory and the Critical Tradition* (Oxford: Oxford University Press).

Ackerman, J.S.

1987   'Numbers', in *The Literary Guide to the Bible* (ed. R. Alter and F. Kermode; London: Collins) 78-91.

Ackroyd, P.

1968   *Exile and Restoration* (London: SCM Press).

Ahuis, F.

1983   *Autorität im Umbruch: Ein formgeschichtlicher Beitrag zur Klärung der literarischen Schichtung und der zeitgeschichtlichen Bezüge von Num 16 und 17. Mit einem Ausblick auf die Diskussion um die Ämte in der Kirche* (Calwer theologische Monographien, 13; Stuttgart: Calwer Verlag).

Allen, D.

1978   *Structure and Creativity in Religion: Hermeneutics in Mircea Eliade's Phenomenology and New Directions* (Religion and Reason, 14; The Hague: Mouton).

Alliband, T.

1980   Review of *History of Religious Ideas*, vol. 1, by M. Eliade, *Reviews in Anthropology* 7: 249-54.

Alter, R.

1979   'A New Theory of Kashrut', *Commentary* 68.6: 46-52.

1981   *The Art of Biblical Narrative* (New York: Basic Books).

Amorim, N.D.

1986   *Desecration and Defilement in the Old Testament* (PhD dissertation, Andrews University).

Anderson, B.W.

1988   *The Living World of the Old Testament* (Harlow, Essex: Longman, 4th edn; also published as *Understanding the Old Testament* [Englewood Cliffs, NJ: Prentice–Hall 1986]).

Anderson, G.A.

1987   *Sacrifices and Offerings in Ancient Israel: Studies in their Social and Political Importance* (HSM, 41; Atlanta: Scholars Press).

Andreasen, N.-E.A.
1972   *The Old Testament Sabbath* (SBLDS, 7; Missoula, MT: Scholars Press).
1974   'Recent Studies of the Old Testament Sabbath', *ZAW* 86: 453-69.
1978   *Rest and Redemption* (Andrews University Studies in Religion, 11; Berrien Springs, MI: Andrews University Press).
Ashby, G.
1988   *Sacrifice: Its Nature and Purpose* (London: SCM Press).
Auerbach, E.
1958   'Neujahrs- und Versöhnungfest in den biblischen Quellen', *VT* 8: 337-43.
Auld, A.G.
1980   *Joshua, Moses and the Land: Tetrateuch–Pentateuch–Hexateuch in a Generation since 1938* (Edinburgh: T. & T. Clark).
Baal, J. van
1976   'Offering, Sacrifice and Gift', *Numen* 23: 161-78.
Bacchiocchi, S.
1980   *Divine Rest for Human Restlessness: A Theological Study of the Good News of the Sabbath for Today* (Rome: Pontifical Gregorian University Press).
Bähr, K.C.W.
1837–91   *Symbolik des mosaischen Cultus* (2 vols.; vol. 2 rev. 1874; Heidelberg: Mohr).
Baentsch, B.
1903   *Exodus, Leviticus, Numeri* (HKAT; Göttingen: Vandenhoeck & Ruprecht).
Bailey, J.W.
1951   'The Usage in the Post-Restoration Period of Terms Descriptive of the Priest and High Priest', *JBL* 70: 217-25.
Baker, D.W.
1987   'Leviticus 1–7 and the Punic Tariffs: A Form Critical Comparison', *ZAW* 99: 188-98.
Barnouin, M.
1969   'Remarques sur les tableaux numériques du livre des Nombres', *RB* 76: 351-64.
1977   'Les recensements du livre des Nombres et l'astronome babylonienne', *VT* 27: 280-303.
Barr, J.
1961   *The Semantics of Biblical Language* (Oxford: Oxford University Press).
1972   'Semantics and Biblical Theology—A Contribution to the Discussion', in *Congress Volume, Uppsala 1971* (VTSup, 22; Leiden: Brill) 11-19.
1973   *The Bible in the Modern World* (London: SCM Press).
Barton, J.
1979   'Natural Law and Poetic Justice in the OT', *JTS* NS 30: 1-14.
1983   'Old Testament Theology', in *Beginning Old Testament Study* (ed. J.W. Rogerson; London: SPCK) 90-112.
1984a   *Reading the Old Testament: Method in Biblical Study* (London: Darton, Longman & Todd).
1984b   'Clarifying Biblical Criticism', *JSOT* 29: 19-35.

1986   *Oracles of God: Perceptions of Ancient Prophecy in Israel after the Exile* (London: Darton, Longman & Todd).

Baudissin, W. von
1878   *Studien zur semitischen Religionsgeschichte*, II (Leipzig: Grunow).

Baumgarten, J.M.
1958   'The Beginning of the Day in the Calendar of Jubilees', *JBL* 77: 355-60.

Beauchamp, P.
1969   *Création et séparation: Etude exégétique du chapitre premier de la Genèse* (Paris: Desclée de Brouwer).

Becker, J.
1983   Review of Hurvitz (1982), *Bib* 64: 583-86.

Beckwith, R.T.
1971   'The Day, its Divisions and its Limits in Biblical Thought', *EvQ* 43: 218-27.

Beer, G.
1939   *Exodus* (HAT; Tübingen: Mohr).

Beidelman, T.O.
1974   *Robertson Smith and the Sociological Study of Religion* (Chicago: University of Chicago Press).

Benzinger, I.
1927   *Hebräische Archäologie* (Leipzig: Pfeiffer, 3rd edn).

Berger, P.
1967   *The Sacred Canopy: Elements of a Sociological Theory of Religion* (Garden City, NY: Doubleday).

1977   *Facing up to Modernity* (New York: Basic Books).

Bertholet, A.
1901   *Leviticus* (KHAT; Tübingen: Mohr).
1926   *Das Dynamistiche im Alten Testament* (Tübingen: Mohr [Paul Siebeck]).
1948   'Religiongeschichtliche Ambivalenzerscheinungen', *TZ* 4: 1-16.

Bianchi, U.
1975   *The History of Religions* (Leiden: Brill).

Black, M.
1962   *Models and Metaphors* (Ithaca, NY: Cornell University Press).

Blenkinsopp, J.
1976   'The Structure of P', *CBQ* 38: 275-92.

Bloch, A.P.
1978   *The Biblical and Historical Background of the Jewish Holy Days* (New York: Ktav).

Blome, F.
1934   *Die Opfermaterie in Babylonien und Israel* (Rome: Pontifical Biblical Institute).

Blum, E.
1990   *Studien zur Komposition des Pentateuch* (BZAW, 189; Berlin: de Gruyter).

Blythin, J.
1970   'Magic and Methodology', *Numen* 17: 45-59.

Borchert, R.
    1956   *Stil und Aufbau der priesterlichen Erzählung* (Diss. Theol., University of
                Heidelberg).
Botterweck, G.J.
    1974   'ḥazir', *ThWAT*, II, 835-46.
Bourdillon, M.F.C.
    1980   'Introduction', in *Sacrifice* (ed. M.F.C. Bourdillon and M. Fortes; New
                York: Academic Press) 1-27.
Boyer, P.
    1986   'The "Empty" Concepts of Traditional Thinking: A Semantic and Pragmatic
                Description', *Man* NS 21: 50-64.
Bratsiotis, N.P.
    1973   'bāśār', *ThWAT*, I, 850-67.
Brett, M.G.
    1991   'Motives and Intentions in Genesis 1', *JTS* NS 42: 1-16.
Brichto, C.B.
    1976   'On Slaughter and Sacrifice, Blood and Atonement', *HUCA* 47: 19-55.
Briend, J.
    1984   'Sabbat', *DBSup*, X, 1132-70.
Brongers, H.A.
    1966   'Die Zehnzahl in der Bibel und in ihren Umwelt', in *Studia Biblica et
                Semitica: Theodoro Christiano Vriezen qui munere Professoris Theologiae
                per XXV annos functus est, ab amicis, collegis, discipulis dedicata* (ed.
                W.C. van Unnik and A.S. van der Woude; Wageningen, Netherlands)
                30-45.
    1977   'Fasting in Israel in Biblical and Post-Biblical Times', *OTS* 20: 1-21.
Brown, P.
    1971   'The Rise and Function of the Holy Man in Late Antiquity', *Journal of
                Roman Studies* 61: 80-101.
Brueggemann, W.
    1976a   'The Kerygma of the Priestly Writer', in *The Vitality of Old Testament
                Traditions* (ed. W. Brueggemann and H.W. Wolff; Atlanta: John Knox)
                101-13, 143-51 (originally *ZAW* 84 [1972] 397-413).
    1976b   'Presence of God, Cultic', *IDBSup*, 680-83.
    1980   'A Convergence in Recent Old Testament Theologies', *JSOT* 18: 2-18.
    1982   *The Creative Word: Canon as a Model for Biblical Education* (Philadelphia:
                Fortress Press).
    1984   *The Message of the Psalms* (Augsburg Old Testament Studies;
                Minneapolis: Augsburg).
Buck, A. de
    1951   'La fleur au front du Grand-Prêtre', *OTS* 9: 18-29.
Budd, P.J.
    1984   *Numbers* (WBC; Waco, TX: Word).
    1989   'Holiness and Cult', in *The World of Ancient Israel* (ed. R.E. Clements;
                Cambridge: Cambridge University Press) 275-98.
Bulmer, R.
    1967   'Why is the Cassowary not a Bird? A Problem of Zoological Taxonomy
                among the Karan of the New Guinea Highlands', *Man* NS 2: 5-25 (repr. in

Rules and Meanings [ed. M. Douglas; Harmondsworth: Penguin Books, 1973] 167-93).

Bunzel, U.
1914   *Der Begriff der Heiligkeit im Alten Testament: Eine ideologische Untersuchung* (Lauban: Max Baumeister).

Burton, J.W.
1974   'Some Nuer Notions of Purity and Danger', *Anthropos* 69: 517-36.

Caird, G.B.
1980   *The Language and Imagery of the Bible* (Philadelphia: Westminster Press).

Campbell, A.F.
1990   *The Study Companion to Old Testament Literature: An Approach to the Writings of Pre-Exilic and Exilic Israel* (Wilmington, DE: Michael Glazier).

Cansdale, G.
1970   *Animals in Bible Lands* (Exeter: Paternoster Press).

Carmichael, C.M.
1976   'On Separating Life and Death: An Explanation of Some Biblical Laws', *HTR* 69: 1-7.
1982   'Forbidden Mixtures', *VT* 32: 394-415.

Carpenter, J.E., and G. Harford
1902   *The Composition of the Hexateuch: An Introduction with Select Lists of Words and Phrases by J.E. Carpenter and an Appendix on Laws and Institutions by G. Harford* (London: Longmans, Green & Co.).

Carroll, M.P.
1978   'One More Time: Leviticus Revisited', *AES* 19: 339-46 (repr. in *Anthropological Approaches to the Old Testament* [ed. B. Lang; London: SPCK, 1985] 117-26).

Cassuto, U.
1961   *The Documentary Hypothesis and the Composition of the Pentateuch: Eight Lectures* (Jerusalem: Magnes Press).
1967   *A Commentary on the Book of Exodus* (trans. I. Abrahams; Jerusalem: Magnes).

Cazelles, H.
1966   'Pentateuque', *DBSup*, VII, 708-858.
1975   'Pureté et impureté', *DBSup*, IX, 491-508.
1985   'Sacré', *DBSup*, X, 1342-46, 1393-1432.
1986   'mōšeh', *ThWAT*, V, 28-46.

Childs, B.S.
1962a   *Memory and Tradition in Israel* (SBT, 37; London: SCM Press).
1962b   'Orientation', *IDB*, III, 609-10.
1974   *Exodus* (OTL; London: SCM Press).
1979   *Introduction to the Old Testament as Scripture* (London: SCM Press).
1985   *Old Testament Theology in a Canonical Context* (London: SCM Press).

Cholewinski, A.
1976   *Heiligkeitsgesetz und Deuteronomium: Eine vergleichende Studie* (AnBib, 66; Rome: Biblical Institute Press).

Clamer, A.
1940   *Lévitique–Nombres–Deutéronome* (La sainte bible; Paris: Gabalda).
1956   *L'Exode* (La sainte bible; Paris: Gabalda).

Clements, R.E.
    1965   *God and Temple* (Oxford: Oxford University Press).
    1976   *A Century of Old Testament Study* (Guildford: Lutterworth).
    1977   'Patterns in the Prophetic Canon', in *Canon and Authority: Essays in Old Testament Religion and Theology* (ed. G.W. Coats and B.O. Long; Philadelphia: Fortress Press) 42-55.
Clines, D.J.A.
    1974   'The Evidence for an Autumnal New Year in Pre-Exilic Israel Reconsidered', *JBL* 93: 22-40.
    1978   *The Theme of the Pentateuch* (JSOTSup, 10; Sheffield: JSOT Press).
    1990   *What Does Eve Do to Help? And Other Readerly Questions to the Old Testament* (JSOTSup, 94; Sheffield: JSOT Press).
Cody, A.
    1969   *A History of Old Testament Priesthood* (AnBib, 35; Rome: Biblical Institute Press).
Cohen, C.
    1969   'Was the P Document Secret?', *JANESCU* 1: 39-44.
Collins, J.J.
    1977   'The Meaning of Sacrifice: A Contrast of Methods', *BR* 22: 19-34.
Comstock, W.R.
    1981   'A Behavioural Approach to the Sacred: Category Formation in Religious Studies', *JAAR* 49: 625-43.
Costecalde, C.-B.
    1985   'Sacré', *DBSup*, X, 1346-93.
Cross, F.M.
    1947   'The Tabernacle: A Study from an Archaeological and Historical Approach', *BA* 10: 45-68.
    1973   *Canaanite Myth and Hebrew Epic* (Cambridge, MA: Harvard University Press).
Culley, R.C.
    1981   'Anthropology and Old Testament Studies: An Introductory Comment', *Semeia* 21: 1-5.
    1985   'Exploring New Directions', in *The Hebrew Bible and its Modern Interpreters* (ed. D.A. Knight and G.M. Tucker; Chico, CA: Scholars Press) 167-200.
Damrosch, D.
    1987   'Leviticus', in *The Literary Guide to the Bible* (ed. R. Alter and F. Kermode; London: Collins) 66-77.
Danby, H.
    1933   *The Mishnah: Translated from the Hebrew with Introduction and Brief Explanatory Notes* (Oxford: Oxford University Press).
Davies, D.
    1977   'An Interpretation of Sacrifice in Leviticus', *ZAW* 89: 387-99 (repr. in *Anthropological Approaches to the Old Testament* [ed. B. Lang; London: SPCK, 1985] 151-62).
Davies, G.I.
    1983a   'The Wilderness Itineraries and the Composition of the Pentateuch', *VT* 33: 1-13.

1983b   Review of Friedman (1981), *JTS* NS 34: 222-26.
1987   Review of Hurvitz (1982), *VT* 37: 117-18.
Davies, P.R., and D.M. Gunn
1984   'Pentateuchal Patterns: An Examination of C.J. Labuschagne's Theory', *VT* 34: 399-406.
De Vries, S.J.
1961   'Calendar', *IDB*, I, 483-88.
1987   'Tradition History of the Pentateuch', *SBLSP* (Atlanta: Scholars Press) 459-502.
Dillmann, A.
1880   *Exodus und Leviticus erklärt* (KHAT; Leipzig: Hirzel, 2nd edn; incorporates parts of Knobel's commentary of 1857 [which are distinguished by inverted commas]).
1886   *Numeri, Deuteronomium, und Josua* (Leipzig: Hirzel).
1892   *Genesis* (Kurzgefasstes exegetisches Handbuch zum Alten Testament; Leipzig: Hirzel, 6th edn).
Döller, J.
1917   *Die Reinheits- und Speisegesetze des Altes Testaments* (ATAbh, 7.2-3; Münster: Aschendorff).
Douglas, M.
1966   *Purity and Danger* (London: Routledge & Kegan Paul).
1970   *Natural Symbols: Explorations in Cosmology* (New York: Barrie & Rockcliffe; cited from Harmondsworth: Penguin Books, 1973).
1973   'Critique and Commentary', in *The Idea of Purity in Ancient Judaism: The Haskell Lectures, 1972–1973*, by J. Neusner (SJLA, 1; Leiden: Brill) 137-42.
1975   *Implicit Meanings* (London: Routledge & Kegan Paul).
1978a   *Cultural Bias* (London: Royal Anthropological Institute).
1978b   'Introduction', in J.G. Frazer, *The Illustrated Golden Bough* (abridged and illustrated by S. MacCormack; London: Macmillan).
Dressler, H.H.P.
1982   'The Sabbath in the Old Testament', in *From Sabbath to Lord's Day: A Biblical, Historical and Theological Investigation* (ed. D.A. Carson; Grand Rapids: Eerdmans) 21-42.
Driver, G.R.
1955   'Birds in the Old Testament', *PEQ* 87: 5-20, 129-40.
Driver, S.R.
1902   *A Critical and Exegetical Commentary on Deuteronomy* (ICC; Edinburgh: T. & T. Clark, 3rd edn).
1911   *The Book of Exodus* (CBSC; Cambridge: Cambridge University Press).
1913   *An Introduction to the Literature of the Old Testament* (Edinburgh: T. & T. Clark, 9th edn).
Dumont, L.
1980   *Homo Hierarchicus: The Caste System and its Implications* (trans. B. Gulati; Chicago: University of Chicago Press).
Dumont, L., and D. Pocock
1959   'Pure and Impure', *Contributions to Indian Sociology* 3: 9-39.

Durham, J.I.
    1963   *The Senses Touch, Taste, and Smell in Old Testament Religion* (DPhil dissertation, University of Oxford).
    1987   *Exodus* (WBC; Waco, TX: Word).
Durkheim, E., and M. Mauss
    1963   *Primitive Classification* (trans. R. Needham; London: University of Chicago Press).
Dussaud, R.
    1921   *Les origines cananéennes du sacrifice Israélite* (Paris: E. Leroux).
Edwards, A.
    1970   'The Earthbound Pangolin', *New Blackfriars* 51: 424-32.
Ehrlich, E.L.
    1959   *Kultsymbolik im Alten Testament und in nachbiblischen Judentum* (Symbolik der Religionen, 3; Stuttgart: Hiersemann).
Eichrodt, W.
    1961   *Theology of the Old Testament*, I (trans. J. Baker; London: SCM Press).
    1964   *Theology of the Old Testament*, II (trans. J. Baker; London: SCM Press).
    1970   *Ezekiel: A Commentary* (OTL; London: SCM Press).
Eilberg-Schwartz, H.
    1990   *The Savage in Judaism: An Anthropology of Israelite Religion and Ancient Judaism* (Bloomington, IN: Indiana University Press).
Eissfeldt, O.
    1965   *The Old Testament: An Introduction* (trans. P.R. Ackroyd; Oxford: Basil Blackwell).
Eliade, M.
    1961   *The Sacred and the Profane: The Nature of Religion* (trans. W.R. Trask; New York: Harcourt Brace Jovanovich).
Ellen, R.F.
    1979   'Introductory Essay', in *Classifications in their Social Context* (ed. R.F. Ellen and D. Reason; London: Academic Press) 1-32.
Elliger, K.
    1952   'Sinn und Ursprung der priesterlichen Geschichtserzählung', *ZTK* 49: 121-42.
    1966   *Leviticus* (HAT, 4; Tübingen: Mohr [Paul Siebeck]).
Emerton, J.A.
    1967   'The Meaning of קדש אישי in Lamentations 4 1', *ZAW* 79: 233-6.
    1976   'An Examination of a Recent Structuralist Interpretation of Genesis XXXVIII', *VT* 26: 79-98.
Epsztein, L.
    1986   *Social Justice in the Ancient Near East and the People of the Bible* (trans. J. Bowden; London: SCM Press).
Evans-Pritchard, E.E.
    1956   *Nuer Religion* (Oxford: Oxford University Press).
    1965   *Theories of Primitive Religion* (Oxford: Oxford University Press).
Evens, T.M.S.
    1982   'On the Social Anthropology of Religion', *JR* 62: 376-91.

Feldman, E.
    1977   *Biblical and Post-Biblical Defilement and Mourning: Law as Theology*
                (New York: Yeshiva University Press).
Feleppa, R.
    1986   'Emics, Etics, and Social Objectivity', *CurAnth* 27: 243-55.
Fernandez, J.W.
    1977   'The Performance of Ritual Metaphors', in *The Social Use of Metaphor:*
                Essays on the Anthropology of Rhetoric (ed. J.D. Sapir and J.C. Crocker;
                Philadelphia: University of Philadelphia Press) 100-31.
Ferro-Luzzi, G.E.
    1974   'Women's Pollution Periods in Tamilnad (India)', *Anthropos* 69: 113-61.
Finegan, J.
    1964   *Handbook of Biblical Chronology: Principles of Time Reckoning in the*
                Ancient World and Problems of Chronology in the Bible (London: Oxford
                University Press).
Finnegan, R., and R. Horton (eds.)
    1973   *Modes of Thought: Essays on Thinking in Western and Non-Western*
                Societies (London: Faber & Faber).
Finn, A.H.
    1914   'The Tabernacle Chapters', *JTS* 16: 449-82.
Firmage, E.
    1990   'The Biblical Dietary Laws and the Concept of Holiness', in *Studies in the*
                Pentateuch (ed. J.A. Emerton; VTSup, 41; Leiden: Brill) 177-208.
Firth, R.
    1963   'Offerings and Sacrifice: Problems of Organization', *JRAI* 93: 12-24.
    1973   *Symbols: Public and Private* (SMRit; Ithaca, NY: Cornell University
                Press).
Fishbane, M.
    1971   *Studies in Biblical Magic: Origins, Uses and Transformations of*
                Terminology and Literary Form (PhD dissertation, Brandeis University).
    1975   'The Sacred Center: The Symbolic Structure of the Bible', in *Texts and*
                Responses: Studies Presented to Nahum N. Glatzer on the Occasion of his
                Seventieth Birthday by his Students (ed. M.A. Fishbane and P.R. Flohr;
                Leiden: Brill).
Fohrer, G.
    1970   *Introduction to the Old Testament* (trans. D. Green; London: SPCK).
Fortes, M.
    1980   'Preface', in *Sacrifice* (ed. M.F.C. Bourdillon and M. Fortes; New York:
                Academic Press) v-xv.
    1983   *Rules and the Emergence of Society* (London: Royal Anthropological
                Institute).
Fowler, M.D.
    1984   'Excavated Incense Burners', *BA* 47: 183-86.
Fox, M.V.
    1974   'The Sign of the Covenant: Circumcision in the Light of the Priestly '*ôt*
                Etiologies', *RB* 81: 557-96.

Fraser, R.
 1990 *The Making of 'The Golden Bough': The Origins and Growth of an Argument* (London: Macmillan).

Frazer, J.G.
 1903 'Taboo', *Encyclopaedia Brittanica* (9th edn), XXIII, 15-18.
 1922 *The Golden Bough* (London: Macmillan, abridged edn).

Freedman, D.N., and M. O'Connor
 1984 '*kerûb*', *ThWAT*, IV, 322-34.

Fretheim, T.E.
 1968 'The Priestly Document: Anti-Temple?', *VT* 18: 313-29.
 1977 'Theology of the Major Traditions in Genesis–Numbers', *RevExp* 74: 301-20.

Fridrichsen, A.
 1916 *Hagios-Qadosh: Ein Beitrag zu den Voruntersuchungen zur christlichen Begriffsgeschichte* (Videnskapsselskapets Skrifter, 3; Kristiana: Jacob Dybwad).

Friedman, R.E.
 1980 'The Tabernacle in the Temple', *BA* 43: 241-8
 1981 *The Exile and Biblical Narrative: The Formation of the Deuteronomistic and Priestly Works* (HSM, 22; Chico, CA: Scholars Press).

Frymer-Kensky, T.
 1983 'Pollution, Purification, and Purgation in Biblical Israel', in *The Word of the Lord Shall Go Forth: Essays in Honor of David Noel Freedman in Celebration of his Sixtieth Birthday* (ed. C.L. Meyers and M. O'Connor; Winona Lake, IN: ASOR/Eisenbrauns) 399-414.
 1987 'Biblical Cosmology', in *Backgrounds for the Bible* (ed. M.P. O'Connor and D.N. Freedman; Winona Lake, IN: Eisenbrauns) 231-40.

Fuchs-Kreimer, N.
 1981 'Christian Old Testament Theology: A Time for New Beginnings', *JES* 18: 76-92.

Füglister, N.
 1977 'Sühne durch Blut—Zur Bedeutung von Leviticus 17, 11', in *Studien zum Pentateuch: Walter Kornfeld zum 60. Geburtstag* (ed. G. Braulik; Wien: Herder) 143-64.

Gabriel, J.
 1933 *Untersuchungen über das alttestamentliche Hohepriestertum* (Theologische Studien der Östereichischen Leo-Gesellschaft, 33; Wien: Mayer).

Gammie, J.G.
 1989 *Holiness in Israel* (OBT; Minneapolis, MN: Fortress Press).

Gaster, T.H.
 1962 'Sacrifices and Offerings', *IDB*, IV, 147-59.

Gaster, T.H. (ed.)
 1959 *The New Golden Bough: A New Abridgment of the Classic Work* (ed. with notes and forward; New York: Criterion Books).

Geertz, C.
 1973 *The Interpretation of Cultures: Selected Essays by Clifford Geertz* (New York: Basic Books).

Gennep, A. van
    1960   *The Rites of Passage* (trans. M.B. Vizedom and G.L. Caffee; Chicago: University of Chicago Press).

Gese, H.
    1977   *Zur biblischen Theologie: Alttestamentliche Vorträge* (BEvT, 78; Munich: Kaiser Verlag; English edn *Essays on Biblical Theology* [trans. K. Crim; Minneapolis: Fortress Press, 1981]).

Gilbert, M.
    1978   'Le monde biblique: Le sacré dans l'Ancien Testament', in J. Ries, H. Sauren, G. Kestemont, R. Lebrun and M. Gilbert, *L'expression du sacré dans les grandes religions*. I. *Proche-Orient ancien et traditions bibliques* (Louvain-la-Neuve: Centre d'Histoire des Religions) 205-89.

Gispen, W.H.
    1948   'The Distinction between Clean and Unclean (Lev. 11–15)', *OTS* 5: 190-96.

Gnuse, R.
    1985   'Jubilee Legislation in Leviticus: Israel's Vision of Social Reform', *BTB* 15: 43-48.

Goldingay, J.
    1984   'Diversity and Unity in Old Testament Theology', *VT* 34: 156-68.
    1987   *Theological Diversity and the Authority of the Old Testament* (Grand Rapids: Eerdmans).

Gombrich, E.H.
    1977   *Art and Illusion: A Study in the Psychology of Pictorial Representation* (London: Phaidon, 5th edn).

Goode, W.J.
    1949   'Magic and Religion: A Continuum', *Ethnos* 14: 172-82.

Gooding, D.W.
    1959   *The Account of the Tabernacle* (Texts and Studies, 6; Cambridge: Cambridge University Press).

Goody, J.
    1977   *The Domestication of the Savage Mind* (Cambridge: Cambridge University Press).

Gordon, B.L.
    1971   'Sacred Directions, Orientation, and the Top of the Map', *HR* 10: 211-27.

Gorman, F.H.
    1990   *The Ideology of Ritual: Space, Time and Status in the Priestly Theology* (JSOTSup, 91; Sheffield: JSOT Press).

Goshen-Gottstein, M.
    1975   'Christianity, Judaism and Modern Bible Study', in *Congress Volume, Edinburgh 1974* (VTSup, 28; Leiden: Brill) 69-88.

Gottwald, N.K.
    1970   'W. Eichrodt, Theology of the Old Testament', in *Contemporary Old Testament Theologians* (ed. R.B. Laurin; London: Marshall) 3-62.
    1979   *The Tribes of Yahweh: A Sociology of the Religion of Liberated Israel 1250–1050 BCE* (New York: Orbis Books).

Goudoever, J. van
    1959   *Biblical Calendars* (Leiden: Brill).

Gradwohl, R.
    1963   'Das "Fremde Feuer" von Nadab und Abihu', *ZAW* 75: 288-96.
Graham, M.P.
    1990   *The Utilization of 1 and 2 Chronicles in the Reconstruction of Israelite History in the Nineteenth Century* (SBLDS, 116; Atlanta: John Knox).
Gray, G.B.
    1902   'The Lists of the Twelve Tribes', *Expositor* 6.5: 225-40.
    1903   *A Critical and Exegetical Commentary on Numbers* (ICC; Edinburgh: T. & T. Clark).
    1925   *Sacrifice in the Old Testament: Its Theory and Practice* (Oxford: Clarendon Press).
Greenberg, M.
    1959   'The Biblical Conception of Asylum', *JBL* 78: 125-32.
    1971   'Sabbath', *EncJud*, XIV, 557-62.
Greenstein, E.L.
    1989   'Deconstruction and Biblical Narrative', *Prooftexts* 9: 43-71.
Grimes, R.L.
    1982   *Beginnings in Ritual Studies* (Lanham, MD: University Press of America).
    1985   *Research in Ritual Studies: A Programmatic Essay and Bibliography* (London: Scarecrow).
Groves, J.W.
    1987   *Actualization and Interpretation in the Old Testament* (SBLDS, 86; Atlanta: John Knox).
Gruber, M.I.
    1987   'Women in the Cult according to the Priestly Code', in *Judaic Perspectives on Ancient Israel* (ed. J. Neusner, B.A. Levine and E.S. Frerichs; Philadelphia: Fortress Press) 35-48.
Gunneweg, A.H.G.
    1965   *Leviten und Priester: Hauptlinien der Traditionsbildung und Geschichte des israelitisch-jüdischen Kultpersonals* (FRLANT, 89; Göttingen: Vandenhoeck & Ruprecht).
Gurney, O.R.
    1977   *Some Aspects of Hittite Religion* (Oxford: Oxford University Press).
Hage, P., and F. Harary
    1981   'Pollution Beliefs in Highland New Guinea', *Man* NS 16: 367-75.
Hahn, H.F.
    1966   *The Old Testament in Modern Research* (Philadelphia: Fortress Press).
Hall, E.T.
    1966   *The Hidden Dimension* (Garden City, NY: Doubleday).
Hallo, W.W.
    1977   'New Moons and Sabbaths: A Case-Study in the Contrastive Approach', *HUCA* 48: 1-18.
    1980   'Biblical History in its Near Eastern Setting: The Contextual Approach', in *Scripture in Context: Essays on the Comparative Method* (ed. C.D. Evans, W.W. Hallo and J.B. White; Pittsburgh: Pickwick Press) 1-26.
Hallpike, C.R.
    1979   *The Foundations of Primitive Thought* (Oxford: Clarendon Press).

Halverson, J.
    1976   'Animal Categories and Terms of Abuse', *Man* NS 11: 505-16.
Hanson, P.D.
    1979   *The Dawn of Apocalyptic: The Historical and Sociological Roots of Jewish Apocalyptic Eschatology* (Philadelphia: Fortress Press).
Har-El, M.
    1981   'Orientation in Biblical Lands', *BA* 44: 19-20.
    1982   'Geographical Orientation in the Lands of the Bible' (Hebrew), in *Proceedings of the Eighth World Congress of Jewish Studies* (Jerusalem: Magnes) 11-16.
Haran, M.
    1962   '*mattānôt hakkôhᵃnîm*', *EM*, IV, 39-45.
    1969   'The Divine Presence in the Israelite Cult and the Cultic Institutions', *Bib* 50: 251-67.
    1970   *Biblical Research in Hebrew: A Discussion of its Character and Trends* (Jerusalem: Magnes).
    1971   'Priests', *EncJud*, XIII, 1069-86.
    1976   '*mimmᵒ ḥᵉrat haššabbāt*', *EM*, VII, 517-21.
    1978   *Temples and Temple-Service in Ancient Israel* (Oxford: Clarendon Press).
    1979   'The Law Code of Ezekiel XL–XLVIII and its Relation to the Priestly School', *HUCA* 50: 45-71.
    1981   'Behind the Scenes of History—Determining the Date of the Priestly Source', *JBL* 100: 321-33.
    1983a   'The Character of the Priestly Source: Utopian and Exclusive Features', in *Proceedings of the Eighth World Congress of Jewish Studies* (Jerusalem: Magnes) 131-38.
    1983b   'Priesthood, Temple, Divine Service: Some Observations on Institutions and Practices of Worship', *HAR* 7: 121-35.
Harris, M.
    1977   *Cows, Pigs, Wars, and Witches* (Glasgow: Collins; orig. pub. New York: Random House, 1974).
    1985   *Good to Eat: Riddles of Food and Culture* (London: Allen & Unwin).
Harrison, R.K.
    1980   *Leviticus* (TOTC; Leicester: IVP).
Hasel, G.F.
    1982   *Old Testament Theology: Basic Issues in the Current Debate* (Grand Rapids: Eerdmans, 3rd edn).
    1985   'Major Issues in Old Testament Theology 1978–83', *JSOT* 31: 31-53.
Haulotte, R.P.E.
    1966   *Symbolique du vêtement selon la Bible* (Théologie, 65; Paris: Editions Montaigne).
Hayes, J.H., and F.C. Prussner
    1985   *Old Testament Theology: Its History and Development* (London: SCM Press).
Hayter, M.
    1987   *The New Eve in Christ: The Use and Abuse of the Bible in the Debate about Women in the Church* (London: SPCK).

Hecht, R.D.
1976   *Sacrifice: Comparative Study and Interpretation* (PhD dissertation, University of California at Los Angeles).
1982   'Studies on Sacrifice, 1970–1980', *RelSRev* 8: 253-58.
Heinemann, J.
1971   'Profile of a Midrash: The Art of Composition in Leviticus Rabba', *JAAR* 39: 141-50.
Heller, J.
1970   'Die Symbolik des Fettes im Alten Testament', *VT* 20: 106-108.
Henninger, J.
1975   'Pureté et impureté', *DBSup*, IX, 398-430, 459-70, 473-91.
Henton Davies, G.
1962   'Tabernacle', *IDB*, IV, 498-506.
Heschel, A.J.
1951   *The Sabbath: Its Meaning for Modern Man* (New York: Farrar, Straus & Giroux).
1955   *God in Search of Man: A Philosophy of Judaism* (New York: Farrar, Straus & Giroux).
Heusch, L. de
1985   *Sacrifice in Africa: A Structural Approach* (Bloomington, IN: Indiana University Press).
Hillers, D.R.
1985   'Analyzing the Abominable: Our Understanding of Canaanite Religion', *JQR* 75: 253-69.
Hönig, H.W.
1957   *Die Bekleidung des Hebräers: Eine biblisch-archäologische Untersuchung* (Zürich: Brunner, Bodmer & Co.).
Hoenig, S.B.
1968   'Sabbatical Years and the Year of Jubilee', *JQR* 59: 222-36.
1979   'The Jubilees Calendar and the "Days of Assembly" ', in *Essays on the Occasion of the Seventieth Anniversary of the Dropsie University (1909–79)* (ed. A.I. Katsch and L. Nemoy; Philadelphia: The Dropsie University) 189-207.
Hoffmann, D.
1905   *Das Buch Leviticus*, I (Berlin: Poppelauer).
1906   *Das Buch Leviticus*, II (Berlin: Poppelauer).
Holzinger, H.
1898a   *Exodus* (KHAT; Leipzig: Mohr [Paul Siebeck]).
1898b   *Genesis* (KHAT; Leipzig: Mohr [Paul Siebeck]).
1903   *Numeri* (KHAT; Tübingen: Mohr [Paul Siebeck]).
1922   *Leviticus* (HSAT; Leipzig: Mohr [Paul Siebeck]).
Honigmann, J.J. (ed.)
1973   *Handbook of Social and Cultural Anthropology* (Chicago: Rand McNally).
Hooke, S.H.
1952   'The Theory and Practice of Substitution', *VT* 2: 1-17.
Horbury, W.
1983   'The Aaronic Priesthood in the Epistle to the Hebrews', *JSNT* 19: 43-71.

Houston, W.J.
  forthcoming *Purity and Monotheism: Clean and Unclean Animals in Biblical Law*
              (JSOTSup, 140; Sheffield: JSOT Press).
Houtman , C.
  1984   'Another Look at Forbidden Mixtures', *VT* 34: 226-28.
Howe, J.
  1981   'Fox Hunting as Ritual', *American Ethnologist* 8: 278-300.
Hubert, H., and M. Mauss
  1964   *Essay on Sacrifice* (trans. W.D. Halls; Chicago: Cohen & West).
Hübner, U.
  1989   'Schweine, Schweineknocken und ein Speiseverbot im Alten Israel', *VT*
              39: 225-36.
Hughes, J.
  1990   *Secrets of the Times: Myth and History in Biblical Chronology* (JSOTSup,
              66; Sheffield: JSOT Press).
Hulse, E.V.
  1975   'The Nature of Biblical "Leprosy" and the Use of Alternative Medical
              Terms in Modern Translations of the Bible', *PEQ* 107: 87-105.
Humbert, P.
  1940–41   'Die literarische Zweiheit des Priester-Codex in der Genesis', *ZAW*
              58: 30-57.
Hunn, E.
  1977   *Tzeltal Folk Zoology: The Classification of Discontinuities in Nature* (New
              York: Academic Press).
  1979   'The Abominations of Leviticus Revisited: A Commentary on Anomaly in
              Symbolic Anthropology', in *Classifications in their Social Context* (ed.
              R.F. Ellen and D. Reason; London: Academic Press) 103-16.
Hurowitz, V.
  1985   'The Priestly Account of the Building of the Tabernacle', *JAOS* 106:
              21-30.
Hurvitz, A.
  1974   'The Evidence of Language in Dating the Priestly Code: A Linguistic Study
              in Technical Idioms and Terminology', *RB* 81: 24-56.
  1982   *A Linguistic Study of the Relationship between the Priestly Source and the
              Book of Ezekiel: A New Approach to an Old Problem* (Cahiers de la Revue
              Biblique, 20; Paris: Gabalda).
  1983   'The Language of the Priestly Source in its Historical Setting—The Case
              for an Early Date', in *Proceedings of the Eighth World Congress of Jewish
              Studies* (Jerusalem: Magnes) 83-94.
Hyatt, J.P.
  1971   *Exodus* (NCB; London: Nelson).
Ikenga-Metuh, E.
  1985   'Ritual Dirt and Purification Rites among the Igbo', *Journal of Religion in
              Africa* 15: 3-24.
Isenberg, S.R., and D.E. Owen
  1977   'Bodies, Natural and Contrived: The Work of Mary Douglas', *RelSRev*
              3: 1-17.

Janowski, B.
1982   *Sühne als Heilsgeschehen: Studien zur Sühnetheologie der Priesterschrift und zur Wurzel KPR im alten Orient und im Alten Testament* (WMANT, 55; Neukirchen: Neukirchener Verlag).
Jaubert, A.
1957   'Le calendrier des Jubilés et les jours liturgiques de la semaine', *VT* 7: 35-61.
Jenni, E.
1956   *Die theologische Begründung des Sabbatgebotes im Alten Testament* (Zürich: Evangelischer Verlag).
1968   *Das Hebräische Pi'el: Syntaktisch-semasiologische Untersuchung einer Verbalform im Alten Testament* (Zürich: EVZ Verlag).
1976   ''ānān Wolke', *THAT*, II, 351-53.
Jennings, T.W.
1982   'On Ritual Knowledge', *JR* 62: 111-27.
Johnson, M.D.
1988   *The Purpose of the Biblical Chronologies with Special Reference to the Setting of the Genealogies of Jesus* (SNTSMS, 8; Cambridge: Cambridge University Press, 2nd edn).
Jones, L.B.
1981   *The Rise and Development of the Kerygmatic Approach to Pentateuchal Criticism* (diss. Southwestern Baptist Theological Seminary).
Kaufmann, Y.
1960   *The Religion of Israel* (trans. and abridged from original Hebrew by M. Greenberg; New York: Schocken Books).
Kearney, P.J.
1977   'Creation and Liturgy: The P Redaction of Exodus 25–40', *ZAW* 89: 375-87.
Kedar-Kopfstein, B.
1977a   'dām', *ThWAT*, II, 248-66.
1977b   'zāhāb', *ThWAT*, II, 537-40.
1977c   'hag', *ThWAT*, II, 730-44.
Keesing, R.M.
1984   'Rethinking Mana', *Journal of Anthropological Research* 40: 137-56.
1985   'Conventional Metaphors and Anthropological Metaphysics: The Problematic of Cultural Translation', *Journal of Anthropological Research* 41: 201-18.
Keil, C.F.
1887–88 *Manual of Biblical Archaeology* (2 vols.; Edinburgh: T. & T. Clark).
1881   *The Pentateuch*, I (trans. J. Martin; repr. Grand Rapids: Eerdmans).
1882   *The Pentateuch*, II (trans. J. Martin; repr. Grand Rapids: Eerdmans).
1880   *The Pentateuch*, III (trans. J. Martin; repr. Grand Rapids: Eerdmans).
Kellermann, D.
1973   'gûr', *ThWAT*, I, 979-91.
1987   ''olāh', *ThWAT*, VI, 105-24.
Kennedy, A.R.S.
1899   'Fringes', *HDB*, II, 68-70.
1902   'Tabernacle', *HDB*, IV, 653-8.

Kessler, R.
1986 'Silber und Gold', *BN* 31: 57-69.
Kidner, D.
1982 'Sacrifice—Metaphor and Meaning', *TB* 33: 119-36.
Kilian, R.
1963 *Literarische und formgeschichtliche Untersuchung des Heiligkeitsgesetzes* (BBB, 19; Bonn: Peter Hanstein Verlag).
1966 'Die Hoffnung auf Heimkehr in der Priesterschrift', *BibLeb* 7: 39-51.
Kingsbury, E.C.
1963 'A Seven Day Ritual in the Old Babylonian Cult at Larsa', *HUCA* 34: 1-28.
Kirk, G.S.
1981 'Some Methodological Pitfalls in the Study of Ancient Greek Sacrifices', in *Sacrifice* (1981) 41-80.
Kiuchi, N.
1987 *The Purification Offering in the Priestly Literature: Its Meaning and Function* (JSOTSup, 36; Sheffield: JSOT Press).
Klein, R.W.
1979 *Israel in Exile: A Theological Interpretation* (OBT; Philadelphia: Fortress Press).
1981 'The Message of P', in *Die Botschaft und die Boten: Festschrift für Hans Walter Wolff zum 70. Geburtstag* (ed. J. Jeremias and L. Perlitt; Neukirchen: Neukirchener Verlag) 57-66.
Knierim, R.
1967 *Die Hauptbegriffe für Sünde im Alten Testament* (Gütersloh: Gütersloher Verlaghaus, 2nd edn).
1981 'Cosmos and History in Israel's Theology', *HBT* 3: 59-123.
Knohl, I.
1987 'The Priestly Torah versus the Holiness School: Sabbath and the Festivals', *HUCA* 58: 65-117.
Koch, K.
1958 'Die Eigenart der priesterlichen Sinaigesetzgebung', *ZTK* 55: 36-51.
1959 *Die Priesterschrift: Von Exodus 25 bis Leviticus 16: Eine überlieferungsgeschichtliche und literarische Üntersuchung* (FRLANT, 71; Göttingen: Vandenhoeck & Ruprecht).
1966 'Sühne und Sündenvergebung um die Wende von der exilischen zur nachexilischen Zeit', *EvT* 26: 217-39.
1977 'ḥāṭā', *ThWAT*, II, 857-70.
1984 'môʿed', *ThWAT*, IV, 744-50.
Koch, K. (ed.)
1972 *Um das Prinzip der Vergeltung im Religion und Recht des Alten Testaments* (Wege der Forschung, 125; Darmstadt: Wissenschaftliche Buchgesellschaft).
Köhler, L.
1957 *Theology of the Old Testament* (trans. A.S. Todd; London: Lutterworth).
Kornfeld, W.
1965 'Reine und unreine Tiere im Alten Testament', *Kairos* 74: 134-47.

Kristeva, J.
    1982   'Semiotics of Biblical Abomination', in *Powers of Horror: An Essay on Abjection* (trans. L.S. Roudiez; New York: Columbia University Press) 90-112.

Kurtz, J.H.
    1863   *Sacrificial Worship of the Old Testament* (trans. J. Martin; Edinburgh: T. & T. Clark).

Kutsch, E.
    1952   'Die Wurzel *'ṣr* im Hebräischen', *VT* 2: 57-69.
    1953   *'miqrā'* ', *ZAW* 65: 247-53.
    1961   'Der Kalendar des Jubiläumsbuch und das Alte und Neue Testament', *VT* 11: 39-47.
    1985   *Die chronologischen Daten des Ezechielbuches* (Göttingen: Vandenhoeck & Ruprecht).

Labuschagne, C.J.
    1982   'The Pattern of the Divine Speech Formulas in the Pentateuch', *VT* 32: 268-96.
    1984a   'On the Structural Use of Numbers as a Composition Technique', *JNSL* 12: 87-99.
    1984b   'Pentateuchal Patterns: A Reply to P.R. Davies and D.M. Gunn', *VT* 34: 407-13.
    1985   'The Literary and Theological Function of Divine Speech in the Pentateuch', in *Congress Volume, Salamanca 1983* (ed. J.A. Emerton; VTSup, 36; Leiden: Brill) 154-73.

Lagrange, M.-J.
    1903   *Etudes sur les religions sémitiques* (Paris: Lecoffre).

Lakoff, G., and M. Johnson
    1980   *Metaphors We Live By* (Chicago: University of Chicago Press).

Lamberty, B.D.
    1986   *Natural Cycles in Ancient Israel's View of Reality* (PhD dissertation, Claremont Graduate School).

Landersdorfer, S.
    1924   *Studien zum biblischen Versöhnungstag* (Münster: Aschendorff).

Lang, B.
    1982   '*kpr*', *ThWAT*, III, 303-18.
    1983   'Old Testament and Anthropology: A Preliminary Bibliography', *BN* 20: 37-46.

Lang, B. (ed.)
    1985   *Anthropological Approaches to the Old Testament* (London: SPCK).

Langer, S.K.
    1957   *Philosophy in a New Key: A Study in the Symbolism of Reason, Rite, and Art* (London: Harvard University Press, 3rd edn).

Larsson, G.
    1983   'The Chronology of the Pentateuch: A Comparison of the MT and LXX', *JBL* 102: 401-409.
    1985   'The Documentary Hypothesis and the Chronological Structure of the Old Testament', *ZAW* 97: 310-33.

Laughlin, J.C.H.
    1976   'The "Strange Fire" of Nadab and Abihu', *JBL* 95: 559-65.
Lawson, E.T.
    1976   'Ritual as Language', *Rel* 6: 123-39.
Leach, E.R.
    1964   'Animal Categories and Verbal Abuse', in *New Directions in the Study of Language* (ed. E.H. Lenneberg; Cambridge, MA: MIT Press) 23-63 (repr. in *Reader in Comparative Religion: An Anthropological Approach* [ed. W.A. Lessa and E.Z. Vogt; New York: Harper & Row, 4th edn] 153-66).
    1970   *Genesis as Myth, and Other Essays* (London: Jonathan Cape).
    1971   'Mythical Inequalities', *New York Review of Books* 16.1: 44-45.
    1976   *Culture and Communication* (Cambridge: Cambridge University Press).
    1982   *Social Anthropology* (Glasgow: Collins).
    1983   'Anthropological Approaches to the Study of the Bible during the Twentieth Century', in *Structuralist Interpretations of Biblical Myth* (ed. E.R. Leach and D.A. Aycock; Cambridge: Cambridge University Press) 7-32.
    1985   'The Anthropology of Religion: British and French Scholars', in *Nineteenth-Century Religious Thought in the West*, III (ed. N. Smart, J. Clayton, S. Katz and P. Sherry; Cambridge: Cambridge University Press) 215-62.
Leenhardt, F.J.
    1929   *La notion de sainteté dans l'AncienTestament: Etude de la racine Q D^H S^H* (Paris: Fischbacher).
Lemaire, A.
    1973   'Le sabbat à l'époque royale israélite', *RB* 80: 161-85.
Levenson, J.D.
    1985   *Sinai and Zion: An Entry into the Jewish Bible* (New York: Winston).
    1987   'Why Jews are not Interested in Biblical Theology', in *Judaic Perspectives on Ancient Israel* (ed. J. Neusner, B.A. Levine and E.S. Frerichs; Philadelphia: Fortress Press) 281-307.
Lévi-Strauss, C.
    1966   *The Savage Mind* (London: Weidenfeld & Nicholson).
Levine, B.A.
    1963   'Ugaritic Descriptive Rituals', *Journal of Cuneiform Studies* 17: 105-11.
    1965   'The Descriptive Tabernacle Texts of the Pentateuch', *JAOS* 85: 307-18.
    1971a   'Cult', *EncJud*, V, 1155-62.
    1971b   *Prolegomenon* to reprint of G.B. Gray, *Sacrifice in the Old Testament: Its Theory and Practice* (New York: Ktav [orig. pub. 1925]) vii-xliv.
    1974   *In the Presence of the Lord* (SJLA, 5; Leiden: Brill).
    1976   'Priestly Writers', *IDBSup*, 683-87.
    1979   'Major Directions in Contemporary Biblical Research', *JJS* 30: 179-91.
    1983   'Late Language in the Priestly Sources: Some Literary and Historical Observations', in *Proceedings of the Eighth World Congress of Jewish Studies* (Jerusalem: Magnes) 69-82.
    1987   'The Language of Holiness: Perceptions of the Sacred in the Hebrew Bible', in *Backgrounds for the Bible* (ed. M.P. O'Connor and D.N. Freedman; Winona Lake, IN: Eisenbrauns) 241-55.

1989	*Leviticus* (JPS Torah Commentary; Philadelphia: Jewish Publication Society).

Levine, B.A., and W.W. Hallo
1967	'Offerings to the Temple Gates at Ur', *HUCA* 38: 17-58.

Lewis, G.
1987	'A Lesson from Leviticus: Leprosy', *Man* NS 22: 593-612.

Lipinski, E.
1970	'Urîm and Tummîm', *VT* 20: 495-96.

Loader, J.A.
1984	'The Exilic Period in Abraham Kuenen's Account of Israel's Religion', *ZAW* 96: 3-23.

Lohfink, N.
1978	'Die Priesterschrift und die Geschichte', in *Congress Volume, Göttingen 1977* (VTSup, 29; Leiden: Brill) 189-225.
1982	*Great Themes from the Old Testament* (trans. R. Walls; Edinburgh: T. & T. Clark).

Lund, N.W.
1929–30	'The Presence of Chiasmus in the Old Testament', *AJSL* 46: 104-26.

Lyons, J.
1977	*Semantics* (2 vols.; Cambridge: Cambridge University Press).

Mace, D.R.
1953	*Hebrew Marriage: A Sociological Study* (London: Epworth Press).

Macht, D.I.
1933	'A Scientific Appreciation of Leviticus 12, 1-5', *JBL* 52: 253-60.

McEvenue, S.
1970	'Word and Fulfilment: A Stylistic Feature of the Priestly Writer', *Semitics* 1: 104-10.
1971	*The Narrative Style of the Priestly Writer* (AnBib, 50; Rome: Biblical Institute Press).
1974	'The Style of a Building Instruction', *Semitics* 4: 1-9.

McEwan, G.J.P.
1983	'Distribution of Meat in Eanna', *Iraq* 45: 187-98.

McKay, J.W.
1972	'The Date of Passover and its Significance', *ZAW* 84: 435-47.

McKeating, H.
1975	'The Development of the Law on Homicide in Ancient Israel', *VT* 25: 46-68.

McKenzie, J.L.
1974	*A Theology of the Old Testament* (New York: Macmillan).

Magonet, J.
1982	'The Korah Rebellion', *JSOT* 24: 3-25.

Maier, J.
1985	*The Temple Scroll: An Introduction, Translation and Commentary* (trans. R.T. White; JSOTSup, 34; Sheffield: JSOT Press).

Malina, B.J.
1981	*The New Testament World: Insights from Cultural Anthropology* (Atlanta: John Knox).

1986   *Christian Origins and Cultural Anthropology: Practical Models for Biblical Interpretation* (Atlanta: John Knox).

Mandelbaum, K.
1982   *A History of the Mishnaic Law of Agricutlture: Kilayim* (Atlanta: John Knox).

Martin-Achard, R.
1974   '*gûr* als Fremdling weilen', *THAT*, I, 409-12.

Marx, A.
1989   'Sacrifice pour les péchés ou rite de passage? Quelques reflexions sur la fonction du *ḥaṭṭā't* ', RB 96: 27-48.

Mayes, A.D.H.
1979   *Deuteronomy* (NCB; London: Oliphants).

Médébielle, A.
1938   'Expiation dans l'Ancien Testament', *DBSup*, III, 48-112.

Meiggs, A.S.
1978   'A Papuan Perspective on Pollution', *Man* NS 13: 304-18.

Mettinger, T.N.D.
1982   *The Dethronement of Sabaoth: Studies in the Shem and Kabod Theologies* (Lund: Gleerup).

Meyer, R.
1965   'Cleanness and Uncleanness outside the NT: Part II: Judaism', *TDOT*, III, 418-23.

Meyers, C.L.
1976   *The Tabernacle Menorah: A Synthetic Study of a Symbol from the Biblical Cult* (ASORDS, 2; Missoula, MT: Scholars Press).

Milgrom, J.
1970a   *Studies in Levitical Terminology. I. The Encroacher and the Levite: The Term 'Avoda* (Berkeley: University of California).
1970b   'The Shared Custody of the Tabernacle and a Hittite Analogy', *JAOS* 90: 204-209.
1971a   'Fasting and Feast Days', *EncJud*, VI, 1189-91.
1971b   'Nazirite', *EncJud*, XII, 907-909.
1971c   '*Leviticus*', in *The Interpreter's One-Volume Commentary on the Bible* (ed. C.M. Layman; Nashville: Abingdon Press) 68-84.
1976a   *Cult and Conscience* (SJLA, 18; Leiden: Brill).
1976b   'Atonement in the OT; Atonement, Day of', *IDBSup*, 78-83.
1980   'Further Studies in the Temple Scroll', *JQR* 71: 1-17, 89-106.
1981a   'Sancta Contagion and Altar/City Asylum', *Congress Volume, Vienna 1980* (ed. J.A. Emerton; VTSup, 32; Leiden: Brill) 278-310.
1981b   'Korah's Rebellion: A Study in Redaction', in *De La Torah au Messie: Mélanges Henri Cazelles* (ed. M. Carrez, J. Dore and P. Grelot; Paris: Desclée) 135-46.
1981c   Review of Haran (1978), *JAOS* 101: 261-64.
1982   'The Levitic Town: An Exercise in Realistic Planning', *JJS* 33: 185-88.
1983a   *Studies in Cultic Theology and Terminology* (SJLA, 36; Leiden: Brill).
1983b   'The Graduated *ḥaṭṭā't* of Leviticus 5.1-13', *JAOS* 103: 249-54.
1983c   'Of Hems and Tassels', *BARev* 9.3: 61-65.
1983d   'The Two Pericopes of the Purification Offering', in *The Word of the Lord*

Shall Go Forth: Essays in Honor of David Noel Freedman in Celebration of his Sixtieth Birthday (ed. C.L. Meyers and M. O'Connor; Winona Lake, IN: Eisenbrauns) 211-15.

1985a 'The Chieftains' Gifts: Numbers Chapter 7', *HAR* 9: 221-25.

1985b Review of Janowski (1982), *JBL* 104: 302-304.

1986 'The Priestly Impurity System', in *Proceedings of the Ninth World Congress of Jewish Studies* (Jerusalem: Magnes), 118-19, 121-25.

1990a 'Ethics and Ritual: The Foundations of the Biblical Dietary Laws', in *Religion and Law: Biblical-Judaic and Islamic Perspectives* (ed. E.B. Firmage, B.G. Weiss and J.W. Welch; Winona Lake, IN: Eisenbrauns) 159-91.

1990b *Numbers* (JPS Torah Commentary; Philadelphia: Jewish Publication Society).

1991 'The *ḥaṭṭā't* : A Rite of Passage?', *RB* 98: 120-24.

Milgrom, J., and D.P. Wright

1986 '*niddāh*', *ThWAT*, V, 250-53.

Miner, H.

1956 'Body Ritual among the Nacirema', *AmAnthr* 58: 503-507.

Moberly, R.W.L.

1983 *At the Mountain of God* (JSOTSup, 22; Sheffield: JSOT Press).

Morgan, D.

1974 *The So-Called Cultic Calendars in the Pentateuch: A Morphological and Typological Study* (PhD dissertation, Claremont Graduate School).

Morris, B.

1987 *Anthropological Studies of Religion: An Introductory Text* (Cambridge: Cambridge University Press).

Mowinckel, S.

1953 *Religion und Kultus* (Göttingen: Vandenhoeck & Ruprecht).

Müller, H.-P.

1978 '*qdš* heilig', *THAT*, II, 589-609.

Münderlein, G.

1977 '*ḥelœb*', *ThWAT*, II, 951-58.

Muilenberg, J.

1962 'Holiness', *IDB*, II, 616-25.

Murphy, R.E.

1990 *The Tree of Life: An Exploration of Biblical Wisdom Literature* (Anchor Bible Reference Library; New York: Doubleday).

Murray, S.O.

1983 'Fuzzy Sets and Abominations', *Man* NS 18: 396-99.

Navone, J.

1971 'Time in the Old Testament', *The Bible Today* 9: 423-26.

Needham, R.

1975 'Polythetic Classification: Convergences and Consequences', *Man* NS 10: 349-69.

1977 'Skulls and Causality', *Man* NS 11: 71-78.

1979 *Symbolic Classification* (Santa Monica, CA: Goodyear Publishing).

1980 *Reconnaissances* (Toronto: University of Toronto Press).

1981 *Circumstantial Deliveries* (Berkeley: University of California Press).

Needham, R. (ed.)
1973   *Right and Left: Essays on Dual Symbolic Classification* (with Introduction pp. xi-xxxix; Chicago: University of Chicago Press).

Neufeld, E.
1944   *Ancient Hebrew Marriage Laws: With Special Reference to General Semitic Laws and Customs* (London: Longmans Green).
1971   'Hygienic Conditions in Ancient Israel (Iron Age)', *BA* 34: 42-66.

Neusner, J.
1973   *The Idea of Purity in Ancient Judaism: The Haskell Lectures, 1972–1973* (SJLA, 1; Leiden: Brill).
1979   'Anthropology and the Study of Talmudic Literature', in *idem*, *Method and Meaning in Ancient Judaism* (BJS, 10; Missoula, MT: Scholars Press) 21-40.
1981   'Defining Israel in the Priestly Codes of Scripture and Mishnah', in *idem*, *Method and Meaning in Ancient Judaism: Third Series* (BJS, 16; Missoula, MT: Scholars Press) 15-24.
1985   'From Exegesis to Syllogism: How Leviticus Rabbah Makes Intelligible Statements', *Conservative Judaism* 37: 42-55.

Newton, J.
1985   *The Idea of Purity at Qumran and in the Letters of Paul* (SNTSMS, 53; Cambridge: Cambridge University Press).

Ngubane, H.
1976   'Some Notions of "Purity" and "Impurity" among the Zulu', *Africa* 46: 274-84.

Nielsen, K.
1986   *Incense in Ancient Israel* (VTSup, 38; Leiden: Brill).

Nixon, H.D.
1984   *Typology of the Mosaic Tabernacle and its Artifacts as Interpreted by Authors of the Nineteenth and Twentieth Centuries* (PhD dissertation, Drew University).

Noordtzij, A.
1982   *Leviticus* (trans. R. Togtman; Grand Rapids: Zondervan).
1983   *Numbers* (trans. E. van der Maas; Grand Rapids: Zondervan).

North, C.R.
1951   'Pentateuchal Criticism', in *The Old Testament and Modern Study* (ed. H.H. Rowley; Oxford: Clarendon Press) 48-83.

North, R.
1954   *Sociology of the Biblical Jubilee* (AnBib, 4; Rome: Biblical Institute Press).
1955   'The Derivation of Sabbath', *Bib* 36: 182-201.

Noth, M.
1948   *Überlieferungsgeschichte des Pentateuch* (Stuttgart: Kohlhammer; ET *A History of Pentateuchal Traditions* [trans. B.A. Anderson; New Jersey: Prentice–Hall, 1972]).
1962   *Exodus* (trans. J.S. Bowden; OTL; London: SCM Press).
1965   *Leviticus* (trans. J.S. Bowden; OTL; London: SCM Press).
1968   *Numbers* (trans. J.D. Martin; OTL; London: SCM Press).

Nowack, W.
  1894   *Lehrbuch der hebräischen Archäologie* (2 vols.; Freiburg: Mohr [Paul
            Siebeck]).
Olson, D.T.
  1985   *The Death of the Old and the Birth of the New: The Framework of the
            Book of the Numbers and the Pentateuch* (BJS, 71; Chico, CA: Scholars
            Press).
Oppenheim, A.L.
  1977   *Ancient Mesopotamia: Portrait of a Dead Civilization* (rev. E. Reiner;
            Chicago: University of Chicago Press).
Ortner, S.B.
  1973   'Key Symbols', *AmAnthr* 75: 1338-93.
  1973   'Sherpa purity', *AmAnthr* 75: 49-63.
Otto, R.
  1926   *The Idea of the Holy* (trans. J.W. Harvey; London, 1926;   repr.
            Harmondsworth: Penguin Books, 1959).
Paran, M.
  1989   *Forms of the Priestly Style in the Pentateuch: Patterns, Linguistic Usages,
            Syntactic Structures* (in Hebrew; Jerusalem: Magnes).
Parker, R.
  1983   *Miasma: Pollution and Purification in Early Greek Religion* (Oxford:
            Oxford University Press).
Paschen, W.
  1970   *Rein und Unrein* (SANT, 25; Munich: Kösel).
Patrick, D.
  1986   *Old Testament Law* (London: SCM Press).
  1989   'Studying Biblical Law as a Humanities', *Semeia* 45: 27-47.
Pedersen, J.
  1926   *Israel: Its Life and Culture I–II* (London: Oxford University Press).
  1940   *Israel: Its Life and Culture III–IV* (London: Oxford University Press).
Peters, E.L.
  1968   'Smith, William Robertson', in *ISSE*, XIV, 329-35.
Pfeiffer, R.H.
  1948   *Introduction to the Old Testament* (New York: Harper & Brothers, rev.
            edn).
Philsooph, H.
  1971   'Primitive Magic and Mana', *Man* NS 6: 182-203.
Pilch, J.J.
  1981   'Biblical Leprosy, Body Symbolism', *BTB* 11: 108-13.
Polhemus, E. (ed.)
  1978   *Social Aspects of the Human Body: A Reader of Key Texts*
            (Harmondsworth: Penguin Books).
Porter, J.R.
  1965   'The Legal Aspects of the Concept of "Corporate Personality" in the Old
            Testament', *VT* 15: 361-80.
  1976   *Leviticus* (CBC; Cambridge: Cambridge University Press).

Portnoy, S.L., and D.L. Petersen
    1991   'Statistical Differences among Documentary Sources: Comments on "Genesis: An Authorship Study" ', *JSOT* 50: 3-14.

Proksch, O.
    1964   'ἅγιος', *TWNT*, I, 88-97.

Rad, G. von
    1931   'Zelt und Lade', *NKZ* 42: 476-79 (repr. in *Gesammelte Studien* [TBü, 8; Munich: Kaiser, 3rd edn, 1965] 100-29; trans. 'The Tent and the Ark', in *The Problem of the Hexateuch* [trans. E.W. Trueman Dicken; London: SCM Press, 1966] 103-24).
    1934   *Die Priesterschrift im Hexateuch* (BWANT, 65; Stuttgart: Kohlhammer).
    1962   *Old Testament Theology*, I (trans. D.M.G. Stalker; London: SCM Press).

Radday, Y.T., and H. Shore
    1985   *Genesis: An Authorship Study* (AnBib, 103; Rome: Biblical Institute Press).

Rainey, A.F.
    1970   'The Order of Sacrifices in Old Testament Ritual Texts', *Bib* 51: 485-98.

Rattray, S.
    1987   'Marriage Rules, Kinship Terms and Family Structure in the Bible', in *SBLSP* (Atlanta: Scholars Press) 537-44.

Rendsburg, G.
    1980   'Late Biblical Hebrew and the Date of "P" ', *JANESCU* 12: 65-80.
    1982   'Dual Personal Pronouns and Dual Verbs in Hebrew', *JQR* 73: 38-58.

Rendtorff, R.
    1963   *Die Gesetze in der Priesterschrift: Eine gattungsgeschichtliche Untersuchung* (FRLANT, 44; Göttingen: Vandenhoeck & Ruprecht, 2nd edn).
    1967   *Studien zur Geschichte des Opfers im alten Israel* (WMANT, 24; Neukirchen: Neukirchener Verlag).
    1990a   *Leviticus* (BKAT, 3.1-2; Neukirchen: Neukirchener Verlag)
    1990b   *The Problem of the Process of Transmission in the Pentateuch* (trans. J.J. Scullion; JSOTSup, 89; Sheffield: JSOT Press).

Reventlow, H.G.
    1985   *Problems of Old Testament Theology in the Twentieth Century* (trans. J. Bowden. London: SCM Press).

Ricoeur, P.
    1967   *The Symbolism of Evil* (trans. E. Buchanan; Boston: Beacon).
    1976   *Interpretation Theory: Discourse and the Surplus of Meaning* (Fort Worth, TX: Texas Christian University).
    1978   *The Rule of Metaphor: Multi-Disciplinary Studies of the Creation of Meaning in Language* (trans. R. Czerny with K. McLaughlin and J. Costello; London: Routledge & Kegan Paul).

Rigby, P.
    1980   'A Structural Analysis of Israelite Sacrifice and its Other Institutions', *Église et théologie* 11: 299-351.

Ringgren, H.
    1948   *The Prophetical Conception of Holiness* (Uppsala: Almqvist & Wiksells).

Rivkin, E.
    1976   'Aaron, Aaronides', *IDBSup*, 1-3.
Rodriguez, A.M.
    1979   *Substitution in the Hebrew Cultus and in Cultic-Related Texts* (Andrews
                University Seminary Doctoral Dissertation Series, 3; Michigan: Andrews
                University Press).
Rogerson, J.W.
    1978   *Anthropology and the Old Testament* (Oxford: Basil Blackwell).
    1979   'W.R. Smith: Religion of the Semites', *ExpTim* 90: 228-33.
    1980   'Sacrifice in the Old Testament: Problems of Method and Approach', in
                Sacrifice (ed. M.F.C. Bourdillon and M. Fortes; New York: Academic
                Press) 45-60.
    1985   'The Use of Sociology in Old Testament Studies', in *Congress Volume,
                Salamanca 1983*, 245-56 (ed. J.A. Emerton; VTSup, 36; Leiden: Brill.
    1989   'Anthropology and the Old Testament', in *The World of Ancient Israel* (ed.
                R.E. Clements; Cambridge: Cambridge University Press) 17-37.
Rogerson, J.W. (ed.)
    1983   *Beginning Old Testament Study* (London: SPCK).
Roth, J.
    1954   'La tradition sacerdotale dans le Pentateuque', *NRT* 80: 696-721.
Rowley, H.H.
    1967   *Worship in Ancient Israel: Its Forms and Meaning* (London: SPCK).
Runciman, W.G.
    1983   *A Treatise on Social Theory. I. The Methodology of Social Theory*
                (Cambridge: Cambridge University Press).
Sabourin, L.
    1985   'Sacrifice', *DBSup*, X, 1483-1545.
Sacrifice
    1981   *Le sacrifice dans l'antiquité: Huit exposés suivis de discussions,
                Vandoeuvres–Genève, 25-30 août 1980; par J.-P. Vernant et al.; entretiens
                preparés et presidés par Jean Rudhardt et Olivier Reverdin* (Entretiens sur
                l'antiquété classique, 27; Geneva: Fondation Hardt).
Saebø, M.
    1980   'Priestertheologie und Priesterschrift: Zur Eigenart der priesterlichen
                Schicht im Pentateuch', *Congress Volume, Vienna 1980* (ed.
                J.A. Emerton; VTSup, 32; Leiden: Brill) 357-74.
Sanders, E.P.
    1977   *Paul and Palestinian Judaism: A Comparison of Patterns of Religion*
                (London: SCM Press).
Sandmel, S.
    1961   'The Haggada within Scripture', *JBL* 80: 105-22 (repr. in *Old Testament
                Issues* [ed. S. Sandmel; London: SCM Press, 1969] 94-118).
Sarna, N.M.
    1986   *Exploring Exodus* (New York: Schocken Books).
Sawyer, J.F.A.
    1972   *Semantics in Biblical Research* (London: SCM Press).
Scheehan, J.F.X.
    1977   'The Pre-P Narrative: A Children's Recital', in A.L. Merril and

W. Overholt, *Scripture in History and Theology: Essays J. C. Rylaarsdam* (Pittsburg: Pickwick Press) 25-46.

Scheftelowitz, J.
1921   'Das Opfer der roten Kuh', *ZAW* 39: 113-23.

Schenker, A.
1981   *Versöhnung und Sühne: Wege gewaltfreier Konfliktlösung im Alten Testament mit einem Ausblick auf das Neue Testament* (Biblische Beiträge, 15; Freiburg: Verlag Schweizerisches Katholisches Bibelwerk).
1983   'Das Zeichen des Blutes und die Gewissheit der Vergebung im Alten Testament: Die sühnende Funktion des Blutes auf dem Altar nach Lev. 17.10-12', *MTZ* 34: 195-213.

Schiffman, L.H.
1985   'Exclusion from the Sanctuary and the City of the Sanctuary in the Temple Scroll', *HAR* 9: 301-20.

Schmid, H.H.
1974   *Altorientalische Welt in der alttestamentliche Theologie* (Zürich: Theologischer Verlag).
1976   *Der sogenannte Jahwist: Beobachtungen und Fragen zur Pentateuchforschung* (Zürich: Theologischer Verlag).
1981   'Auf der Suche nach neuen Perspektiven für die Pentateuchforschung', in *Congress Volume, Vienna 1980* (ed. J.A. Emerton; VTSup, 32; Leiden: Brill) 375-94.

Schmidt, W.H.
1983   *The Faith of the Old Testament* (trans. J. Sturdy; Oxford: Basil Blackwell).
1984   *Introduction to the Old Testament* (London: SCM).

Schwartz, D.R.
1986   'Viewing the Holy Utensils (P. Ox. V, 840)', *NTS* 32: 153-59.

Scott, J.A.
1965   *The Pattern of the Tabernacle* (PhD dissertation, University of Pennsylvania).

Seebass, H.
1985   'Josua', *BN* 28: 53-65.

Segal J.
1957   'Intercalation and the Hebrew Calendar', *VT* 7: 250-307.

Seidl, T.
1982   *Tora für den 'Aussatz'- Fall: Literarische Schichten und syntaktische Strukturen in Levitikus 13 und 14* (ATS, 18; Munich: EOS).

Seow, C.L.
1984   'The Designation of the Ark in Priestly Theology', *HAR* 8: 185-98.

Shea, M.O.
1983   'The Small Cuboid Incense-Burners of the Ancient Near East', *Levant* 15: 76-109.

Shiner, L.E.
1972   'Sacred Space, Profane Space, Human Space', *JAAR* 40: 425-36.

Silva, M.
1983   *Biblical Words and their Meaning: An Introduction to Lexical Semantics* (Grand Rapids: Zondervan).

Smith J.Z.
    1972a   'I am a Parrot (Red)', *HR* 11: 391-413 (repr. in Smith 1978: 265-88).
    1972b   'The Wobbling Pivot', *JR* 52: 134-44; (repr. in Smith 1978: 88-103).
    1973   'When the Bough Breaks', *HR* 12: 342-71 (repr. in Smith 1978: 208-39).
    1978   *Map is not Territory: Studies in the History of Religions* (SJLA, 23; Leiden: Brill).
    1980   'The Bare Fact of Ritual', *HR* 20: 112-27.
Smith, W.R.
    1927   *Lectures on the Religion of the Semites: The Fundamental Institutions* (London: A. & C. Black, 3rd edn [1889]).
Snaith, N.H.
    1944   *The Distinctive Ideas of the Old Testament* (London: Epworth Press).
    1947   *The Jewish New Year Festival: Its Origins and Development* (London: SPCK).
    1967   *Leviticus and Numbers* (NCB; London: Nelson).
Snijders, L.A.
    1984   '$m\bar{a}\,l\,\bar{e}$' ' *ThWAT*, IV, 876-86.
Söderblom, N.
    1913   'Holiness (General and Primitive)', *ERE*, VI, 731-41.
Soggin, J.A.
    1975   'Ancient Israelite Poetry and Ancient "Codes" of Law, and the Sources "J" and "E" of the Pentateuch', in *Congress Volume, Edinburgh 1974* (VTSup, 28; Leiden: Brill) 185-95.
    1980   *Introduction to the Old Testament: From its Origins to the Closing of the Alexandrian Canon* (London: SCM Press, 2nd edn).
Soler, J.
    1973   'Sémiotique de la nourriture dans la Bible', *Annales Economies, Sociétés, Civilisations* 28: 443-55 (ET 'The Semiotics of Food in the Bible', in *Food and Drink in History: Selections from the Annales Economies, Societés, Civilisations*, V [ed. and trans. R. Forster and O. Ranum; Baltimore: Johns Hopkins University Press, 1979]; repr. as 'The Dietary Prohibitions of the Hebrews', *New York Review of Books* 26, 14th June, 1979, 24-30).
Spencer, J.R.
    1984   'The Tasks of the Levites; *šmr* and *ṣb'* ', *ZAW* 96: 267-71.
Sperber, D.
    1975   *Rethinking Symbolism* (Cambridge: Cambridge University Press).
Spronk, K.
    1986   *Beatific Afterlife in Ancient Israel and in the Ancient Near East* (AOAT, 219; Neukirchen: Neukirchener Verlag).
Steiner, F.
    1956   *Taboo* (London: Cohen & West; repr. Harmondsworth: Penguin Books, 1967).
Stroes, H.R.
    1966   'Does the Day Begin in the Evening or Morning? Some Biblical Observations', *VT* 16: 460-75.
Struppe, U.
    1988   *Die Herrlichkeit Jahwes in der Priesterschrift* (Osterreichische Biblische Studien, 9; Klosterneuberg: Osterreichisches Katholisches Bibelwerk).

Sturdy, J.
    1972   *Numbers* (CBC; Cambridge: Cambridge University Press).
Talmon, S.
    1958   'Divergencies in Calendar-Reckoning in Ephraim and Judah', *VT* 8: 48-74.
Tambiah, S.J.
    1968   'The Magical Power of Words', *Man* NS 3: 175-208 (also in Tambiah
                1985: 17-59).
    1969   'Animals are Good to Think and Good to Prohibit', *Ethnology* 8: 423-59
                (repr. in *Rules and Meanings* [ed. M. Douglas; Harmondsworth: Penguin
                Books, 1985] 169-211).
    1973   'Form and Meaning of Magical Acts', in *Modes of Thought: Essays on
                Thinking in Western and Non-Western Societies* [ed. R. Finnegan and
                R. Horton; London: Faber & Faber] 199-229; repr. in Tambiah 1985: 60-
                86).
    1985   *Culture, Thought and Social Action: An Anthropological Perspective*
                (Cambridge, MA: Harvard University Press).
Tawil, H.
    1980   'Azazel, the Prince of the Steppe: A Comparative Study', *ZAW* 92:
                43-59.
Terrien, S.
    1978   *The Elusive Presence: Toward a New Biblical Theology* (San Francisco:
                Harper & Row).
    1982   'The Numinous, the Sacred and the Holy in Scripture', *BTB* 12: 99-108.
Thiel, W.
    1969   'Erwägungen zum Alter des Heiligkeitsgesetzes', *ZAW* 81: 40-73.
Thiselton, A.C.
    1974   'The Supposed Power of Words in the Biblical Writings', *JTS* NS 25:
                283-99.
Thompson, R.J.
    1970   *Moses and the Law in a Century of Criticism Since Graf* (VTSup, 19;
                Leiden: Brill).
Thornton, R.
    1982   'Modelling of Spatial Relationships in a Boundary-making Ritual of the
                Iraqw of Tanzania', *Man* NS 17: 528-45.
Toorn, K. van der
    1985   *Sin and Sanction in Israel and Mesopotamia: A Comparative Study* (Studia
                Semitica Neerlandica, 22; Assen, Netherlands: Van Gorcum).
Tsarpati, G.B.-A.
    1968   *'mispār'*, *EM*, V, 170-85.
Tsevat, M.
    1972   'The Basic Meaning of the Biblical Sabbath', *ZAW* 84: 447-59.
    1974   'Common Sense and Hypothesis in Old Testament Study', *Congress
                Volume, Edinburgh 1974* (VTSup, 28; Leiden: Brill) 217-30.
Turner, V.
    1967   *The Forest of Symbols* (Ithaca:, NY Cornell University Press).
    1969   *The Ritual Process: Structuralism and Anti-Structuralism* (Ithaca, NY:
                Cornell University Press).

1974   *Dramas, Fields, and Metaphors: Symbolic Action in Human Society* (Ithaca, NY: Cornell University Press).

1977   'Sacrifice as Quintessential Process: Prophylaxis or Abandonment', *HR* 16: 189-215.

Uffenheimer, B.

1979   'Utopia and Reality in Biblical Thought', *Immanuel* 9: 5-15.

Van Seters, J.

1979   'Recent Studies on the Pentateuch: A Crisis in Method', *JAOS* 99: 663-73.

Vaux, J. de

1972   *Les Nombres* (La sainte bible; Paris: Gabalda).

Vaux, R. de

1961   *Ancient Israel: Its Life and Institutions* (London: Darton, Longman & Todd).

1971   *The Bible and the Ancient Near East* (trans. D. McHugh; London: Darton, Longman & Todd).

Vink, J.G.

1969   'The Date and Origin of the Priestly Code in the Old Testament', *OTS* 15: 1-144.

Vivian, A.

1978   *I campi lessicali della 'separazioni' null' ebraico biblico, di Qumran e della Mishna: Ovvero, applicabilita della teoria dei campi lessicale all' ebraico* (QSem, 4; Florence: Istituto di Linguistica e di Lingue Orientali).

Vos, C.S.

1968   *Women in Old Testament Worship* (Delft: Judels and Brinkman).

Wacholder, B.Z., and D.R. Weisberg

1971   'Visibility of the Moon in Cuneiform and Rabbinic Sources', *HUCA* 42: 227-42.

Wagner, V.

1974   'Zur Existenz des sogenannten "Heiligkeitsgesetztes"', *ZAW* 86: 307-16.

Waltke, B.K., and M. O'Connor

1990   *An Introduction to Biblical Hebrew Syntax* (Winona Lake, IN: Eisenbrauns).

Webster, H.

1942   *Taboo: A Social History* (London: Stanford University Press).

Wefing, S.

1981   'Beobachtungen zum Ritual mit der Roten Kuh (Num 19, 1-10a)', *ZAW* 93: 341-64.

Weimar, P.

1984   'Struktur und Composition der priesterschriftlichen Geschichtsdarstellung', *BN* 32: 81-134; 33: 138-62.

Weinfeld, M.

1972   *Deuteronomy and the Deuteronomic School* (Oxford: Oxford University Press).

1979   *Getting at the Roots of Wellhausen's Understanding of the Law of Israel on the 100th Anniversary of the Prolegomena* (Jerusalem: Institute for Advanced Studies, The Hebrew University).

| 1981 | 'Sabbath, Temple and the Enthronement of the Lord—The Problem of the Sitz im Leben of Genesis 1.1–2.3', in *De La Torah au Messie: Mélanges Henri Cazelles* (ed. M. Carrez, J. Dore and P. Grelot; Paris: Desclée) 501-12. |
| 1983 | 'Social and Cultic Institutions in the Priestly Source against their Ancient Near Eastern Background', in *Eighth World Congress of Jewish Studies* (Jerusalem: Magnes) 95-129. |

Wellhausen, J.

| 1885 | *Prolegomena to the History of Israel* (trans. J.S. Black and A. Menzies from the 2nd German edn of 1883; Edinburgh: T. & T. Clark). |
| 1876–77 | 'Die Composition des Hexateuchs', *Jahrbücher für deutsche Theologie* 21 (1876): 392-450, 531-602; 22 (1877): 407-79 (repub. in 1885 as *Die Composition des Hexateuchs und der historischen Bücher des Alten Testaments* [Skizzen und Arbeiten, 2; Berlin: G. Reimer; 2nd edn 1889; 3rd edn 1899; repr. 4th edn 1963]). |

Wenham, G.J.

1972	'*Bᵉtûlâ* "A Girl of Marriageable Age"', *VT* 22: 326-48.
1978	'Leviticus 27.2-8 and the Price of Slaves', *ZAW* 90: 264-65.
1979a	'The Restoration of Marriage Reconsidered', *JJS* 30: 36-40.
1979b	*The Book of Leviticus* (NICOT; Grand Rapids: Eerdmans).
1981a	'Aaron's Rod (Numbers 17, 16-28)', *ZAW* 93: 280-81.
1981b	'The Theology of Unclean Food', *EvQ* 53: 6-15.
1982a	'Christ's Healing Ministry and his Attitude to the Law', in *Christ the Lord: Studies in Christology Presented to Donald Guthrie* (ed. H.H. Rowden; Leicester: IVP) 115-26.
1982b	*Numbers* (TOTC; Leicester: IVP).
1983	'Why Does Sexual Intercourse Defile (Lev 15 18)?', *ZAW* 95: 432-34.

Westermann, C.

1970	'Die Herrlichkeit Gottes in der Priesterschrift', in *Wort–Gebot–Glaube: Beiträge zur Theologie des Alten Testaments Walter Eichrodt zum 80. Geburtstag* (ed. H.J. Stoebe; ATANT, 59; Zürich: Zwingli Verlag) 227-49 (repr. in *Gesammelte Studien* [TBü, 55; Munich: Kaiser, 1974] II, 115-37).
1978	*Blessing* (trans. K. Crim; OBT; Philadelphia: Fortress Press).
1984	*Genesis 1–11: A Commentary* (trans. J.J. Scullion; Minneapolis: Augsburg).

Wheelock, W.T.

| 1982 | 'The Problem of Ritual Language: From Information to Situation', *JAAR* 50: 49-71. |

Whitekettle, R.

| 1991 | 'Leviticus 15.18 Reconsidered: Chiasm, Spatial Structure and the Body', *JSOT* 49: 31-45. |

Whybray, R.N.

| 1987 | *The Making of the Pentateuch: A Methodological Study* (JSOTSup, 53; Sheffield: JSOT Press). |

Wilkinson, J.
    1977   'Leprosy and Leviticus: The Problem of Description and Identification',
                SJT 30: 153-69.
    1978   'Leprosy and Leviticus: A Problem of Semantics and Translation', *SJT* 31:
                153-66.
Wilson, B.R. (ed.)
    1970   *Rationality: Key Concepts in the Social Sciences* (Oxford: Basil
                Blackwell).
Wilson, R.R.
    1977   *Genealogy and History in the Biblical World* (New Haven: Yale University
                Press).
    1984   *Sociological Approaches to the Old Testament* (London: SCM Press).
Wittgenstein, L.
    1979   *Remarks on Frazer's Golden Bough* (trans. A.C. Miles; rev. R. Rhees;
                Retford, Nottinghamshire: Brynmill Press).
Worgul, G.S.
    1979   'Anthropological Consciousness and Biblical Theology', *BTB* 9: 3-12.
Wright, D.P.
    1985   'Purification from Corpse-Contamination in Numbers xxxi 19-24', *VT* 35:
                213-23.
    1986   'The Gesture of Hand Placement in the Hebrew Bible and in Hittite
                Literature', *JAOS* 106: 433-46.
    1987   *The Disposal of Impurity* (SBLDS, 101; Atlanta: Scholars Press).
Wuthnow, R., J.D. Hunter, A. Bergesen and E. Kurzweil
    1984   *Cultural Analysis: The Work of Peter L. Berger, Mary Douglas, Michel
                Foucault, and Jürgen Habermas* (London: Routledge & Kegan Paul).
Xella, P.
    1981   *I Testi Rituali di Ugarit. I. Testi* (Studi Semitici, 54; Rome: Istituto di studi
                del Vicino Oriente, Universita di Roma).
Yamauchi, E.M.
    1983   'Magic in the Biblical World', *TB* 34: 169-200.
Zatelli, I.
    1978   *Il campo lessicale degli aggetivi di purità in ebraico biblico* (QSem, 7;
                Florence: Istituto di Linguistica e di Lingue Orientali).
Zevit, Z.
    1976   'The Priestly Redaction and Interpretation of the Plague Narrative in
                Exodus', *JQR* 66: 193-211.
    1982   'Converging Lines of Evidence Bearing on the Date of P', *ZAW* 94:
                481-511.
Ziderman, I.
    1987   'First Identification of Authentic *Tekelet*', *BASOR* 265: 25-33.
Zimmerli, W.
    1960   'Sinaibund und Abrahambund: Ein Beitrag zum Verständnis der
                Priesterschrift', *TZ* 16: 268-88.
    1965   *The Law and the Prophets: A Study of the Meaning of the Old Testament*
                (Oxford: Basil Blackwell).
    1980   ' "Heiligkeit" nach dem sogenannten Heiligkeitsgesetz', *VT* 30: 493-512.

Zipor, M.
    1987   'Restrictions on Marriage for Priests', *Bib* 68: 159-67.
Zuesse, E.
    1974   'Taboo and the Divine Order', *JAAR* 42: 482-504.
    1975   'Meditation on Ritual', *JAAR* 43: 517-30.
    1979   *Ritual Cosmos: The Sanctification of Life in African Religions* (Athens, OH: Ohio University Press).
    1987   'Ritual', *EncRel*, XII, 405-22.

INDEXES

INDEX OF REFERENCES

HEBREW SCRIPTURES

JEWISH AND CHRISTIAN SOURCES

INDEX OF AUTHORS

JOURNAL FOR THE STUDY OF THE OLD TESTAMENT

Supplement Series

DATE DUE